BAINISTEOIR

O'Neills

At All Costs

Happy 80th Birthday
Love Breda
x x

At All Costs

Davy Fitzgerald

with Vincent Hogan

Gill Books

Gill Books
Hume Avenue
Park West
Dublin 12
www.gillbooks.ie

Gill Books is an imprint of M.H. Gill & Co.

978 07171 7960 2

Print origination by O'K Graphic Design, Dublin
Copy-edited by Ruairí Ó Brógáin
Proofread by Neil Burkey
Printed by CPI Group (UK) Ltd, Croydon CRO 4YY

This book is typeset in 12.5/16.5 pt Minion
With titles in Frutiger LT.
The paper used in this book comes from the wood pulp of managed forests. For
every tree felled, at least one tree is planted, thereby renewing natural resources.

5 4 3 2 1

CONTENTS

PROLOGUE

I'm a bad loser, that's not something I can hide. Most competitive people are. Bad days can come close to poisoning you.

There have been occasions when I've taken defeat too personally and, maybe, it's left me looking petty and ungracious. I couldn't allow that happen in Cork in July 2018. I wouldn't. Not against my own people, my own family even. So, as our All-Ireland quarter-final slipped into injury-time, I turned to Seoirse Bulfin on the line.

'Hard place to be, Seoirse,' I said. 'But how we carry ourselves is important here.'

He knew what I was getting at. Mike Corry knew. Michael 'Gazzy' Collins knew. They'd all been with me on that five-year roller-coaster ride with Clare, through the good days and the not-so-good. There for the All-Ireland win and, three years later, the slow realisation of a journey coming to the end.

This was uncomfortable for every one of us.

I'd gone to Gaz especially, just before throw-in, and gave him a big hug. I don't think it's possible to know this man without loving him. And, if I'd had a knot in my stomach all week leading into this game, I knew it was probably nothing to what he was feeling. Gaz, you see, was a fixture in the Clare backroom for seven different management teams before being dispensed with in late 2016.

Why they didn't ask him back, I'll never know. Maybe the new management just wanted a completely new broom after my five years there, but Gaz never got a phone call.

When I asked him to come to Wexford with me, maybe I was being selfish in a sense. Gaz is in his seventies, after all. But his personality lifts everybody around him, whether he's banding hurleys, doing the water or just keeping the dressing-room light with his stories.

In March, Gaz and his wife, Patsy, suffered a bombshell with the tragic loss of their son, Ronan. As a group, we were heartbroken for them and I know it meant a lot when Conor McDonald drove down to Gaz's house on behalf of the Wexford players. In the months after, maybe the hurling was a godsend for him and Patsy. I don't know, but I hope so.

They'd come and stay the night before home games, whether in the house in Kilmuckridge or Whites Hotel in Wexford town, and we'd all play cards into the early hours.

I suppose our embrace in Cork was about everything and nothing then. Just something I wanted to do.

'This'll be a tough day, Gaz', I said. 'Just want to say I appreciate everything that you've done for me!'

Make no mistake, I wanted to beat Clare. But I wanted to respect them too. I wanted to be civil and dignified and, maybe above all, adult in how I conducted myself that day in Páirc Uí Chaoimh. I'm a Clare man. I was born in Clare. I live in Clare. I will die in Clare.

So, I did something that day I've never done before.

I went down to the opposition dug-out before throw-in, wishing everybody the best of luck. Shook the hand of John Fall, one of my best friends and an officer of the Clare county board. Then I encountered my dad. We'd been avoiding each other all week and, even now, the circumstance of the day felt incredibly awkward. I held my out hand and, at first, he hesitated.

'Put out your fucking hand,' I said, laughing.

I shook Doc Quinn's hand, before joking, as I turned away, 'Come down this line today Doc and I'll fucking kill ya!'

That was the air of it, the tone. Making light of the discomfort. I shook the hands of Donal Moloney and Gerry O'Connor. 'Best of luck lads!' Out on the field? The two Clare goalkeepers, Pa Kelly and Andy Fahy. Anyone from Clare I came upon, the same smile, the same words.

'Best of luck to ya!'

And when it was over, that couldn't change. The bad loser in me couldn't be allowed to find expression. I made a point of shaking as many Clare hands as I could get to. Some faces, I could see, were a little reluctant. Some, I'd say, were still uncomfortable about how things ended in 2016.

But others were genuinely warm.

Conor Cleary, I knew, had been getting a bit of stick in Clare. 'Stay honest and there'll be no fear of you!' I told him.

Big embraces too with John Conlon and Pat O'Connor. Then a few clowns in Clare jerseys came in and started dancing around me, trying to rub it in. I just looked through them, kept my cool and walked away.

Back in the dressing-room, you'd have heard a pin drop. One thing to lose, another to not perform. I could see the pain in everyone now and felt gutted for them. Mattie Rice came down with me to the Clare room and I broke the ice by joking, 'I'd normally be coming in here to give out!'

Those who were in the showers came out to pay me the respect of a full audience and I appreciated that. So, I said my few words, then back across the corridor to hear Moloney reciprocate on Clare's behalf. He was decent and kind with what he said about my contribution to their story.

We ate back in the Glanmire school where we'd made our base for the day before heading home. No declarations, no big announcements. Just a lot of firm handshakes and bear hugs.

It was near midnight when I got back to Sixmilebridge and I fell asleep to the relentless reel of Sky Sports News. Woke the following morning knowing immediately that Clare probably wasn't the place for me to be that day.

Said it to Sharon. 'C'mon, bring the dogs and let's get out of here!'

I don't know what Brian Cody thinks of me, probably not much. Actually, I doubt he thinks much about me at all.

But he's set the bar for every county hurling manager these past two decades and it's no secret that I've got huge respect for what he has achieved. Wexford got the better of his Kilkenny team twice in massive games in 2017, so I suppose it was no surprise to us that a payback of sorts was coming.

Put it this way, when we won the Walsh Cup final at Nowlan Park in January 2018, it registered as our third consecutive victory against Kilkenny on their own field. You didn't need to be a mind reader to understand how that would hurt them, hurt Brian especially, given that he spent the conclusion of that game banished to the stand.

Little moments shine a light inside even the most private of minds when a game is on the line and I saw a few of them from Kilkenny in 2018. The first was that bitingly cold January Saturday when Cody reacted so fiercely to Richie Reid's dismissal for interfering with Matthew O'Hanlon's helmet. The two players were doing a bit of jostling directly in front of our dug-out when Richie pulled Matthew's helmet clean off. I had sympathy for him, but it was a clear red-card offence, one that the linesman called immediately.

I could see Brian, bull-faced, marching down the whitewash to complain, so I sent Seoirse out with the message, 'Might be important to defend the linesman here, re-assure him he made the right decision!'

As Seoirse began telling the man with the flag not to be 'listening to that shite', I could see that Brian – even on a January Saturday – was now almost fit to be tied. I admire that in him, that competitive dog.

We'd play Kilkenny three more times in 2018, losing every one of them.

The first defeat, in March, signified nothing. We'd already qualified for the National League quarter-finals, so I rested maybe half a dozen players, something I'd imagine few Wexford teams have ever done going to Kilkenny.

But the other two defeats effectively killed our season. In other words, I suppose Cody reset the balance again.

He does that better than anyone I know but, in Wexford, we were left feeling that we hadn't helped ourselves. Because the first truly flat performance of our season arrived on April Fool's Day, when we surrendered a two-year unbeaten record in Wexford Park to a Kilkenny team that just walked through us.

That League semi-final came just a week after we'd squeezed out All-Ireland champions Galway in the quarters and, I suppose, the popular consensus became that the team was simply tired.

I didn't buy it then and I still don't now. We just hit a wall and, I suspect, it was more a psychological one than physical.

Anyway, those little moments?

With about a minute to go in that semi-final and the Cats nine points up, one of our players went down with cramp. Kilkenny defender, Paddy Deegan, stopped to help him ease the lactic acid out of his leg when a member of Kilkenny's backroom staff came running in and roared at Deegan to get up the field.

Nine points up, cruising and still programmed only for the kill.

I'd never seen Cody more animated than he was that day, something that confirmed to me we'd got under Kilkenny's skin. I loved that. But I also knew that to stay there we'd need a level playing field. And that was going to be denied to us.

As we shook hands at the end of the game, I just said to him, 'Well done Brian, but I can assure you that the next time we meet, we'll be a different story!'

He smiled that familiar smile. 'I'm sure ye will,' he said.

From the very announcement of the new championship structures, I'd questioned the fairness of some teams having to play four weeks in succession. The new system was a godsend, but it came spoiled by that one glaring inequity.

Not alone were Wexford one of the teams burdened with that compressed schedule: our last two games would be against Galway and Kilkenny.

To me, that always looked too much to ask. I've heard people arguing there's no reason why, given modern fitness standards, players should have any difficulty playing on four successive weekends. But it isn't about physical fitness. It's the challenge of rebooting the mind.

I'll always remember playing one of my best ever games when Clare drew with Tipperary in the '99 Munster Championship. In the dressing-room afterwards, Ger Loughnane warned me that, psychologically, I'd find the replay a huge challenge six days later.

I thought Ger was raving. I mean, I felt on top of the world, having converted the late penalty that got Clare out of jail. But you know something? Six days later, I felt unbelievably flat in Cork.

Our fourth game of the year against Kilkenny came when, mentally, the lads were operating on fumes. We'd beaten Dublin, devoured Offaly, then run into a brick wall against Galway on successive Championship weekends. It was asking more of us than was fair to ask.

That fourth week became all about tricking the mind in a sense, because self-pity would get us nowhere. The non-performance against Galway had rattled us all to the core. 17,000 people in Wexford Park and we hadn't laid a glove on them.

Ordinarily, the morning after a championship game, the players do a hyperbaric recovery session just across the road from our training centre in Ferns. This involves the players spending maybe an hour and ten minutes wearing oxygen masks in a decompression chamber where the inhalation of 100 per cent oxygen enhances the body's natural healing process.

But after the Galway defeat, we all knew that bodies weren't the problem now.

The players just met up at Curracloe Strand and talked things through amongst themselves. They were hurting bad and just needed to process that hurt in a private session now.

In Wexford Park, we use the weights room to have more space on match days, lining up two rows of chairs facing one another so that people are always looking into one another's faces. There's no hiding place, no quiet corner to steer clear of any hard talking.

But we were ten minutes back in that room after losing to Galway before anyone said a word. The feeling was sickening.

Honestly, I could've taken off any of eight players that day and they'd have had no grounds for complaint. They knew it, I knew it. We just turned up flat and, against Galway, of all teams, a team without manic energy is a team that's going to struggle.

Everybody goes on about their size, but our middle eight are fairly big men themselves. Size shouldn't have been a problem for us. And we knew they were coming down with a score to settle, given two of the three games they'd lost under Micheál Donoghue's management in the last year had been to us. We honestly felt we were ready for that.

But we weren't.

We never attacked the ball. We were passive in contact. We didn't win a single 50/50 contest all day. We never broke a tackle.

Galway got an early goal from a ball that should have been cleared after Mark Fanning's save and, after that, I don't know why, but we pretty much rolled over. It was my job to stop that happening and, clearly, I'd failed to do that.

But the same third-week dip was evident elsewhere too. We weren't on our own here. Tipperary, Waterford and Limerick would all struggle when out for a third successive weekend. The schedule was, as I suspected it would, beginning to squeeze.

It took me ages to say anything in the dressing-room but, eventually, I just went down the line, asking lads individually what they'd thought of their own performance, asked them to be honest in front of everyone. Honest about us in management, honest about themselves. And I asked if there was anything different they felt we needed to be doing in training.

The broad consensus was that they had to figure this out for themselves: this tendency to flat-spot, to leave a performance behind in the dressing-room.

Jack O'Connor's contribution pretty much summed up the mood of the collective.

'Listen, this isn't about tactics,' he said. 'That's not the problem. The problem is us and we need to get to the bottom of it.'

The whole way home, I rang individual players, getting much the same response. They were furious with themselves – sickened – and they were desperate to put things right against Kilkenny.

The following Wednesday night in Ferns, I asked the players to take ownership of the team meeting. Éanna Martin, Kevin Foley and Paul Morris took charge, picking out their own clips, having their own notes prepared.

Éanna encapsulates the honesty of the Wexford dressing-room. He'd seen very little championship action the previous two years, yet remained an incredibly important figure within the group.

I love the bones of men like Éanna because they're not always thinking about themselves. Here's a guy who was on the

Wexford team before I arrived, yet never slackened an inch in his commitment despite not making my starting fifteen. First in every evening, always working himself like a dog.

He just wants Wexford to win, it's that simple.

People can see that. They recognise that honesty, so Éanna has great standing in the dressing room. Same as, say, Paddy Donnellan had in Clare, or Stephen Molumphy in Waterford.

Just men everybody knows can be trusted.

That night's meeting ran for more than an hour, hitting most of the notes I'd hoped it would hit. It would be reflected in the performance against Kilkenny too. In fact, for 40 minutes that Saturday evening, Wexford hurled as well as any team I've managed.

We had Kilkenny on the ropes, and if it had not been for a couple of poor decisions by referee James McGrath, we'd have been well clear.

I'd get lambasted in some quarters for saying that afterwards, one Sunday newspaper journalist pointing out how the official match stats recorded us being awarded more frees that day than Kilkenny.

This is something that wrecks my head, journalists commenting on what you've said when they've not actually taken the trouble to listen.

My comments about McGrath concerned the fact that he'd done our League semi-final meeting too and, over the two games, Kilkenny had been awarded 17 frees inside our 65-yard line, while we'd been awarded just five inside theirs. That's an extraordinary imbalance.

I subsequently got an independent referee to go through tapes of the two games and that imbalance was inexplicable to him. I could show him shirt tugs, helmet pulls, a moment when Rory O'Connor was thrown to the ground right beside McGrath and zero action was taken.

Bear in mind this was a game we'd end up losing by a single point. A game in which even a draw would have been good enough to put us in the Leinster final. But, having been nine points up at one stage and playing absolutely out of their skins, the players just ran into a wall.

And that wall was psychological.

I mean, though we were seven up at half-time, I was worried going out for the second half. I remember saying as much to my selectors, JJ Doyle and Páraic Fanning, who were sitting in the dug-out. 'Guys, we're going to run out of gas here. It's only a matter of when!'

And the truth is it happened too soon. Our last score from play would be a 37th-minute Lee Chin point, after which Kilkenny just began coming – rolling off seven scores in a row – to leave us fighting for our lives.

The players were magnificent, digging in, hanging tough, just trying to get over the line. But, in a hugely intense game, we couldn't buy a free inside the Kilkenny 65.

That's what exasperated me: the sense that a foul at one end of the field didn't seem to be a foul at the other.

I kicked a bin over when I reached the dressing-room after. Kilkenny had got us again, but I remained adamant that my players simply hadn't been given a fair crack. It was my conviction then and it's still my conviction now.

Between our schedule and the frees that never came, the life had just been squeezed out of us.

I like good people and two of the best I've met in hurling are Wexford's joint captains, Matthew O'Hanlon and Lee Chin.

Solid men, decent, absolutely trustworthy. And I needed them when we went back training last winter as I ran into a blizzard of excuses from different lads now slow to get back into the beat of an inter-county lifestyle. It came to a head one November Sunday morning in Ferns when two lads turned up to train a little the worse for wear.

Páraic Fanning and I could smell the drink on their breaths immediately, but I decided not to go to war with them in front of the group. Our numbers were already low for a variety of reasons and I couldn't really do with further depletion.

But once I'd got both to confirm that they'd been on the beer the night before, I called the group into a circle, declaring to no-one in particular, 'If anyone ever turns up here again with a few pints on them, trust me, it'll be the last time they'll come through that gate!'

Afterwards, I rang Lee, told him I wasn't happy.

He immediately sent out a WhatsApp message, describing the lack of commitment as 'a load of bollocks'. Lee sets a serious example, living his life like a professional athlete. Almost instantly the attitude of the group improved. But that morning was a warning to me that 'Second Season Syndrome' might become a problem here.

Both Matt and Lee travelled to Singapore with the All-Stars in December 2017 and, much as I'd have preferred them to be at home, I was never going to deny them the trip, given how few Wexford men had got the honour in recent years.

Everything back then was a process of building for a decent crack at the National League and, to that end, beating Kilkenny in that Walsh Cup final – the game uniquely settled by a free-taking competition in the end – re-assured me that we were on the right road.

Our subsequent survival in Division 1A meant the league campaign had to be deemed a success too. But did we put too much into it?

Well, life in 1A is worth a hell of a lot more to the county board than would be the case if Wexford dropped back into 1B.

So winning three of our first four games and, then, that quarter-final against Galway certainly helped GAA matters in Wexford financially.

That said, the Galway game was played at almost championship intensity, and I do believe the lads were drained psychologically by the effort required to win.

And so, for the second year running, our season pretty much ran out of gas.

It hit a brick wall.

The morning after our loss to Galway in the Leinster Championship, I woke to that familiar sick feeling, and decided to be on the golf course around the time the Waterford v Tipperary game was throwing in at the Gaelic Grounds. I pitched up at Dromoland with two friends but, halfway through our round, I got the game up on my phone in the buggy and the three of us ended up watching it.

Tipp were steeped to get the draw and were, clearly, struggling with their schedule. But you had to admire their fight too. For the second game in a row, they'd got up off their knees to dig out a result.

It reiterated to me the need for teams to stay honest, even when it seems the whole world might be against them. And, no question, there would have been times in 2018 when some of our players felt that.

The Friday after our championship defeat by Clare, Jackie Tyrrell dedicated his *Irish Times* column to Lee's struggle to replicate the form of 2017, particularly the kind of display he summoned during Wexford's first championship victory against Kilkenny in 13 seasons.

Jackie hurled for me at LIT and, I suppose, will forever stand as the human embodiment of commitment on a hurling field. His theory on Lee seemed to be that, as a 'full-time hurler', he might simply have too much time on his hands and not enough distractions. That, maybe, a normal day job would actually complement the training load rather than run in conflict with it.

Now I'd say Lee regrets the day that term 'full-time hurler' ever came into his life because it conveys that very idea of someone with nothing to do but go to the gym and maybe watch *Jeremy Kyle* for the afternoon.

Trust me, nothing could be further from the truth. Trouble is, Lee is such an innately straight guy he cannot help but give straight answers. And, sometimes, those answers put him under pressure.

He's become a magnet for attention and that attention brings its own pressures too. Sometimes, I think that means – if anything – he ends up trying too hard. Almost forcing things when the wiser approach is just to go with the flow of a game.

After the Galway defeat, I invited him over to Sixmilebridge for a couple of days. I just wanted to take him away from the pressure-cooker of Wexford, to unwind. He'd spoken brilliantly in the dressing-room, was shirking absolutely nothing and, yet, just couldn't find his form.

We played pool. We played golf. We ate good food. We talked about anything and everything.

And you know something? For those 40 minutes we had wind in our sails the following Saturday against Kilkenny. No man stood taller for us than Lee Chin. He was magnificent.

Chin epitomises so much that is good about Wexford men and women, so much that is appealing about them as people.

I've encountered all sorts in my career as hurler and manager. I've had every insult imaginable thrown at me. The day we played Offaly in May 2018, a couple of clowns positioned themselves directly behind our dug-out and began giving me their best shot.

For the whole of the first half, the bullshit was unrelenting.

'Ah you're always whinging over something Davy?'

'Still sore over '98 Davy?'

They were so determined to draw a response from me, they seemed completely oblivious to the fact that their team was getting absolutely destroyed by some of the best hurling this Wexford team has produced.

Honestly, I couldn't believe that adults could behave so sadly. At one stage, I turned around to the bench, and said, 'Aren't they some fucking clowns?'

That drew an explosion of laughter from our subs and seemed, finally, to get the message across. The fools were long gone before the final whistle.

The 2018 Kilkenny defeat bought us time that we didn't entirely welcome.

The only thing we did over the next ten days was two yoga sessions with Treasa, a teacher from Wexford town. The players arrived both nights with their hurleys, mad for road, but I wouldn't let them near the field. I wanted them manically hungry.

Then we did a two-week block of proper training before meeting the defeated Joe McDonagh finalists, Westmeath, in Mullingar. That game was always going to be a relative formality, meaning I now knew I was on another collision course with my own.

We'd played Clare in the League in February, winning by four points and I'd found that experience uncomfortable too. Largely, I left the dressing-room to the players beforehand.

There was a moment in the game when Donal Moloney actually stepped across the line, colliding heavily with our midfielder, Kevin Foley. The linesman went absolutely apoplectic, lecturing him about his conduct.

And me?

I just stood there with my arms apart, as if to say, 'Lord Jesus, catch yourself on Donal!'

If it had been a manager of any other county against us, I know I'd have gone to war at that moment. But not against Clare. I wasn't looking for trouble against my own. Not that day. Not any day.

So, my stomach was in a knot for the whole week before our All-Ireland quarter-final. Just this heavy, sickly feeling. As always, the people I'm closest to were the ones who suffered most. I was hugely irritable at home, just willing the week away.

Apparently, some sections of the media took to billing the game as 'The Davy Derby', but I honestly didn't know that. I'd shut myself away from media, even side-stepping a question about the game the evening we beat Westmeath.

I wasn't trying to be difficult. I just felt anything I might say could become the story. And, hand on heart, I really didn't want to be the story that week.

The couple of times I slipped down to Crowe's Centra for bread or milk, the slagging was all light-hearted. People actually wishing me well. 'Can't say I hope you win, but …' That sort of thing.

In our preparation, I made a point of not talking about any specific Clare players. My approach was that, if one of the Wexford lads wanted specific information, they could come to me individually. But no way was I going to be bad-mouthing men I had been through so much with.

Yes, of course, we targeted certain things and my big frustration was that we never really implemented those things.

Why that happened, I honestly cannot say.

But I remain adamant that physical freshness wasn't a problem. We always monitor tiredness and all of the readings were where we needed them to be. My suspicion is that, maybe, the panel wasn't deep enough for the intensity of our schedule.

Like, I probably used the same 19 to 20 players most of the time in a season that brought us maybe 14 games played at championship or near championship intensity. I mean, from the Walsh Cup game against Dublin, we were pretty much on a war footing in every game, bar Westmeath, right up to that All-Ireland quarter-final.

During their time in 1B, and under the old championship structures, Wexford might have been used to four, maximum five, games of that ilk in a season.

Maybe that drained lads emotionally. Maybe it meant we went to the well too often and, somewhere along the way, lost that necessary mental edge. Wexford need to turn up every day to be competitive. They need to be aggressive.

And the simple reason I didn't use more of the extended panel is I didn't think that they were ready. It's a call you have to make. And I'm sure some of the lads who didn't play would tell you it's one I got wrong.

The morning of the quarter-final I was up before dawn to do a 5 kilometre walk to raise funds for a young Sixmilebridge girl, Aoife Sage, I'd read about some months back in the *Clare Champion*.

Aoife suffers from a rare illness causing the partial dislocation of her joints, as well as that dreadful condition, chronic pain syndrome. I'd read in the *Champion* how her family were trying to raise funds for a vital operation that would help and, so, decided to organise this walk.

If anything, it became the perfect distraction for me.

Maybe 150 of us met at 6 a.m. in the Shannon Industrial Estate, starting the walk from Starbucks, which had a Wexford flag flying outside courtesy of the manager.

It was slagging the whole way around and, honestly, I loved every minute of it. When you hear a story like Aoife's, you quickly realise how irrational sport can make us become. The plain silliness of being a bad loser.

I suppose I'm learning that all the time. And, still, this game of hurling puts life in us too that I hope I never lose. I'll admit straight up that I'm a dreamer. I believe nothing is impossible. My view is that every last one of us can make our own history.

And you know something? I'm a long way from finished making mine.

Davy Fitzgerald, July 2018

1

'TRY NOT TO GET TOO WOUND UP!'

Within a few weeks of taking the Wexford job I was diagnosed with sleep apnoea.

It was just the latest in what felt like a succession of psychological kicks to take. The diagnosis meant wearing a mask in bed at night connected to a small mobile ventilator. I must have looked like Darth Vader with it on and, to begin with, struggled to get even a couple of hours' proper sleep, between the noise of the machine and the discomfort of the mask.

The diagnosis pitched me into a serious depression.

My heart issues were well known by now, but this was an unexpected complication. To be honest, I'd been feeling dreadful for some time, and, after two days of extensive tests in the Galway Clinic Dr Bláithín Murtagh confirmed the need for a mask and gum-shield to be worn at night.

I was shattered. Essentially, your breathing repeatedly stops and starts because of, in my case, a relaxation of the throat muscles. In extreme cases the brain and other organs can become deprived of oxygen, with, naturally, grave consequences.

So just when I needed to be coming at the Wexford job with huge energy, I was on the floor. Honestly, it felt as if I'd made a terrible mistake. There were days I'd feel so jaded I could hardly lift my hands. The round trip to Wexford was always going to be an ordeal, but now I was arriving into Ferns just feigning enthusiasm, if I'm honest.

I had absolutely zero energy. Worse, I had zero morale.

Here I was at 45, feeling as if my body was slowly but surely giving up on me. I felt in turmoil, forcing myself into the car for the three-hour drive to training, taking these deep breaths then on arrival, just to summon some kind of artificial energy. Forcing everything.

I felt incredibly down and remember sitting up in bed one night and bursting into tears.

All I could think was, 'Where the fuck is all this heading?'

Sharon, my partner, was brilliant. She just kept reassuring me that things would improve and that this was just a temporary setback. Likewise my family, particularly my mother, Nuala, and sister, Helen. But they were absolutely united in their conviction too that, above all, I needed a break now. To be honest, they'd all been against me taking the Wexford job in the first place, given that my body now needed everything that that commitment would deny me. Rest. Relaxation. Time to myself.

Energy-wise, I'd say I was a two out of ten when I accepted the job and, looking back, it was probably nuts to do so. And yet, in a strange way, I recognised too just how much I needed the hurling now. I'm not good sitting around the house, over-thinking things. I need a project to keep me going. I need people around me.

Trouble was, the week of my final game as Clare manager, an All-Ireland quarter-final defeat to Galway, I'd spent two days in St Vincent's Private Hospital, getting a couple of stents inserted to clear a blockage in an artery.

So every dark thought imaginable was coming into my head now.

You see, I've got lucky with my heart twice. Hugely lucky.

My first incident was while in charge of Waterford in '09. Just a week or so after our All-Ireland semi-final defeat by Kilkenny and I felt something wasn't quite right with me. No pain as such. No obvious telltale signs of any trouble. Just an ongoing feeling of tightness in my chest that I knew I couldn't afford to ignore.

Why?

Because there's a pretty bleak medical history on my mother, Nuala's, side. One of her brothers, Pat, died from a heart attack at 27. Another, John, went in his early forties, then Conor was gone, like their father, in his early fifties.

Like them, I have heart disease. I try not to think about that too deeply, because there's nothing to be gained from it. But I'm not ashamed to say that I'm afraid of dying. I think most people are. And it does come into my head that, with my medical history now, anything could happen at any moment.

In '09 I went up to Dublin, where they found a 95 per cent blockage in one artery. For some reason it was decided to send me home for a week before inserting stents. I'd say that was honestly the longest week of my life. I was so worried I couldn't sleep a wink, and Sharon would wake to find me walking around the house at two or three in the morning.

Basically, I was almost afraid to close my eyes.

That sensation returned in August of 2016 when, just three days before we played Galway, I found myself in a Dublin hospital bed with what felt like a concrete block pressing down on my chest.

In that instance I'd been directing cars into a field for the wake of a dear neighbour in Sixmilebridge, Geraldine Crehan, when suddenly I felt this tightness in my throat. My dad was standing beside me as it happened and I just said to him, 'Not feeling great, might go in and eat a bit.'

Whatever way I looked, he insisted on driving me the 200 yards in from the front gate.

I'd been out on the bike that morning, pushing myself really hard at times over maybe a 40 km spin, so it was in the back of my mind that maybe I'd overdone it. I suppose it's ironic when I think about it now. Geraldine had died of a heart attack, and while organising the parking a few of us got to talking about the importance of regular heart checks.

Now I was about to have an incident of my own.

I ate a bit, still didn't feel right, so rang Doc Quinn. He wanted me to drop down to his surgery, but I was pretty sure I needed to head straight to Galway. 'Will you sort something for me?' I asked.

So he rang John Clarke in the Galway Clinic and, stupidly I suppose, I insisted on driving myself, my son, Colm, in the passenger seat and James 'Bomber' Hickey in the back. Looking back, that was madness. Dad, Sharon and Helen were all offering to drive, but I had it in my head that concentrating on the road would stop me over-thinking what exactly was now happening to me.

That wasn't fair to the two lads; I realise that now. Colm was under instructions to grab the wheel and slip the car out of gear if anything happened. I can still see their faces to this day. Terrified.

On arrival in Galway, Mr Clarke wanted me to do a stress test (a monitored run on a treadmill) but I refused. Deep down, I knew I wasn't capable. So I was brought down to A&E, where they checked my bloods, did an ECG, everything coming back normal.

In a perverse way, this wasn't what I wanted to hear. My body was telling me something was wrong, and the last thing I needed now was to be given some kind of notional all-clear.

'Honestly, I'm not right ...' I kept protesting.

It was then they did the angiogram. I've had eight or nine of these over the years and dislike them hugely. It involves injecting dye into an artery, and sometimes the doctor will put a pressure wire in to check the blood flow, which is horrible. I really struggle to breathe when that's being done.

Anyway, the angiogram soon identified the problem. A 98 per cent blockage.

Soon as I heard that I requested a transfer to Dublin, where I could be put under the care of my regular consultant, Niall Mulvihill. Galway had been brilliant, but Niall is a man I've literally come to trust with my life.

And so, in the week of what would prove my final game as Clare manager, I ended up travelling alone in the back of an ambulance to Vincent's Private.

It would take about an hour and a half of extreme discomfort to insert the stents this time (the job had been done in maybe 20 minutes in '09) and I was pretty uncomfortable afterwards. Niall had to work hard to open things up, leaving the artery walls really sore.

He couldn't give me any definitive answer on why the new blockage had occurred but thought it possible that my blood pressure shot up so high during that bike ride at home that the plaque simply caved in. The theory being then that I'd simply pushed myself too hard.

Again, I felt low after the procedure. The discomfort in my chest made the instinct to question everything unavoidable. Mid-forties in a hospital bed and almost afraid to go asleep again.

Wondering to myself, 'Jesus Christ, is there any real tomorrow for me?'

As I was being released the following day I checked with Niall that it'd be okay for me to be on the line that Sunday in Thurles. 'Yes, but just try not to get too wound up!' he told me.

Now that would be easier said than done.

There's a contradiction in how people who don't actually know me choose to see me.

It seems I'm either a lunatic on the sideline who never shuts up or someone who nearly over-thinks his hurling. In other words, I'm guilty in some eyes of being all heat and no light, in others of being too analytical.

On some level, TV hasn't helped me. I can be absolutely calm and reserved on the line for 70 minutes of a big game, but if I have a 30-second eruption, that becomes the defining image of my day. There's an element of giving a dog a bad name to this, because, trust me, some other managers have far worse tongues than mine.

Most of my players will probably tell you that the public persona isn't accurate, that at times of the highest stress I have a capacity to be even-tempered and clear-cut in delivering instructions.

But I suppose a cartoon tends to entertain people more than flesh and bone.

Like, a YouTube video went almost viral in 2018 when I got into a shouting match with the opposition manager after Limerick Institute of Technology's Fitzgibbon Cup defeat to DCU. And the reaction to that was pretty typical. I was lacerated on Twitter. It was 'Davy making a show of himself again.'

The truth?

We'd been beaten by a single point, and as I was walking off the field this fella started accusing me of running his Wexford players into the ground. He'd been at the same thing weeks earlier when we played them in a League quarter-final, basically suggesting that I'd been abusing the players in my care.

That was his style all through. Full of aggression. Constantly looking to get a rise.

You know, I could nearly accept that when the game was on. But after it? When you've just won by the narrowest margin? This clown was intent on winding me up and, unfortunately, I took the bait.

His accusation was completely bogus.

I had two of his starting players, Aaron Maddock and Paudie Foley, in Wexford. Plus two of his subs, Joe O'Connor and Darren Byrne. Our Fitzgibbon game is on a Monday, so the Tuesday before that the lads ring me looking to be excused from Wexford training because of exam pressure. I agree immediately.

They have a challenge game with DCU the following night, and again I've no problem with them playing that, suggesting they try to limit their involvement to half an hour. They come down that Thursday, when we just do a light session, because we've the Walsh Cup final against Kilkenny coming on the Saturday. That final, of course, goes to extra time.

I use Maddock for the first 70 minutes of it and a small bit of extra time. I use Paudie for maybe 20 minutes in total. The following day I've a challenge organised against Na Piarsaigh, which, because of the weather, is restricted to just 20-minute halves. I use Paudie for one of those halves, meaning he's played 40 minutes of hurling over the whole weekend. I don't use Maddock at all.

That was their entire loading.

So to then get accused of doing something I categorically did not do, at a moment you're fairly raw – well, the DCU manager got exactly the response he was looking to get. And wouldn't you know, someone was there to get it on camera.

But I've only myself to blame for giving them the reaction they wanted. I regret that reaction, if only because it gave them a respect I don't believe they deserved.

That evening I texted Paudie to congratulate him on the win, telling him I found their manager's abuse a little hard to fathom, given the facts. Paudie reassured me that there'd been absolutely no griping from them.

Which, of course, confirmed my suspicion. I'd been set up. And, sadly, gave them exactly what they wanted.

It was around this time too that Darach Honan came out with criticism of his treatment during my time as Clare manager, specifically the county board's refusal to pay a €6,000 bill for an operation he needed on his hip.

Darach chose to imply that the hip issues, which brought about his retirement at just 27, had been down to 'poor load management' and a need for there to be 'more responsibility taken by the people in charge'.

I was hugely disappointed by those comments, because anybody involved in that Clare regime would tell you that Darach would have trained the least amount of anyone in that group. We were always incredibly careful with him, and the county board would have facilitated that care.

To that end, a huge amount of money was spent on different procedures, everybody doing their damnedest to get Darach to full fitness.

In 2013, for example, he would have spent a lot of time with Gerard Hartmann when we were at county training. Who paid for that? Darach got absolutely the best of treatment, and I can assure you it wasn't exactly cheap.

My understanding of the issue over the €6,000 is that he was able to play with his club at the time this supposed overload was occurring, yet it was the county board that got billed.

It's funny, I was routinely criticised in Clare for giving Darach too many chances. I always considered him an exceptional talent, and his size (6'7") made him almost un-markable on the good days. I have to say I always found him a gentleman to deal with too and was delighted that he ended up playing a key role in us winning the 2013 All-Ireland.

I will always have a special bond with those players, and I'd like to think that, to this day, most of them would feel comfortable ringing me if they had a problem. Maybe, in the end, not all showed me the loyalty I might have expected, but we did something extraordinary together. Nobody can take that from us.

And I found it interesting that not one other player came out at the time of Darach's interview to back up what he was saying. The truth is they'd all become too familiar with the sight of him walking around the field, rubbing his leg, while they were training.

In my view, he was hugely unfair with what he said in January 2018. And, deep down, I suspect he knows that.

The bullying of my childhood certainly informed the way I behaved as a player and, if I'm honest, as a manager now. I've always refused to be intimidated in hurling. It's in my DNA to front up, to challenge, to fight if need be.

You see, I know what real bravery is and, honestly, I don't measure it in how hard a man behaves on the hurling field. Some of the toughest opponents I've come across actually showed themselves, at different times, to have damn-all moral courage. There's a distinction between trying to cut the hand off an opponent and real manliness.

I should know.

So the people who inspire me are often physically the weakest you could come across. People cursed by fate to address their own mortality long before it feels either fair or reasonable that they should. One of those people was a young Clareman called Jack Lynch.

Jack lies in Tulla Cemetery today, lost to leukaemia at just 20. I only got to know him during my last year as Clare manager, and I'm not exaggerating when I say I've never encountered a more remarkable human being. The first time we met was at a pub gathering for him in late 2015, myself, David McInerney and Conor Cooney invited along to offer support.

Jack and I got talking and I ended up telling him we'd love to have him along with us for a game in 2016.

And so he was in the dressing-room the day we played Limerick in that year's National League, and a few months later he was there again when we won the Cup itself.

I'd have texted him on and off after that, this lovely, warm, polite young man who – outwardly at least – was forever philosophical about his struggles with a disease that would kill him.

But I'll never forget his call in the late autumn of 2017 telling me that his leukaemia had returned and, basically, that he'd been told he was going to die. I could hardly speak as he told me, and it ended up him almost comforting me on the phone.

'It's okay, Davy, I'll fight away!'

I've often wondered how I'd be in that predicament. Imagine getting that message! Sorry, nothing more we can do for you! Condition terminal! At 20?

I wouldn't want to be told, I can say that categorically. I just think if you tell somebody they're going to die, the natural inclination is to give up. To become resigned to your fate.

Jack, I suppose, challenged that theory.

His positivity was extraordinary. I brought him for lunch in Dromoland one day not long after that call, and I can honestly say we laughed our way through it from start to finish. And only a few weeks before he died there was a fund-raiser for him in Sixmilebridge, a 'waxathon' that I suspected might end badly for me if I hung around too long.

Anyway, Jack and I sat into his car outside Gleeson's pub and we had one of the most open conversations I've had with anybody in my life.

Hand on heart, I told him things I've never told anyone. His openness just had that effect on me. Here he was, gravely ill yet absolutely free of hurt or self-pity.

At least any that I could see.

The day before he died I drove up to the family house in Liscullane, Tulla, with his uncle, John. Jack was lying on the couch, and it was obvious just how weak he had become. But he still made the effort to get up, have some dinner, chat to us for a while.

We exchanged a high five as I was leaving, but 24 hours later everything had become much starker.

His mother, Noeleen, and other family members were around the bed where Jack, now unconscious, was connected to a morphine machine. Noeleen suggested I whispered any last message I had for Jack in his ear.

To begin with, I couldn't get the words out. Honestly, I just felt heartbroken for him, heartbroken for his family, heartbroken for this bright, optimistic boy who was being taken from the people he loved.

Eventually I said a few things and left the family to their privacy, Jack passing away about an hour and a half later.

I remember going to Wexford the following evening and spending maybe the first half hour of training telling my players the story of young Jack Lynch from Tulla. How hard he'd fought for life and how dignified he'd remained throughout that fight.

'There's no pressure in hurling,' I said that night. And I meant every word.

Jack meant a huge amount to an awful lot of people. You could see at his funeral that he was adored, and to this day he comes into my mind a lot. I mean, how do you rationalise what happened him and the devastation it brought to his family? When you have faith, how do you square that with there being a God?

I honestly don't have the answer to that. And I've yet to meet somebody who has.

In February 2018 I finally got around to doing something I probably should have done a long time ago.

With Sixmilebridge under a heavy white blanket, I invited Sharon out to the front of the house, where I'd written a marriage proposal in the snow. We've been together eleven years now and, though we can fight like cats and dogs, I'd be lost without her.

Sharon is the sister of Ger 'Sparrow' O'Loughlin who I hurled with for Clare over more than a decade. I'd known her for years before we became an item, and maybe the great, untold story (until now) of my first summer as Waterford manager in '08 was the effort I put in to getting her to come home from Australia.

Basically, she left two days before I was due to make my debut on *The Sunday Game,* and it's fair to say I was devastated to see her go. It was proving a rotten summer all round for me, having been dropped by Clare, almost losing a finger in a club match, and now seeing the woman I loved head to the far side of the planet.

To begin with, her plan was just to go for two months, but then word came back that she'd decided to stay longer.

And, of course, by now I was in the middle of an adventure with Waterford hurlers that would take us all the way to their first All-Ireland final since 1963. I'd been hoping she'd make it home for that showdown with Kilkenny and was gutted to hear she wouldn't make it.

So the night before the final, staying with the team in Ashbourne's Marriott Hotel, I must have spent four hours on the phone to Brisbane. Just talking over and back, getting nowhere. On the eve of one of the biggest hurling days I've known, my private life was on the floor.

It's history now what happened us against Kilkenny, and it's fair to say I wasn't great company for anyone in the weeks immediately after. I was endlessly replaying the final build-up in my mind, trying to figure out the things I'd got wrong, the lessons I needed to learn. But, if I'm honest, I was brooding a lot about Sharon too. Trying to work out a way of getting her back.

Then around 2 a.m. one Saturday, having just come home from a night out in Ennis, I rang Australia and – inevitably – the conversation ended in an argument.

But Sharon's parting line stayed with me. 'Knowing my luck,' she said in exasperation, 'I'll probably end up with you!'

Soon as I put the phone down I knew exactly what I needed to do. Rang Seán Power the following morning, a great friend of Waterford hurling, who happens to own a travel agency.

'Seán, I need to go to Australia,' I told him.

'When are you thinking of, Davy?' he asked.

'Today.'

'Sorry?'

The following day I was on a red-eye to Frankfurt and from there a Singapore Airlines flight to Brisbane. I booked a round trip of just four days (two of which would be spent in the sky), as I had been invited to Eoin Kelly's wedding the following Friday in the Tower Hotel in Waterford.

On arrival in Australia, the customs people smelt a rat immediately on seeing my arrangements. Nobody flew that distance for a two-day turnaround. So they grilled me about my intentions before letting me through with laughter and good wishes on realising the mission I was on.

Sharon knew nothing of my plans. I'd texted her that Saturday to say there'd be 'something delivered' to her that Monday. She presumed I was sending flowers.

Next thing, I'm standing outside this house in Brisbane that she's sharing with friends, wondering have I made the biggest mistake of my life. So I rang. 'Did you get that thing?'

'No.'

'Well go down and check the front door, I think it's been left there.'

When she saw me, her face lit up with the most brilliant smile.

So we spent two fantastic days together, without, if I'm honest, really resolving anything. And the day I was leaving I decided to bring things to a head. 'Do you want us to get back together?' I asked.

And her reply nearly cut me in two. 'I don't know,' she said.

Here I was after flying from the far side of the world and she was equivocal about whether or not we had a future. I responded, naturally, as you might expect. Threw my clothes into the suitcase and stormed out of the house.

Sharon came after me, telling me one of her friends would give me a lift to the airport, and all she's getting back is 'I don't fucking need a lift!' In my temper, I ended up at Brisbane Airport six hours before my flight!

For me, that was the end of us. I said as much in a text from Singapore Airport on the way home, only to get a call from her three weeks later. 'I'm getting back in a few weeks. Do you still want to try to make a go of this?'

And that's what we did, eventually.

We have our ups and downs, and you know, if you think I'm fiery, Sharon's temper would put me in the shade. I don't know, but maybe that's why it works between us. She's a straight shooter, but a hugely loyal and decent person.

And I know I'm not the easiest person to live with. One day I can be high, the next day very low. Maybe I take too many things to heart. We broke up temporarily about three years ago, and I can honestly say I was miserable while that lasted.

My first marriage, to Ciara Flynn, didn't work out, yet the two of us remain on perfectly civil terms, and it's fair to say we don't have any regrets, given it gave us our son, Colm.

But Sharon's become a massive part of my life now and someone I care about deeply. More than care about, to be honest. So, eleven years on, I finally got around to writing a long-overdue question in the snow.

And, thank God, I got the right answer!

Maybe my public image encourages people to make certain assumptions about me. It's one of the reasons I agreed, against almost all advice, to have the TV presenter Lucy Kennedy come and live with us for a couple of days in 2017 for an episode of *Living with Lucy.*

It happened to coincide with my time suspended for that pitch incursion during the National League semi-final against Tipperary. So Lucy was actually with me heading to Portlaoise for our opening Leinster Championship game against Laois. I've a pretty decent grasp of how television works, through my involvement with *Ireland's Fittest Family,* so I know how a convenient edit can hugely influence a viewer's perception of someone.

So my one request was that they'd be honest and fair in how they edited the footage. If they did that and I came out of the programme badly, then I'd have nobody to blame but myself.

Maybe trusting them to do so was a gamble on my part, but, in fairness, they proved true to their word. And Sharon and I actually enjoyed having Lucy around. She was so down to earth and funny throughout, you could almost forget everything was being filmed, if it wasn't for the two camera people, the producer and a runner following us everywhere.

Why did I do it?

Largely because of the way I'm perceived as a bit of a lunatic. Because of the one-dimensional way so many people see me.

I'll give you an example.

In September of 2017 I attended a fund-raiser for a young Kildare man, Adam Burke, in Twomilehouse. Adam's the 21-year-old whose family were told he might never walk, talk or even recognise them again after suffering a near-catastrophic stroke during a GAA match.

He's fought back incredibly to do all those things but still needs hugely costly therapy if he is to reclaim full speech and mobility. Now, one of the first people I bumped into at that function was

Michael Duignan, someone I'd had a very public run-in with during the summer.

After our All-Ireland quarter-final defeat by Waterford I'd been asked a question about pundits criticising our use of a sweeper system. And I suppose my fairly strong response centred, specifically, on the *Sunday Game* analysts Duignan and Henry Shefflin.

Anyway, Michael took exception to what I said and went on *Morning Ireland* a couple of days later implying that I seemed to be trying to deprive him of a livelihood.

This was our first time meeting since and, fair play to him, he couldn't have been more decent. We actually had a really good conversation and I was glad about that. That criticism of him and Henry goes back to my absolute conviction that a lot of pundits don't quite get the system being deployed either by me or by Derek McGrath for Waterford.

In both our cases we'd been trying to compete on behalf of teams who didn't have a modern tradition of winning. Yet the populist view seems to be that we must always just go toe-to-toe with the Kilkennys and Tipperarys of this world in the interests of entertainment.

Honestly!

Keep trying to meet the traditional giants at their own game and my view is a lot of teams haven't a hope. It's actually beyond stupid to even try.

You know, during the summer of 2017 Wexford were getting an average of between 38 and 40 shots away per game, yet Michael wanted our system outlawed! Meanwhile, a lot of teams that weren't, technically, deploying sweepers routinely operated with no more than two players inside the opposition 65 at any given time.

If you watch most teams out there that don't play a so-called sweeper, their number 6 especially will sit back on the 45-metre line always. Nine times out of ten you won't see him cross the 65. He'll just sit there.

In fact if you look at Kilkenny's great team, Tommy Walsh, JJ Delaney and, say, Brian Hogan would always drop back rather than go forward.

So the minute the ball went in behind you'd have six guys gone back to mind the house. What then happened, their two wing-forwards dropped back. Look at Henry Shefflin. He spent so much of his time back around midfield and his own half-back line to cover precisely that situation.

Kilkenny's midfield would drop back too. So the whole team was effectively adjusting so they could crowd the danger zone.

My view was that I really didn't need that many bodies back. Admittedly, I did that with Waterford in 2010 when we won the Munster final. The minute the ball went in over the half-backs they had to retreat. Likewise the two midfielders, wing-forwards and corner-forwards. Everybody back.

But, over time, my thinking was put just one guy in front of numbers 2, 3 and 4. Because that's the area people are worried about, the danger of conceding goals. Now this guy's not a sweeper. A sweeper is the wrong terminology. What he's actually doing is he's doubling up every time with 2, 3 and 4.

Those three players can now attack the ball with freedom, because they know if they miss it there'll be cover there.

That means that 5, 6 and 7 don't have to be coming back. They're not needed, and, because of that, there's less confusion back there. In fact they're allowed to go the other way, and that means we can often end up with eight attacking players.

The way I see hurling, I don't want my players tied to a 30 square metre piece of ground. I want them to have the licence to go express themselves and play. Honestly, our full-back could end up on the opposition's 65. If he does, what I've told him to do is stay there for a few minutes. Everybody then drops back one, all aware of their role.

I'm constantly telling my players, 'Don't be afraid to express yourselves!' If that's a 20-yard hand-pass, a cross-field ball, whatever, I want them to try everything that this great game allows. To use their imaginations more, their skills more. Of course there'll be times you'll have to fight like dogs to get the ball too, but just use your head when you do get it.

Because you're going to have runners coming.

A wing-forward might have to play wing-back for five minutes, and I don't see anything wrong with that. It just takes work. Like, it's second nature to the Wexford lads now. Paul Morris, for example against Offaly in 2018, spent a period of the game at corner-back. My corner-forward at corner-back! But you know what? He did it perfectly for those two minutes, and a Wexford goal came from our corner-back, Simon Donohue, being 90 to 100 yards up from his normal position.

The point is, Simon then needed time to filter back. You can't look to have him charging back down the field straight away. That shouldn't be a problem.

I honestly think this type of stuff has made hurling more exciting. And yet you hear people talking about me or Derek ruining the game. People see the so-called sweeper system as seven backs. But look at other systems that supposedly more attacking teams deploy: they can have nine or ten defenders back at any given time.

Bottom line: I don't camp my wing-forwards back in our half-back line. I want them to stay up the field. I don't want them to come any further back than midfield, unless someone else has gone bombing forward.

Once players get used to our system you can actually hurl with way more freedom. I don't mind if they go short or long, they can make up their own minds. If they want to horse the ball up the field, fine, so long as it works. Some people just seem too blinkered to see that.

As it happens, I've always liked Duignan and Shefflin on a personal level, but a lot of people take what TV pundits say as gospel. It can actually turn a crowd against you, and sometimes I just think it's important to challenge that assumption.

That was honestly the beginning and end of the message I was trying to get across that day in Cork, so I was glad of the opportunity now to shake hands with Michael and put it all behind us.

But that same evening in Twomilehouse I had a very different experience with another TV pundit.

I'd never particularly liked Joe Brolly's style in front of a camera, because it always struck me as attention-seeking. That said, I like to keep an open mind about people if I've never met them.

And Brolly, I know, has done some really decent things in his time, not least that donation of a kidney to someone he didn't even know.

But he was late to that function in Twomilehouse, and I can honestly say I've never been treated more rudely by anyone in my life. I got the impression he just radiated sarcasm from beginning to end.

Maybe Joe just thinks that kind of stuff is a bit of fun. Maybe he assumes that people will be so impressed by his cleverness with words that they'll overlook his rudeness. Not the first time he'd have been wrong.

There's a perception out there that any kind of involvement in TV is a guarantee of wealth in Ireland, but, trust me, it's a myth.

The concept for *Ireland's Fittest Family* came from a morning coffee I had in the Oakwood in Shannon six years ago with a good friend, James Sexton. James is a brilliant entertainer, one of those people who could put his mind to anything and someone who's well known locally for an uncannily good Neil Diamond tribute act.

We'd been talking about the old RTÉ *Superstars* programme from a few decades back that some people might best remember for Pat Spillane's 'farmer's tan'.

I've always nurtured the idea of GAA teams as extended families, because I don't think there's any more powerful human emotion than the desire to fight for and protect your own. And this morning it was as if a light bulb went on inside my head.

'Jesus, imagine a *Superstars*-type competition designed around families – the most important unit in your life!'

There and then the two of us started working on a potential format and within weeks had a meeting arranged with the then RTÉ Commissioning Editor, Bill Malone, through Paul Byrnes, who was producing *The Sunday Game.*

Looking back, we had some gall striding into Malone's office a few weeks later, neither of us having any real idea how this process worked but both absolute in our conviction that a reality show built around families would be a winner.

Malone was grinning at the end of our presentation. 'Ordinarily, this never really works, but …'

He told us to find a production company, and after meeting with three we chose one called Animo. Why? No real reason, other than the fact that I took an instant liking to their representative, Adrian Lynch, who now works in RTÉ.

And within a year we were making the programme.

Everybody thinks James and I must be minting it when they see our names now in the end-of-programme credits, but the truth is that we only get a small percentage. The dream would be if it ever became a global TV programme because – well, a lot of small percentages might accumulate into something substantial.

I've loved being one of the coaches, starting off with Eddie O'Sullivan, Nicky Symmonds and Kenneth Egan in 2013, right up to today, with Derval O'Rourke, Anna Geary and Donncha O'Callaghan. And it always gets genuinely competitive.

I had war one day in 2017 with Derval in Kilruddery when I accidentally crossed into the path of her team. Honestly, she went through me for a short-cut and, naturally, my instinct was to give it back with interest. It was vicious between us, but I think the more we've competed against one another the more we've realised just how much we have in common.

Suffice to say, Derval's a fighter. I got the impression she hated my guts during her first year on the show and, if I'm honest, I wasn't exactly mad about her either. But we see one another as kindred spirits now.

The work can be intense on filming days, but we have incredible fun too. And, sometimes, we all end up laughing so hard it almost physically hurts. We were on Spike Island one day, just finished filming, and I challenged Egan and programme presenter Mairead Ronan to try to run up the ramp. Kenneth went first, reaching the top no problem. I turned to Mairead, 'You go next and I'll try last.'

So, she takes off up the ramp and Kenneth barely catches her. He's got hold of one of her hands, but his other hand has Mairead grabbed in a compromising position. Trouble is, he can't let go or she'll go tumbling.

Next thing, the two of them get this fit of laughter, realising they can't actually move now. This laughter spreads like wildfire until every last person on set, including Mairead's husband, Louis, is doubled over.

I don't think I've seen so many people, literally, unable to speak because they were laughing so hard. Even now, years later, the very thought of that day on Spike Island gives us all a fit of giggles.

I think because I own the format for the show there's an assumption that I'm always forewarned about what's coming next. Hand on heart, that's simply not the case. The production company decides, and trying to get any advance information out of them is absolutely futile.

That said, I'm really proud of the success of the programme. Everything I thought it could become it has. There's something really special about seeing a family achieve something together. It's as if it taps in to a deeper emotion. Something really intimate and personal.

The programme is hard work, given we're routinely on set from 7 a.m. to 8 p.m. And, trust me, it isn't exactly Hollywood. Nobody has their own trailer or access to fine dining. There can be anything up to thirty people working on set at any given time, be they production staff or people building the course.

Everybody is under pressure of one sort or another. It started out as just six broadcast hours but runs to nearly double that now and has been retained for another season. It crosses generations and seems to have touched a nerve with families.

I just wish it proved the cash cow so many seem to imagine.

2

SHORT FUSE

When I look in the mirror, I'm sure a lot of people imagine I see an illusion.

You don't get up as many people's noses as I plainly do without somehow communicating stuff like pigheadedness and self-importance, and maybe even arrogance, in how you do your business. Actually, come to think of it, I'd say some of the public nearly go looking for a tail and hooves whenever they watch me on the line, bristling over the latest injustice.

On one level, I regret that. I hate the one-dimensional view so many people have formed of me across the years, even if I know too – deep down – that much of it is self-inflicted.

I've certainly had a troubled relationship with referees, especially during my years in management, and, while I'm old enough now to recognise that I wronged some of them in my time, I'm also wise enough to see some value in that famous line 'Just because you're paranoid doesn't mean they're not out to get you!'

So who is it that I see in the mirror? Honestly? A reasonably decent man who's made many mistakes, that's who. But a man – I like to think – who's learnt from most of them.

There was a time around 2014 that I became absolutely convinced that certain referees had a personal agenda against me and, accordingly, against Clare hurling. I'm talking about a very small group here but one that had significant power and wasn't afraid to use it. My concern about this group drew me into regular correspondence in Croke Park with the referees' head, Patrick Doherty, and once even the then Director-General, Páraic Duffy.

My view was that these referees simply weren't giving Clare an even break, that – either by choice or possibly poor judgement – they weren't reffing our games with an even hand.

Whenever I felt this happen I'd always sit down the following week with an independent assessor just to make sure I wasn't fooling myself. Usually their opinion tallied more or less with mine. Trust me, I wasn't looking for them to humour me. I wanted honesty.

But there were days we'd be looking at tapes from a game and the word coming back to me from the assessor was 'bamboozled'. They couldn't understand some of the decisions we were either on the wrong end of or being denied. More especially, they couldn't explain the disparity in frees being awarded within the scoring zone to our opponents but not to us.

To begin with, I felt Doherty was hostile towards me. But could I really blame him? As far as he was concerned I wasn't inclined to show much respect for the very people he oversaw, so why on earth should he entertain me when I came on the phone complaining?

I get all of that now. But at the time I think I saw it as some kind of grand conspiracy against me. One, I suppose, of many.

Now, not in a million years would I swap places with a referee on a hurling field hemmed in by between 40 and 50,000 people. Lord Jesus, that's the definition of pressure. It's a horribly difficult job and one, no doubt, not helped when someone in a manager's bib is giving you grief from the line.

But, sometimes, they don't help themselves. I really believe that. Sometimes I feel they can be a little too outwardly dismissive of someone simply trying to ask a question.

A case in point?

The first game in our 2014 bid to retain the Liam MacCarthy Cup was against Cork in Thurles. We lost by five points in the end, but in my opinion James McGrath had a really shocking first half. The free count was 12-5 to Cork, and I'd challenge anyone to look at the video and see a game that came even close to justifying that statistic.

I was absolutely seething, but I knew full well that I couldn't go anywhere near the referee. Just had a feeling in my blood that he was waiting for me to step out of line, almost willing me to do it. So, as we were coming in at half-time we sent Mike Deegan across to ask James a very simple question. 'Why,' he enquired 'are there so many frees on one side but not on the other for the same offence?'

Now, Mike asked that question in a perfectly civil manner. How do I know? Because he's a man who doesn't work any other way. This is a man who's never been confrontational in his entire life, who never even raises his voice. He communicates in such a calm, matter-of-fact way you'd struggle to ever see inside his mind. I'm cut from different cloth, of course, and I will admit as I walked down the tunnel I did let out a roar, to nobody in particular, *'This isn't right!'*

And there would have been no shortage of Clare bodies leaning down out of the stand, screaming for the referee's blood, as we headed in.

They clearly saw what we were seeing. Our players had become so frustrated with the refereeing in that first half, they started complaining to Seoirse Bulfin, 'We can't do anything here, we're being pulled for everything.'

So there was a lot of roaring and shouting in the tunnel as we went to the dressing-room, and as far as McGrath was concerned I suspected he made no distinction between that general rowdiness and a Clare selector asking a perfectly civil question.

Anyway, I was late out behind the team for the second half, and as I turned the corner there was James McGrath standing by our dug-out, clearly asking my father about my whereabouts.

Soon as I saw him I came to a halt. James clearly wanted to give me a very public dressing-down in front of 40,000 people now, in spite of the fact that there'd been no confrontation between us. And I wasn't having that.

Next thing, a linesman comes in the tunnel, telling me, 'James wants to speak to you.'

And I'm 'If James wants to speak to me, he can come in here and have it out one to one, no problem. But I'm not doing it in front of 40,000 people!' I was completely calm as I spoke.

Eventually McGrath had to restart the game without the satisfaction of making a show of me, and I'll have to admit his handling of the second half was actually significantly better.

Now, when I got that first 35 minutes of hurling studied the following week by an independent assessor he told me he was flabbergasted by what he saw. Maybe James was just having an off-day. We all do. But I had it in my head that he didn't much like me, and the trouble with that being in your head is that every bad decision then becomes a personal attack.

I'm not saying we'd have beaten Cork with a different referee in charge. To be honest, we probably wouldn't. But the players were incredibly frustrated, and that frustration definitely comes against you in a pressure situation.

Now here's the thing. Mike Deegan was given a two-month suspension afterwards, and in all my years of involvement with hurling I can't think of a greater injustice. The moment that suspension was announced I knew in my heart that this would be his last year involved in inter-county management.

It sickened him, and it sickened me. He was suspended for asking a question, essentially. Punished because of the rumpus exploding around McGrath as he asked it. I can say this 100 per cent, what was done to Mike in 2014 was wrong and left a really bitter taste with me. He was the easy option, the fall-guy. It was nonsense.

He'd step down at the end of that campaign, and I knew full well it was because of the suspension. From the same game Joe O'Connor was cited too, even though he'd never said a word.

When I spoke to journalists after the game I told them, 'I knew something was going to happen today even before the game began!'

Again, maybe I'd have been better advised to say nothing. But my head was stewing over a phone call I'd taken from an acquaintance, telling me he'd been speaking to a very prominent GAA official, who told him they were on a mission to 'sort out Davy Fitz!'

Listen, I'm not saying James McGrath was a part of any grand conspiracy. I'm pretty certain he wasn't. It just seemed to me that, for whatever reason, he was especially wound up that day.

James is a decent referee, I can see that. But I'm just trying to bring people to my head space here. At the time I absolutely believed that Clare had begun suffering because of officialdom's dislike of me. I'd be on the phone to Doherty in Croke Park, spitting fire about what was happening.

My argument was never really about the specifics of a decision, because, being honest, a referee could legitimately award a free every ten seconds in championship hurling if he's going to do things to the letter of the law. So I was never questioning specifics, never saying 'This isn't a free …'

The case I'd be putting was always about the absence of consistency. The same infringement being interpreted differently in one game.

And the more I felt I was being dismissed, the deeper it set my anger.

There were other energies testing my patience that summer, most of which I'll return to elsewhere in this book.

But it's fair to say I was a coiled spring most of the time. At the very point I imagined that things would be harmonious in Clare I felt people pulling against us. Against me specifically. And I suppose my short fuse kept getting shorter with each little episode of negativity.

That defeat to Cork pitched us down the All-Ireland qualifier route, and the day Wexford came to Ennis we were well and truly fighting for our lives.

I was hugely proud of the boys digging out a draw with fourteen men, getting us out of jail. But everything felt raw by now. Down in the dressing-room tunnel afterwards I caught sight of a local journalist who'd been giving me a hard time, and that just sent me into overdrive.

I'd granted him a big one-to-one interview for the *Clare Champion* when I took over in 2012 but felt he'd been consistently unfair towards me since. He was constantly questioning our management of things, even through 2013, right up to the point of us winning the All-Ireland.

Why? I had no idea. And, I suppose, therein lay trouble.

I would say that from the time of our first interview to that day in Ennis a lot of what he wrote about the Clare hurling team had what I perceived to be some kind of personal dig at me. It was really getting under my skin.

Looking back, my anger would have been better directed towards the owner and editor of the newspaper. Why were they allowing him do this? We'd won only the fourth All-Ireland in Clare's history the previous September, but here was this local journalist almost constantly having digs.

Let me say categorically, I had no issue with the other hurling writers in the *Champion*. Gerry McInerney was one of my idols as a child, one of Clare's best ever forwards and a man who clearly knew his hurling. In fairness, Séamus Hayes was always straight down the middle too. I never had a problem with him, because while he could be critical it never felt as if he was pulling against us.

Every now and then I might take a little swipe off Joe Ó Muircheartaigh in the *Clare People* too, but nothing sustained. I could live with that.

So encountering him in the dressing-room tunnel was a red rag to a bull now. We were feeling pressure from every angle, and when I saw him by the wall, next to the ladies' toilet, a red mist came straight down. I'll admit I went ballistic, calling him everything under the sun and telling him the only thing his writing was achieving was to hurt Clare hurling.

He started giving it to me back, and unfortunately the exchange was in front of all the national journalists, who would refer to it in their match reports.

I just about had the good sense to turn away from him before it got physical, and accept now that I was wrong to do what I did. But I was absolutely sick of this guy, sick of his personal swiping against me.

Looking back, I think everything was just coming to a head for me. You're All-Ireland champions, yet – within your own county – you get the sense that so many people are trying to undermine you. It's hard enough when opponents are doing their damnedest to pull you off that pedestal, but when your own are pulling against you!

That's certainly how it felt to me back then, and I suppose this journalist just caught me at the wrong time. No question, I shouldn't have attacked him in the manner I did. But do I regret it massively?

Probably not.

And you know something? I doubt he carries too many regrets from the incident either. And when I was finally advised to do another sit-down interview with him, as some kind of peace gesture, he happened to have an RTÉ camera crew following him around that week as part of their series *The Local Eye*, focusing on a selection of provincial newspapers.

Needless to say, the cameras weren't allowed next or near our interview in the Temple Gate, but they were there when he began transcribing an interview that would, apparently, run to over 4,000 words.

Did the granting of that 'exclusive' improve our relationship? Sadly not.

Put it this way. After we won the National League in 2016 I did a fairly wide-ranging interview with *Newstalk*, running to almost half an hour. But during it I was asked about my relationship with local media. My answer, lasting no more than maybe 40 seconds, referred to my lack of regard for some, specifically those who I got the impression had never lifted a hurley in their lives.

Next thing there was a front-page editorial in the *Champion*, written by this guy, saying essentially that I should keep my opinions to myself. All this within a week of us winning only the fourth National League title in Clare's history!

Honestly, I found that hilarious. I felt I'd been getting hammered, but the moment I tossed something back that was the reaction. It told me a lot. Some people could dish it out but they clearly couldn't take it.

That said, none of this did him any harm. In early 2018 he got a promotion and good luck to him. He's clearly very well thought of professionally, so my opinion maybe doesn't amount to a hill of beans.

Of course, one week after that 2014 draw with Wexford our championship defence was over, with a three-point defeat after extra time in the replay, Brendan 'Bugs' Bugler and Jack Browne both shown red cards.

Did I mention how the referee, Johnny Ryan, had a horrible day?

Looking back, the truth is that referees and me pretty much existed in two parallel worlds, neither inclined to see anything from the others' perspective. During my early days in management my attitude was that I was always right. Refs have to get decisions right in a split second, but I had zero sympathy for the difficulty of their job. If I felt my team had been wronged I'd go to war almost on reflex.

Look, I think a lot of the referees know the story. There might have been two or three who wouldn't have been happy that I was being so vocal with them, but I think they know in their heart of hearts that there's no badness in me. If I see something wrong, I'll say it.

Maybe two or three got it into their heads that I had a bit of an attitude. Listen, I'm fighting for my players and probably don't appreciate the pressure I put referees under at times. I'll admit that.

But I have a big respect for the job they do. They won't always get it right, and you've got to understand that and forgive it. I make mistakes every day of the week. It's true, a referee's mistake could cost you a game, but they'll make those mistakes for both sides. You have to get over it.

I've accepted that a lot more. I like to think it's something I've improved on. It doesn't mean I won't still give out to them, but it's not out of a bad place. I can honestly say that.

It's just if you see something wrong you feel compelled to fight against it. And, look, they should hear what I'm getting from the sideline every day I go out. I've long since accepted that that comes with the territory.

People can say whatever they want to me in that environment. I've been listening to it my whole career.

But the thing that would absolutely wreck my head was if I got the impression that there might be something personal in decisions going against us, simply because referees didn't like my attitude on the line. Now, down that road lies madness, I understand that. But it's taken me some time to get there.

Funny, one of the things that changed me was a conversation I had a few years ago with Diarmuid Kirwan. Now, Diarmuid's probably the best referee I've come across in the last ten years. One of the best I've ever seen, actually.

But I gave him dog's abuse during the '08 Fitzgibbon Cup final, when LIT were beaten in extra time by Waterford IT. During the game, after it, I was just roaring at him, giving out.

A few years later we got chatting. 'Davy,' he said, 'I'll make mistakes, you'll make mistakes, we both just have to accept that.' And you know something? It was the first time I'd ever heard a referee acknowledge he made mistakes. Sounds simple, but it was a watershed moment for me.

I mean, Diarmuid was talking *to* me as distinct from *at* me, and there and then it was as if a penny began to drop. You see, the one thing that's always driven me crazy is this attitude of being dismissed. Of being spoken down to. After that chat with Diarmuid I remember thinking, 'Listen, unless it's absolutely blatant, you're just going to have to get over yourself here, learn to live with bad decisions ... once someone's not absolutely hammering you.'

Believe it or not, I've been much better since. For sure, I'll still blow a gasket if I feel my team's been wronged. But I promise you that's not being theatrical for the sake of it. I manage the same way I played, with my heart on my sleeve. It's the only way I know.

But I've learnt to take a deep breath now too. To see the other side.

I mean, one of my worst sideline explosions would have been against the Wexford referee James Owens when Clare lost their final 2015 National League group game by a point against Kilkenny at Nowlan Park, pitching us into a relegation play-off against the same opposition.

Going in at half-time that day, I gave James both barrels. Held absolutely nothing back.

But when I looked back at the game afterwards I found his decisions had actually been on the money mostly. I'd been 100 per cent in the wrong to say what I said. He was doing linesman at one of our games later that year and I made a point of seeking him out beforehand. 'James,' I said, 'I owe you an apology. You got those decisions right the last day. I was completely out of order.'

I've done that a few times, and, to be fair, my apology has generally been met graciously. That said, there's probably a few more I still need to apologise to. The way I behaved towards them, the language I used, I look back now and realise my conduct was unacceptable.

One such case was during my time with Waterford. After Kilkenny beat us by five points in the '09 All-Ireland semi-final my emotions were a mix of pride in the players for the mettle they showed against opponents who'd completely blitzed us the previous September and huge frustration with a couple of Barry Kelly's decisions when we'd begun applying real pressure on the champions.

In my opinion, Barry had given Kilkenny a sequence of soft frees in the scoring zone just as we were coming to grips with the game, and those frees stalled our momentum.

I'd been fine in the immediate aftermath, paying tribute to Brian Cody and his players for a performance adorned by arguably Henry Shefflin's greatest performance in a black-and-amber jersey.

But then, who was in the lift as I went to go upstairs? Yep, Barry. Soon as I saw him, the red mist descended again, and there and then I began tearing shreds off him for his performance. There were other people in the lift, and I had absolutely no business behaving the way I did towards him.

Barry, to be fair, is well able to take it and wasn't shy about telling me where to go with my opinion. Still, it's a big regret of mine that I behaved that way. Again, I would have apologised to him a good while later, but probably nowhere near soon enough.

I mean, I had endless run-ins with Brian Gavin over the years, and it's fair to say our exchanges wouldn't have been suitable for delicate ears. Again, I'd have had it in my head that he didn't like me.

But you know something? I also always understood that he was one of the best referees in the game and, when I think about it, if Brian really had it in for me he had every opportunity to blow up at the 2013 All-Ireland final immediately after Patrick Horgan looked to have nailed a winning injury-time point for Cork.

But history was rewritten in the seconds that followed. Seconds that changed our lives in Clare.

Listen, people who remember my playing days will know I had only one emotional setting going into battle. Well, I'm much the same in management, albeit pretty accomplished nowadays at keeping it inside. There might be one or two moments in a game when I'll overheat, and that tends to be what people fixate upon afterwards. Maybe 30 seconds out of 73 or 74 minutes.

I'm pretty sure a lot of those who then race to judgement have absolutely no idea what it's like being on the line in those big games, dog's abuse coming at you through the wire. It can feel as if you're in a war zone at those moments, your biggest obligation to hang tough.

The trouble is you're still pretty raw in the minutes after a championship defeat, every small detail of the game playing out in your head. That's not an excuse. I just hate being beaten, and sometimes that brings an over-reaction if the wrong person crosses my path at the wrong time.

At that moment you're just thinking, 'Lord Jesus, those frees killed us …'

If I looked back honestly, the frees might have been soft but, technically, probably legitimate. And that kind of outburst hasn't done me any favours across the years. In fact I'm sure anyone reading this would be inclined to think, 'Davy, if a small group of referees did have it in for you, could you honestly blame them?'

Maybe I was digging my own grave through my temper.

I was certainly creating this persecution complex, whereby I'd sense subsequent decisions going against me would be some form of payback. And that was really dangerous territory. The moment you start thinking that way, the moment you become open to the idea of some kind of personal agenda playing out against you, you're in trouble. It starts to eat you up. It poisons you.

That's why I eventually sought a meeting with Páraic Duffy in 2014.

In my head, Clare were suffering because influential people disliked me. You could argue that that dislike was no more than human nature, given my record of tearing strips off referees. But that didn't make it right. A referee's neutrality should be sacrosanct.

I appreciated Duffy giving me the time. An independent assessor came with me to our meeting, and we went through a DVD of different examples where it was crystal-clear that we'd been on the wrong end of poor refereeing decisions.

Páraic, naturally, didn't commit one way or the other. I knew he couldn't. But he was at least open to the idea that this was a conversation worth having, that – maybe – I wasn't just this raving lunatic who needed to be shouted down.

Páraic told me that he'd communicate my concerns, and, to be perfectly honest, that's all that I was asking.

I felt better immediately after our meeting, if only for the fact that the man at the top of our organisation hadn't waved me away. Hadn't dismissed me.

I didn't go to him looking for a favour, because I knew he couldn't promise anything. But I just needed that chance to express my concern about how Clare games were being refereed. I wanted that concern to register at the highest level.

My frustration that things were getting personal between me and certain referees at the time was, I will always suspect, well founded. I felt I had no option but to articulate it.

And I like to think I've been a slightly calmer presence on the sideline since. Sure, I've had a few run-ins, and people will obviously point to Wexford's 2017 National League semi-final against Tipperary and my incursion on the pitch that led to a suspension.

Listen, I got what I deserved that day, but Diarmuid Kirwan would tell you that I wasn't abusing anybody when I went on the field. That's not to defend it. In a split second I just got drawn into trying to stand up for one of my players, and – well, it spiralled into something bigger.

I'm still no angel. I accept that. But I'm learning to be less of a devil.

3

BROKEN FRIENDSHIPS

E arly in November 2017 Frank Lohan emailed me about a coming golf day in Lahinch for the Clare squad of '95 and '97.

I didn't reply. I should have, and on some bizarre level I think I made a mental note to do so at a later date. A date that never materialised. I regret that now, because my silence probably seemed ignorant and I'd never intended to communicate that towards Frank, someone I've always liked.

But it's as if this psychological barrier just comes down the minute anybody comes to me these days with talk of another Clare reunion. Why? I don't want confrontation. I hate it. But, increasingly, I find it hard to see how it could be avoided, given how some of my old Clare comrades have become so openly unsupportive of me in recent years.

Like, in 2015 Clare County Council honoured the '95 team with a twentieth-anniversary function in Ennis. I felt incredibly awkward going, because I knew there'd be a few faces there that I simply didn't want to see.

One of them was Brian Lohan's. It'd be fair to say we'd fallen out big-time, Brian having made the unprecedented call for 'an independent review' of Clare hurling after that year's championship exit to Cork. He wanted the review conducted under the chairmanship of Ger Loughnane and, essentially, sought to have the county board excluded from the process, as it was 'not independent enough'.

This I took as an obvious dig at my dad, albeit Loughnane had been on the war path that summer too, declaring the position of the board chairman, Michael McDonagh, to be 'utterly untenable'.

This I found incredible given my own experience of Michael, someone I considered exceptional in his job and a man utterly committed to the Clare cause. And he will surely be judged kindly by history given the success Clare had on his watch.

Anyway, I was at home when I got the call from a close friend, wondering had I heard 'what Lohan's after coming out with?'

I was absolutely disgusted and texted Lohan straight away. I mean, these are the guys you played with, and it feels as if they're setting you up. I just couldn't understand it. How could he be looking for a review?

'What are you at?' I asked in the text. 'Do you not think I'm getting enough stick without you jumping on the bandwagon?'

His response was incredible. 'The Review will help you,' he said.

My reply to that was pretty strong, and I won't repeat it. But I basically told Brian what I thought of him. To me, I should have been getting more loyalty from these guys, but I was getting none. On the contrary, I just got the impression they were determined to undermine me.

It's hard enough to beat other counties without feeling that your own are on your back. Think about it. We'd spent sixteen years in Clare winning nothing before I took over. Now, two years after collecting only our fourth ever senior All-Ireland, I was getting it from my own crowd. I found that incredibly hard to take.

Worse, one of the best county chairmen I ever worked with was constantly getting grief too. Trust me, you need your chairman and your board to back you 100 per cent when you're managing a county team. I was getting that from Michael and also from

Bernard Keane as treasurer, a man who always recognised what we were bringing into Clare financially.

But so much of what was happening now gave the impression of something fundamental being wrong with how Clare GAA was being run. It was crazy. Crazy and deeply unfair.

My relationship with Lohan had never quite recovered from a row between us over a Fitzgibbon Cup game the previous year and – Sod's Law – who was walking by now just as I was getting out of my car for that county council function?

Now, it's fair to say he was about as pleased to see me as I was him and, being honest, there was a hugely childish dimension to what followed. We actually walked in just yards apart, flanking our old physio, Colm Flynn, on either side.

People might find this hard to believe, but not a single word passed between Lohan and me, not as much as a nod of the head. Poor Colm tried to feign normality, speaking to us separately as if some invisible screen prevented Lohan and me from actually communicating with one another.

Bearing in mind that just three years earlier I'd asked Lohan to be one of my Clare selectors, you'll get an idea of just how spectacularly our relationship had collapsed here.

There was a time he was as close to me as a brother. As Clare goalkeeper and full-back for the most momentous decade in the county's history, I think it's fair to say we had an almost telepathic relationship.

But, more than that, I believed we were really tight, regularly golfing together, doing business together, all the time bouncing ideas off one another about hurling and what it was that made a winning dressing-room.

Even in his role as University of Limerick's hurling manager I gave Brian loads of detail of what we did at LIT in terms of fund-raising and general organisation.

But it's fair to say Brian wasn't the only man I had no interest in meeting that day in Ennis.

Why? I just felt any polite courtesy between a few of us would be insincere, one of whom was Jamesie O'Connor.

In their very different ways, both Brian and Jamesie had been cutting the back off me since I took over Clare. Why Jamesie especially chose to do that I don't know. I actually phoned him a couple of times early on in my term as manager to ask him why he seemed so consistently negative towards my leadership of the team, given I was hardly a wet weekend in the job.

No more than with Lohan, I felt I'd had a great relationship with Jamesie when we were teammates. Virtually every night at county training we'd have free-taking competitions. But he just never seemed to warm to the idea of me as the Clare hurling manager, and pretty soon I became used to friends ringing, asking me, 'Lord God, what did you ever do to Jamesie?'

To this day, I haven't got the answer.

Loughnane was a different kettle of fish. I wasn't long in the door of that function when he was straight across with that familiar beaming smile, chatting away as if nothing had changed from the '90s. Fair play to him, that's Ger's style. He fronts up every time.

When I think of his greatness as a manager I'd say that very strength of personality is the first thing that comes to mind. Ger could cut you to pieces one minute but talk away normally to you the next, all the time radiating complete indifference to any idea that what he's just said might have upset you.

Maybe I'm a hopeless innocent in that regard. Maybe my natural instinct of loyalty to old friends and teammates seems a little quaint and old-school now to the modern GAA pundit, whose main priority is to keep his gig.

When Ger was going through the worst of treatment for his leukaemia a few years back I made a point of regularly texting him a message of support. A simple enough gesture, I know, but one I felt it important to make, given what the man had done for all of us as hurlers and people.

And you know, on some level I can take the digs Ger aims at me, because he'll always still do what he did that day in Ennis. That is, he'll always push out that big hand in whatever it is that his concept of friendship happens to be.

But, hand on heart, I can't see the same thing happening with Brian Lohan any time soon.

The beginning of the end of our relationship was the Fitzgibbon Cup quarter-final of 2014 between my team, LIT, who started 6/1 outsiders to beat Brian's team, UL.

We were generally seen as having our weakest hand for a decade that year, while UL could call on county players like Jack Browne, Conor Ryan, Pádraig Walsh, Pádraic 'Podge' Collins, Jason Forde and Johnny Glynn. They even had inter-county players on the bench, so the odds being offered were realistic. I knew that.

But I had a plan, and that plan involved taking the gamble of setting up as a straight fifteen – something I almost never do – in our final group game against GMIT, a game I knew would be closely watched by UL's management. And, as we fell over the line that day, everything they saw was a lie.

As soon as the players came back into the dressing-room I went straight into quarter-final mode, going through the system and the match-ups I had in mind for UL.

Now, when you play UL at their place they put you in these tiny cramped dressing-rooms that would make the old Páirc Uí Chaoimh seem palatial. The idea, I suspect, is to split you up. So I knew this was coming and decided we'd only use the rooms at half-time, that we'd go straight from the bus into a warm-up on the pitch.

This involved stepping in through bushes at the top end of the field, and as we did so I noticed that, unusually, it was the end UL set out all their training cones on for a warm-up. Straight away, a light bulb went on in my head.

We'd reached the field before them, so why not rattle a few cages here?

So, sending down the hurley-carriers just to make sure the dressing-rooms would be accessible at half-time, I told everybody else to stay where they were. 'Right, we're warming up here,' I said. 'We don't need any cones!'

I knew there'd be confrontation and, in many ways, maybe that was my intention.

Next thing we had people roaring at us to 'Fuck off back down to the other end …' but I wouldn't let us take a backward step. I remember looking into the square at one stage, four goalies on the line, trying to stop shots in a scene of absolute chaos. I knew Brian was fuming but pointedly never made eye contact.

That was my message to the whole group: ignore them, keep doing what you're doing, do not step back a single inch here.

In my head, they'd gone against their normal routine of warming up at the bottom end just to make the statement that this was their field, and on it we'd be expected to do what we were told. And I wouldn't countenance that. I couldn't.

I wanted us to show in everything we did that day that, however much we might end up outclassed on the field, we'd be standing up for ourselves. That we weren't going to lie down in front of anyone.

There were a few jostles exchanged, and the language was fairly choice at times, but they got the message eventually, retreating to the bottom end of their own field. To me, that was our first victory.

But you could cut the tension with a knife now too, and by throw-in time the place was an absolute cauldron. There's always an edge between the colleges, but that day it was wild. Maybe 3,000 people in the place, every last one of them screaming blue murder.

I instructed one of my players, a Tipperary lad, Philly Ivors, to just position himself on the sideline, making absolutely zero effort to join the play until I told him otherwise. His job basically was to take one of their defenders out of the game.

I did not play a single forward inside the UL 45, and from the throw-in you could see they were struggling to cope with how we had set up with so many bodies around the middle third. On top of that, my lads worked like men possessed, chasing, harrying, forcing turnovers by pure force of will.

And Ivors? He hit 1-3, while a second-year Tony Kelly was absolutely unplayable the same day, scoring 1-10 as we won by six points. It was an incredible victory for us, one the *Limerick Leader* match report subsequently put down to 'a tactical master-class'.

Brian never came near me afterwards. I didn't need to be told he was absolutely bulling.

When the dust had settled a couple of months later (we'd lost our semi-final to Waterford IT by a point) I decided to ring Lohan. Had just pulled in to the Clare Abbey car park and was killing time before a meeting. The silence between us had been playing on my mind and I wanted to put an end to it.

But it soon became clear that Brian wasn't in any mood for a handshake and fresh start. He told me that he couldn't accept 'some of the stuff' that had gone on in that quarter-final, suggesting that – in his eyes – I'd been personally responsible for the worst of it.

My response was 'Brian, my job is to win for LIT. I've to do what I have to do, just as you have to do what you have to do for UL. You know me long enough, you know I'd do anything for you.

'But when we're on opposite sides in a game, it's war. It has to be. You need to get over this.'

It was at that point he made a comment to me I have no intention of ever repeating. Let's just say the comment was poor, that's as far as I'll go.

The following year UL beat us in the Fitzgibbon semi-final and I just stood there at the end, waiting to see if he'd come over. Maybe I should have actively sought him out myself, but – again – the day passed without a handshake.

And, again, maybe I should have been the person to seek one.

Anyway, from 2014 on, my friendship with Lohan was never the same again.

The following year he would call for that 'independent review', something I honestly couldn't get over. It was only two years since we'd won the All-Ireland, and people seemed to be forgetting that, when I became manager, Clare couldn't get out of Division 1B and hadn't won a serious championship game in ages.

Out relationship then sank to an all-time low in 2016 when Tony Kelly picked up a bad ankle injury during Clare training that would rule him out of the Fitzgibbon Cup. Tony by now had left LIT to join UL in pursuit of a teaching career, and, though we'd been gutted to lose him, he'd given us everything and left with my blessing.

But Brian always seemed paranoid about his UL players training with Clare.

I can say categorically that I treated all the college players exactly the same and have always been particularly mindful of the physical load they encounter early in the year.

My routine is that if they have a practice game with the college they are excused county training that evening. But they're not allowed train with the college, because you simply can't have them being flogged from pillar to post.

On this particular Tuesday evening I wanted all the college players to train with Clare, even though they had Fitzgibbon games that Thursday. The deal was that everybody would do half an hour – everybody. This immediately caused ructions, a call coming through from UL to say that Tony would be training with them that night.

I said he couldn't, that we were closing in on the start of the National League and I needed a full complement of players at Clare training.

Now, we'd had issues with UL the year before too when Tony had a hamstring injury and I wouldn't play him in the first two rounds of the League. That was a League campaign that would end up with us being relegated, but our physio, Ger Keane, was adamant that neither Kelly nor David McInerney were fit to play.

Lohan seemed to get it in his head that I was specifically stopping UL players, and he went to Gerard Hartmann to have Tony's injury assessed.

Now that same paranoia was kicking in again. But we had a League game against Offaly just a couple of weeks away and I felt it important to have all the Clare players together this particular Tuesday evening. We had war on the phone with UL before Tony pitched up and – Sod's Law – he wrecked ankle ligaments during a tackling drill when his leg got tangled up with one of the younger lads, Shane McNamara.

The injury was bad enough for him to miss most of the League and, of course, UL's entire Fitzgibbon campaign.

Lohan was furious. In interviews he more or less implied that Tony's injury had been down to us asking the players to do 'too much', describing it as 'a very messy situation, but that doesn't happen with all managers'. Those interviews would even continue into 2017, Lohan all but insinuating that Tony's injury was down to something malicious on my part.

As if we'd injured our own star player deliberately.

Anyway, that's why I found that county council gig, initially at least, so uncomfortable. I walked in thinking, 'Jesus, I'll be glad when this is over!' But then I got talking to the likes of Frank Lohan, Sparrow, 'Tuts' and Kenny Morrissey, and I really enjoyed their company.

But, looking back, it would strike me as fundamentally sad that that kind of gathering could be so uncomfortable.

Because Lohan and Jamesie are two men I used go to war with. They'll always be up there as two of the greatest Clare hurlers ever, because they were so important to what we achieved with the county in '95 and '97. Maybe I'm naïve, but I just think Clare men shouldn't be cutting other Clare men down.

Which is why I will always be so disappointed by how they treated me while I was Clare manager.

All that said, maybe they felt they had good reasons for criticising my management of the county. And maybe I should have been more accepting of that.

For men who had such incredible experiences together, I'd love to think that some day we could just get back to the way we used to be. Wishful thinking? Maybe it might start with me answering the next email about an upcoming Clare golf day.

4

THE COLD SHOULDER

had a sixth sense that trouble might be coming my way when Tony Considine was appointed Clare manager at the end of 2006.

Somewhere in the back of my mind I could remember a disparaging remark I'd made about his role within the Ger Loughnane management team. Something along the lines that 'Sure he was a good man to sing a song.' For the life of me, I'm not even sure of the forum or the context.

All I know is that it was a dismissive line which, if I'm honest, was unfair. Tony was actually a big part of that Clare story in the '90s, always available for one-to-one chats with players, making sure they were in the right head-space. He knew his hurling too, was well capable of taking a session. But we always felt he was so unfailingly loyal to Ger, it pretty much became accepted that anything you might say to Tony would be communicated straight to the top.

Of all the people involved in Clare's All-Ireland wins of '95 and '97, I'd say Tony was the only one who would never, ever have taken even remote issue with Loughnane.

He became his most faithful servant.

There had been talk that Cyril Farrell or Louis Mulqueen might be in the frame to take over from Anthony Daly that October, but when Considine was confirmed in the job I just couldn't help wonder if that line about singing would come back to haunt me.

Why did I say it?

I think on some level I'd become pissed off with some of the stuff he was writing in the *Examiner*, where he was inclined to have little pops off men, me included, he once soldiered with. To me, that was disloyal. We'd been struggling as a group to get back to the heights of the late '90s, and I think Dalo especially could have done with a little more support at the time.

Instead he had Considine in the *Examiner* and Loughnane in the *Star* regularly having goes at Clare.

He never said much publicly, but Dalo was constantly giving out about Loughnane's stuff especially. He felt he was being routinely undermined and that that really made life more difficult for him than it needed to be.

It was probably at its worst around '04, when people almost felt compelled to take sides. You were either on Dalo's side or Loughnane's, plenty of good men being caught in the middle.

Shortly after Tony's appointment I went to Australia with a friend, Brian Culbert. We were staying in this hotel in Brisbane and I made a point of going to the gym every single day of our stay. Now, I hated the gym, but I remember saying to Brian I felt I was going to be in trouble fitness-wise when I rejoined the Clare squad.

Soon as we got home I decided to test the water in my relationship with Considine, driving out to his house in Quin. 'Tony,' I said, 'I hope nothing from the past will get in the way of us working together now.'

His response seemed pretty clear-cut.

'It won't, Fitzy,' he said. 'I'm professional in what I do. What's in the past is in the past. You'll be treated the same as everyone else. I'll keep a track of everything on the laptop.'

But Tony's early priority was, at least as far as most of us could ascertain, to run the crap out of everybody.

He brought us to Cratloe Woods, the idea being – it seemed – to build character. I think he wanted to make some kind of statement, maybe something along the lines that Clare would return to old principles on his watch. The principles established by being the hardest-working team in hurling and, accordingly, the fittest.

I hated every minute of it and, if I'm honest, reckoned it was borderline idiotic making me – a goalkeeper in my mid-30s – do the same gruelling runs as the outfield players. Under Dalo I'd always been left to calibrate my own fitness so that I'd be peaking by early April. I'd work like a dog to achieve that, was never in the habit of cutting corners, and I don't think I ever let Clare down while working to those arrangements.

Trouble was, a lot of the work I'd do would go unseen by the others. Dalo was probably ahead of his time, in that he would let the goalkeepers off the running some nights, because we'd be doing different drills specific to our position. I knew full well this pissed some of the others off. I could sense them looking over, complaining, 'Fitzy did fuck all tonight!'

Previously I'd do all the runs and reckon I'd have been as fit as any member of the Clare panel from the mid-'90s to 2000. Even on non-training nights I'd go for a run myself on the beach in Lahinch. But over time you need to adjust to what your body is telling you. I knew I couldn't sustain that.

That said, I was still working relentlessly on my goalkeeping skills. Often monotonous work, dealing with high deliveries, low deliveries, shot-stopping. I had my own personal trainer too, who I'd do a session with before I even got to training. You'd actually be wrecked after a session, but I suspect others wouldn't have seen it like that.

If I'm honest, that pissed me off. There was just this lazy perception that goalkeepers didn't want to work. It was bullshit. But maybe Tony bought in to it.

Because now, under his regime, I was being left to slog with everyone else, enduring the same winter grind, in other words, as a 20-year-old whose game might have been built around running power and stamina.

On some level, I wondered even then if Tony was looking to humiliate me.

Every night I'd come home last in the runs, feeling a mix of embarrassment and anger.

Of our first fifteen sessions under Considine I missed just one. And Tony chose to make a big deal out of that missed session, even though I'd explained to him in detail the importance of a financial meeting that had kept me away. I'd told him about it well in advance too, but all I kept hearing was, 'This isn't good enough ...'

The next night we were training in Ennis, on the Lee's Road Astroturf, when he just seemed to decide to make me a target for the night.

Nothing I brought to that evening seemed good enough for him. Not my energy, not my touch. All I kept hearing was the same bark, over and over: 'Fitzy, for fuck's sake ...'

I thought I was training well and knew my touch was as good as anyone's. But he just kept hammering me, giving me this horrendous abuse in front of everybody. On some level, I started to wonder if he was trying to make a show of me.

Now, I will admit my thinking was influenced by something a reasonably close acquaintance had said a few weeks earlier about meeting Considine in a bookies' office. They'd been chatting away about the year ahead, and he claimed Tony made a declaration to him that he'd 'sort Davy Fitz out!'

While I'd no idea at the time whether it was true or not, it certainly got inside my head. And maybe, on some level, it closed a door for me on ever seeing eye-to-eye again with Tony Considine.

I certainly felt he'd been massively out of order this particular night in Ennis and, though I said nothing there and then, I sought the advice afterwards of certain people who I'd trust.

One of them was one of Tony's own selectors, Ger Ward, a man I'd have had many massive battles with over the years whenever Sixmilebridge were playing Clarecastle.

Ger had great success as the Magpies' manager, but neither of us would have been the shyest of types in the heat of championship. For all that, I regarded Ger as straight and honourable. I knew he wasn't a bullshit merchant.

So we met in Dromoland, and I told him everything I was feeling, adding the context of that reputed conversation from the bookies'.

That meeting felt like a breath of fresh air to me, because here was one of Tony's own management team actually listening to things from my point of view and saying he fully understood why I might be pissed off.

'Fitzy, you need to have it out with Tony, man to man,' Ger advised me.

One of my big regrets about how the whole Clare regime would unravel over the next few months was that Ger Ward almost fell into the category of collateral damage, becoming one of those who chose to resign. I was gutted over that, because Ger was a man with a hell of a lot to offer Clare. But that was his one and only chance at that level, and in the end I know my situation became a factor in him walking away.

I did what Ger suggested, rang Considine, and we agreed to meet an hour before the next training session in Crusheen.

The venue was the kitchen, a cold enough setting yet perfectly appropriate for the exchange about to follow.

Basically, I told Considine I was getting the impression he didn't want me there. That he was constantly on my case without any good reason. That I knew I wasn't the fittest member of the group but I'd been a long time playing inter-county hurling and had a fairly good idea of what was required to get me right for the summer.

I also chose to tell him of that suggested bookies' exchange, something – in fairness – that he completely denied.

'Tony, I'm finding it fair hard to enjoy any of this the way you're constantly having a dig at me,' I told him.

And that's when Considine pretty much told me I was surplus to his requirements. 'Fitzy,' he said, 'if you don't like what I'm doing, there's the door. It's your decision.'

I was devastated. The coldness of his response hit me like a punch in the stomach. Nothing that had gone before counted for anything here. It was as if he was looking through me now as he spoke. *'Your decision'*!

I'd say I almost visibly shuddered there and then in front of him. There was nothing left to be said here. As I turned for the door he said behind me, 'You think about that now, and do what you have to do.'

At that moment he might as well have been handing me a page of A4 on which to write my retirement statement.

I remember my car was parked right at the corner of the dressing-room entrance, and I literally lurched out to it like someone close to physical collapse. Was this really how things were going to end for me as a Clare hurler? After seventeen seasons?

Sitting into the car I remember seeing my son, Colm, around the side, filling the water bottles with Gazzy (Michael Collins), a man who would serve seven different Clare managers before coming to Wexford with me in 2016. No more than ten yards away, the two of them oblivious to what had just happened inside. My head was completely spinning now, so I took two minutes to catch my breath before climbing back out and walking over to them.

Gaz could see immediately that there was something wrong.

'Fuck it, Davy, you look like you've seen a ghost!'

I looked at him, tears stinging my eyes now. 'Gaz, it's all over!' I said.

GAZZY: 'I knew something was wrong before that. As I was heading down the field with water I saw the two of them in the kitchen having a chat, and I just knew from the shape of them it wasn't about sending one another Christmas cards. I didn't want to be eavesdropping, but at one stage I was close to the door.

'They were arguing about the session Fitzy had missed. I could hear Davy saying that he had to make a living and Considine telling him, "Sure I've a living to make too!" They were going at it hammer and tongs, and the last thing I heard Considine say was, "Well, if you can't make up your mind, I'll make it up for you."

'It was a few minutes later that Davy came over, put out his hand and told me he was "out of here." Pat Fitz had arrived at that stage and was standing on my left-hand side, young Colm to the right. I couldn't speak, honestly couldn't open my mouth. I thought this was an argument that would just blow over.

'I go back a long way with the Fitzgeralds, played junior hurling with Davy's uncle, John, in the '50s. At that moment I'd say I went into shock. Pat and I exchanged glances, but I couldn't say anything, so I just turned on my heel and went off down the field with my water.

'And all I could think was, "Is this really happening?"'

Gazzy understood immediately what I meant, and I could see the emotion well up inside of him. But before the conversation could go any further I went walking out into the middle of the field, where Considine was now chatting with one of his selectors, Kieran O'Neill. The exchange proved brutally short.

'Tony, I'll go so.'

'Best of luck, Fitzy!'

I can't honestly explain the physical pain I felt turning away at that moment and walking the breadth of the field again, not another word coming from behind to soften the blow. Just 'Best of luck, Fitzy!'

I got into the car, pulled out the gate towards Ennis, but knew immediately that I was in no fit state to drive. Honestly, I felt as if my head was about to explode. Pulling in to the side of the road, I burst out crying. My whole life had been so wrapped up for so long in hurling for the Bridge and for Clare, I couldn't really process what was just after happening.

One thing to have my Clare career end so suddenly. Another to have it done so coldly.

I rang Sharon first, asking her to see if she could get someone to give her a lift out to Crusheen so that she could drive me home. Then, waiting in the car, I began making other calls. Two of them, I will admit, were to county board officials. My own father, Pat, the county secretary. And the county chairman, Michael McDonagh.

Both said almost the exact same thing to me: 'Let's try to sort this out.'

Were they wrong to interfere? You'll have to make up your own mind there. All I will say is that if Tony felt I was finished as an inter-county goalkeeper, I honestly don't believe there was much evidence to back up his viewpoint.

Bear in mind that I was the All-Star goalkeeper in '05 and, in my opinion at least, hadn't let those standards slip in '06, a season in which I made arguably my greatest ever save from Joe Deane.

A three-man delegation consisting of two county board officials, Michael O'Neill and Bernard Keane, and a Sixmilebridge delegate, John Corbett, went to the management in an effort to sort out the impasse. Considine rejected their intervention.

To be fair, he was entitled to do that. I just felt I was entitled to a hearing he hadn't really granted me.

There would be a lot of behind-the-scenes efforts at diplomacy over the following weeks, and the chairman did, eventually, arrange a meeting aimed at some kind of reconciliation.

Trouble was, people from both sides of the argument were having their say now, the atmosphere curdling into a virtual civil war within the county. And I do remember a quote from Tim Crowe, another of Tony's selectors, in the *Clare Champion* around the time Michael McDonagh was trying to bring both sides back to the table.

Now, Tim was a Bridge man, like myself, but when he said something along the lines that people who can't stand the heat should get out of the kitchen it became pretty plain to me he wouldn't be arguing my case at any coming management meetings.

The comment disappointed and entertained me in equal measure.

My disappointment was obvious. We were Bridge people and neighbours, yet here he seemed to be implying that I wasn't tough enough for whatever challenge playing for Clare now presented.

But in another sense that's what entertained me too. People could have thrown lots of criticism my way during my playing career, but not being able to stand the heat? Honestly, Tim?

Deep down, I suppose I sensed there were other issues at play here, which I'll go into elsewhere. Suffice to say a distance had grown between Tim and me by then which was now, clearly, only widening.

That said, his comment pretty much confirmed to me that there really wasn't any way back now, even though efforts at some kind of reconciliation were ongoing.

Those efforts led to another meeting back in Crusheen in mid-February, me accompanied by the county chairman, Considine accompanied by Kieran O'Neill.

The chairman got out of my car to let Considine into the passenger seat and leave us to it.

And you know something? I suddenly thought there was light at the end of the tunnel. Considine just sounded softer in his tone towards me. He told me I'd just been getting the wrong signals. That nobody in the camp wanted to see the back of me.

'Listen,' I said, 'I still want to hurl for Clare. The last thing I want to do is retire. But, like I said, I just feel under attack all the time …'

'Fitzy, I'm not picking on you at all.'

'Well, that's how it's looked to me, Tony.'

'No way, not a chance, you picked that up wrong …'

'Well, Tony, I still want to play for Clare.'

And that's when Considine offered what I thought was an indication that we were about to resolve things. He told me not to say anything to the newspapers, or anybody in the media. To lie low, in other words, and wait till I heard back from him.

I thought it was over. I thought we'd reached some kind of peace arrangement and that I was back as a member of the Clare panel. Said as much to the chairman when he got back into the car. 'You'd never know …' I smiled.

When I got back home I rang my father. 'Think we might be able to sort this …'

And the following day?

A big article in the *Examiner*, in which Considine was trumpeted as speaking 'for the first time' about why I was gone from the Clare panel. In it he basically said that I had left of my own volition. 'I'd like to emphasise one thing,' his own paper quoted him as saying now. 'Davy Fitzgerald has not been dropped from the Clare panel, he withdrew, opted out, as did several other players. It was entirely his own decision, made for his own reasons, that's something he's going to have to sort out for himself. He walked out of his own accord, he knows the way back and I'll say no more about that.'

In the same article Gerry Quinn was quoted as saying, 'We're not getting involved, it's between the two of them,' as well as 'I think Tony Considine has our interests, Clare's interests, at heart.'

Quinn, incidentally, was confirmed in the piece as Clare's new vice-captain.

It was staggering. Tony had made a complete fool out of me.

My reflex was to cut loose, and that's exactly what I subsequently did in a few newspaper interviews. I regret that now. Because the next few weeks just descended into a tit-for-tat squabble over my predicament when I knew the situation now was utterly irretrievable. The focus should have been on Clare, not me. But there was a lot of upheaval at county board level now, a lot of different parties articulating disquiet over how the whole thing had been handled.

It dragged on for months and, in hindsight, maybe I was partly responsible. If I was asked about it I just wasn't inclined to deliver a 'No comment' response. I found it hard to let go. I was hurting too much. I felt bitter.

Opportunities kept presenting themselves to give my side of the story, and I was only too happy to oblige. Hand on heart, did I manipulate some of the coverage? I probably did.

Looking back, maybe I should have said to the reporters ringing me, 'Listen, forget about it. It's over!' But I didn't, and it all descended into a kind of circus.

By mid-February, Dave Mahedy stepped away as trainer in frustration at what he felt had been continuous efforts by management to undermine his methods. Even that was handled appallingly.

It was claimed that he would be attending a Down game in Portaferry, despite Dave having already resigned. He agreed to a statement suggesting his decision was based on 'family and work commitments,' yet it was subsequently spun by management that he'd only been a short-term appointment to give the team access to UL's facilities.

When journalists enquired about Ger Ward's absence from that Down game, Considine's response was, 'The last I heard from Ger was that he was going away for the weekend.' Ger, by then, had expressed his reservations about the machinations of the Clare management team and had indicated that he was considering his position.

When he agreed to meet Considine in the Old Ground Hotel a week later, Tony reputedly never showed up.

The next Ger heard, apparently, was a call from a local journalist looking for a comment, given that his resignation had been accepted by the management team.

In March, county board delegates received a letter from Considine declaring me to be no longer a member of the Clare panel and requesting 'Could we now get on with playing hurling?'

If only life could have been so simple.

So, that summer became torture for me.

I got signed up by the *Star* to write a column, replacing Ger Loughnane, who'd gone to manage Galway. But, if I'm honest, I hated being on the outside looking in. I'd been to every single championship game Clare played from 1977 to 2007 but honestly couldn't bring myself to go now to the Munster opener against Cork in Thurles.

It was a game that would go down in infamy, the teams becoming involved in a scuffle coming out the tunnel that spilled onto the field. The incident became known as 'Semplegate', a total of eight players provisionally suspended for their involvement in the row.

I watched the game on television, feeling completely empty.

If I'm brutally honest, I was torn in my feelings for Clare that day. The atmosphere around the team just felt utterly toxic, and my father, as county secretary, had to bear the brunt of it.

Earlier in the year a story did the rounds that I was behind a complaint made about UL playing an illegal player in an intermediate game against LIT, whose senior team I managed. Brendan Bugler, the UL secretary at the time, came under pressure for the mistake.

I knew absolutely nothing about the story until word came filtering through that I was being held responsible for Bugs now getting the heat.

I got the impression that the picture of me and my father being presented to the Clare players had become increasingly poisonous. It honestly felt as if there was hatred in the air.

At the end of April, a challenge match against Tipperary was organised in Thurles without anybody telling my father. Think about that. The county team playing a game without the county secretary even knowing.

They didn't even have jerseys, playing instead in shirts borrowed from a Limerick school. Apparently the players travelled to Killaloe by cars unaware of what was even planned until they boarded a bus there. With no county board involvement there was, presumably, no proper insurance cover for the team. They had no team doctor.

Clare's management was pushing Dad away now, treating him like dirt. In Meelick one day Considine caused embarrassment by asking three people, my father, Padraic Quinn, the team doc, and Pat O'Donnell, team sponsor, to leave the dressing-room.

It had to be excruciating for Dad working in those circumstances, but he's one of the most principled people I know. If I'm honest, I can't even imagine what he was going through, walking into that dressing-room, being civil with people he knew were doing their damnedest to undermine him.

We spoke about it often. I remember saying to him one day, 'Listen, no matter how bad you feel, you still have to do your job.' To be honest, I didn't have to say that. Pat Fitzgerald is far too loyal a Clareman to see things any other way.

What was Tony trying to achieve?

Some felt he was looking to re-create the kind of ruthless edge with which Loughnane had transformed Clare's fortunes in the '90s. They've always been very close, and it was obvious they'd be in regular contact now. But I felt Loughnane's style was already outdated by then. Because Ger dogged people in a way that you could no longer dog people.

You could be playing a training match, get busted with a wound that clearly needed stitching, and Ger would just bellow, 'Play on!'

There were times he'd openly belittle people in front of the group, just looking to flick the right switches to get an angry reaction. If I'm honest, he was a master of this tactic. His thing was to make people toughen up. Man up, if you like.

That said, I always felt he could be needlessly ignorant with people too.

Now, I say that, acknowledging that probably nobody could have got out of Clare hurlers what Ger Loughnane got out of us in the '90s. The belief he instilled in us was just incredible. He trained us harder than any team had trained before. He changed our lives.

Could anyone else have done that?

The only other man who comes to mind is Father Harry Bohan, who brought Clare to two National League titles in the '70s. Both men, obviously, had something special about them.

I've always said that I'll never forget the influence Loughnane had on my hurling life. It was immeasurable. I just don't believe that that should mean we all bow and scrape in his presence for ever more. I've always refused to do that. And, rightly or wrongly, I came to the conclusion that that refusal would come against me in '07.

Because, as Tony tried to flex his managerial muscle, it was hard not to believe that he wanted, on some notional level, to become another Loughnane.

When I think about it, the issue with me could have been resolved quite easily. Tony could have brought me back, just left me sitting on the bench all year and told anyone who asked that he wasn't seeing enough in training to justify starting me.

How could anyone argue with that? Tony could, effectively, have declared me over the hill.

Instead he just seemed intent on making a more overt point. One that left the county almost split down the middle.

Just a couple of weeks before the Cork game a 'no confidence' motion against the management team was brought to a county board meeting by the Smith O'Briens Club (Killaloe) but was eventually withdrawn, on the basis of it being so close to championship.

I will admit it disappointed me that only a small handful of Clare players bothered to get in touch with me when this story was still raging. I'd soldiered for years with some of them, yet they seemed indifferent now to what I was going through. That said, I honestly don't know what version of events they were being given and can only presume it wouldn't have been one that looked kindly on me.

I certainly had no personal issues with the starting goalkeeper, Philip Brennan from Tulla. He'd been my number one when I was Clare's under-21 manager, a guy I genuinely had great time for yet someone whose attitude towards me seemed to change profoundly during that time.

Clare were well beaten by Cork that day in Thurles, the defeat bouncing them into a round-robin qualifier group in which they won their games against Antrim, Galway and Laois.

Naturally, there was great fanfare around the Galway fixture, Loughnane returning to Ennis for a championship game against his native county. The story goes that he only named his starting fifteen about five minutes before they left the dressing-room. My suspicion is that Ger simply couldn't envisage Galway being beaten by a Clare team showing very little form.

Whatever his thought processes, Galway never got out of the blocks that day, losing a poor game in the end by two points.

I didn't go. I couldn't. Instead I made sure to be playing golf in Dromoland come throw-in time. Sharon was with me, but if I thought the golf might offer some kind of escape I was gravely mistaken. My head was all over the place. I couldn't concentrate. My sense of displacement was still far too acute for me to pretend everything was fine.

Clare's reward for topping that qualifier group was an All-Ireland quarter-final against Limerick. It was a game they'd be well beaten in, essentially ending Considine's reign as manager.

I didn't see a single second of the action, having plenty to occupy myself with much closer to home in Lahinch.

I'd got my golf handicap down to two that summer (amazing what can be achieved with time on your hands) and finally managed to win my first ever match in the South of Ireland Championship. In fact I managed to win two, the second coming the day of Clare's quarter-final against an Irish international, Cian Curley.

I was like someone possessed, winning with a birdie on eighteen against a man who works today as a professional in America.

That was my release from the ugliness of Clare's hurling summer.

On the very day the sky fell in on our hurlers I had my greatest day on a golf course. To me, it almost felt like karma. Trouble was, I'd invested so much energy and emotion into the win I went out the following day and couldn't hit the ball out of my way against the experienced Tipperary veteran Arthur Pierse.

Looking back, I had emptied myself against Curley. The rhythm was gone completely from my swing, and I remember pulling my drive so badly on the sixth I almost took the head off Arthur's caddy. Needless to say, he won easily.

Less than a month after their defeat by Limerick, Considine would respond to his sacking as Clare manager by likening the Clare GAA scene to Chicago under Al Capone. It was colourful stuff in which he declared that he'd been removed from office by 'a kangaroo court with willing assassins'.

He branded county delegates 'muppets', insisting 'Everyone deserves a trial. Even Saddam Hussein got a trial.'

Looking back, it was a rotten time for all concerned. Such a pity, given how Tony and I had previously soldiered together on some of Clare's greatest days.

5

A LOW BLOW

There's something in my psychological make-up that means I'm hopelessly drawn towards proving people wrong.

It's how I'm wired. Sharon would tell you I often end up in tears watching *The X Factor* if someone seemingly low on self-esteem produces a performance to bring the judges to their feet. I adore that, the triumph of the underdog. It just makes me fill up when I see it happen, because I can't think of anything better in sport or in life than somebody defying the odds.

In a sense, that was the energy that always underpinned my hurling career. A determination to prove people wrong.

It's not particularly that I see something of myself in the underdog. If anything, I have nearly too much belief in my own ability. It's something that rubs certain people up the wrong way too. I recognise that.

But I just love seeing people step outside their comfort zone and achieving. I've never been motivated by medals. In fact I actually have no idea where mine are at home. I think my mother has them, but I'm not entirely sure.

The human story is what drives me on. Medals are the bonus.

So Tony Considine's decision to retire me as a county man filled me with defiant energy in '07. Now I was the underdog and I suppose I wanted to prove I was still the best goalkeeper in Clare.

My form was decent in the club championship, but when we got to a semi-final against Crusheen I knew there'd be needle in the game.

I'd had ongoing verbal run-ins with one of their forwards over the years, and on this day in Cusack Park we were at it again even before the ball was thrown in. To say we didn't like one another would have been an understatement.

He'd been doing the usual, promising to 'get' me. I fully expected that. What I hadn't expected, I suppose, was that he'd deliver on the promise.

I was guarding the town-end goal in the first half when a ball came dropping close to my feet. My two hands were on the top of the hurley when, all of a sudden, he pulled high, hitting my left hand about two feet above the ball.

I knew instantly I was in trouble.

The pain was so excruciating I was actually incapable of speech. It was like an explosion in my body. The referee blew for a free, taking no further action. The clearest red-card offence imaginable, and the only penalty was a free out to the Bridge.

Just as well I couldn't speak!

Looking down at my left hand, I could see part of the fourth finger hanging off. Instinctively, I reached down to try to reconnect it. As I did so I went sprinting off the field, not even waiting for a doctor. I didn't need one to tell me I was headed for hospital now.

I'll never forget going in the tunnel to where the old kitchen used to be and having to wait there 20 minutes for the ambulance. Doc Quinn met me going in, took one look and I could almost see the blood draining from his face.

Others came in, like my father, like Helen, like my old teammate and friend Danny Chaplin, every one of them looking queasy.

DANNY CHAPLIN: 'I was in the stand and went down to see how he was. Everybody thought he just had a broken bone. But Davy was screaming, "They tried to cut off my fucking finger!" He was adamant that he'd been done.

'The top of his finger was hanging down, connected by only the back piece of skin. The finger had nearly been cut clean through. You could see the white of the bone. He was in a bad way. Doc Quinn went away to get some morphine. I'd never seen Davy react the way he reacted to that pain, but he had good reason.

'I got into a fight about it in the stand when I went back up.'

They brought me to Ennis General, gave me two injections on the top of the finger to numb it a little, then announced that I'd have to go to Galway for surgery.

And as long as I live I don't think I'll ever endure a longer journey.

Sharon was in the back of the ambulance with me, and every single pothole on the road seemed to communicate a message to my screaming finger now. The pain was shocking.

In Galway, I honestly couldn't wait for them to give me a general anaesthetic. I just wanted to be asleep now, to be free of it. The surgeon, Dr O'Sullivan, warned me he couldn't guarantee I'd ever get full feeling back in the finger, because surgery would be complicated.

Basically, they had to reattach nerves, and that's never a straightforward process.

Waking up was horrendous, because instantly the pain was with me again. I have this memory of being home a few days after, getting out of bed and slumping to my knees, my good hand holding the broken one. I was literally roaring with the pain.

That lasted for more than a week, my finger bearing no resemblance to what it had been before. There was a big ball positioned at the top of it, basically holding everything together. From that ball, a long pin ran down inside the centre of my finger.

Maybe six weeks after the operation I had to go back in to get the ball removed, and O Sweet Jesus, the agony of it.

The Crusheen lad who put me through all that was never man enough to apologise. No remorse, no phone call – nothing. For all he knew, my hurling career was over, but he hadn't the guts to ring.

Actually, I heard subsequently that he was bragging about it in the pub, doing this John Wayne thing that 'a man's got to do what a man's got to do.'

In fairness to Crusheen club, they were on the phone that evening, making it clear that they could not condone what had been done to me. But to this day the big man has had nothing to say.

Funny, four years later I came back in a one-off game for the Bridge against Crusheen, again in a county semi-final. I was back on the bench for the final and, as we were coming off the field after our warm-up, there he was walking out past me.

And I'll admit I wasn't exactly statesmanlike in what I said to him. You see, I regard his type as the ultimate cowards, and he proved as much now, just walking sheepishly past, eyes glued to his boots.

I've never minded taking a slap on the field when someone's man enough to apologise after. Trust me, I've taken plenty. But, bottom line, you take responsibility for what you've done. If an apology is in order, you deliver one.

One of the worst blows I took hurling for Clare had been from Tipperary's Paul Shelly in the replayed Munster Championship game of '99. I'd played a blinder in the drawn game, and I think Tipp decided they'd try to rattle me.

So, first ball in, Shelly flakes straight down on my hand. Was probably close to breaking it.

There and then, you'd be fit to be tied. But soon as the game was over Shelly made a point of coming across to me and apologising for the belt. I appreciated that. We'd hammered Tipp the same day, so he probably couldn't wait to get out of Cork. But he took the time to do what needed to be done.

While my playing career was hanging by a thread now, I was determined to keep broadening my horizons on the coaching front.

One of the teams I'd got involved with was the Confey senior hurlers in Kildare, a commitment that was supposed to extend to just a single night's training but would extend to a friendship I now treasure. It developed on the back of a call from Galway's Joe Connolly in the spring of '06, asking if I'd help out an old friend of his from UCG, Liam Dowd.

I agreed to take a session but found myself returning to Leixlip maybe ten times that year as they tried to win their first-ever county senior title. On nights I couldn't make it, Bertie Sherlock – a great character and a good Tipp man who Seán Stack had brought in to the Bridge and somebody I always liked having around a dressing-room – would travel on my behalf. Dowd's view was that Confey had the hurlers but simply lacked natural leadership in the dressing-room.

I liked him from our first meeting in the Springfield Hotel, just his commonsense view of looking at things. He saw himself as an organiser, no more. And to get Confey over the line Liam felt he needed the voices of men with the kind of hurling experience he himself simply couldn't draw on.

To that end, he'd involved Limerick's Pat Herbert for a while and managed to get the likes of Eamonn Cregan and Michael Duignan to take individual sessions too.

Confey would get to that year's county final in '06, but a disastrous opening ten minutes blew their chances against Ardclogh in Newbridge. I could see that Liam was absolutely devastated afterwards and agreed to stay involved in '07, meeting up in the Phoenix Park, where they were doing their pre-season running. I did out a full training programme for them, and that would be the year they'd finally reach their Promised Land, beating Coill Dubh in the final. I couldn't have been happier for Dowd that day, because I knew that title meant more to him than if he'd been handed a million quid. I'd also seen enough of the man to know he had far more to offer a hurling set-up than he himself ever realised.

He was just a smart guy, always thinking, always planning.

We used go down to the Springfield for chicken and chips after a Confey training session, and two hours would pass in an eye-blink when we got chatting. I really liked how he saw things that weren't always obvious.

And I just remember thinking, 'I like having this guy around me.'

LIAM DOWD: 'I'd never met Davy Fitz until that first night in the Springfield, and my impression of him up to then was of a bit of a lunatic. You know, this fella banging hurleys off walls. But I was impressed straight away that he wanted to meet us maybe two hours before taking the session, wanted to know about the group he was coming in to train.

'Then, when we got up to the field, he asked me to come around with him as he began laying out cones. The whole way round, he was interrogating me about this Confey team, constantly making eye contact.

'As we were walking back in I remember looking back at the field, and the cones were set up for about a dozen different drills. That was a striking moment for me, because it told me something about his brain-power.

'I remember thinking, "Right, this fella has a bit between his ears!"

'And the intensity of that session, physically and mentally, was incredible. We were blown away by it. So much so, I couldn't help but go to him with bare-faced cheek at the end and say, "Davy, any chance of getting you for another night?"

'Davy wouldn't take a cent, not one euro. Never. And I was uneasy about that when he started coming regularly. I remember saying it to him one evening, "Davy, you can't be doing this for nothing. You can't be out of pocket for diesel and the like. If this keeps up I won't ask you any more, because it just won't feel right."

'And his reply caught me completely off guard.

'He said, "No, I don't want a thing now. But what I will ask is, when I take over a county team I want you in the back-room set-up."

'There was a lot of talk at the time connecting him with the Dublin job, and that's what I assumed he had in mind now. "Jesus," I said, "I'm not sure I'd have anything to contribute."

'And his reply was, "Liam, that's for me to decide."'

I did wonder in '07 if I'd ever hurl again and, basically, set out on a mission that winter to defy the odds.

You see, the Bridge had lost that semi-final by a couple of points, Crusheen then losing the final to Tulla by just one. There was nothing between the best clubs in Clare, I knew that. I'd just had the year from hell, effectively getting dropped from the county squad and now almost losing a finger. I simply couldn't let that be the end of things.

But it took me ages to be able to even bend the finger again, and, despite loads of physio, I found I couldn't wrap it completely around the hurley. There was also the psychological bridge to cross. The very thought of a sliotar hitting the top of the finger almost brought me out in a cold sweat, and, to begin with, it felt really awkward trying to catch balls with my left hand.

I also had unexpected options opening to me now, in terms of management positions. One arrived that November with a call from the Kerry County Board chairman, looking for a meeting. And I met Jerome Conway in the Woodlands in Adare, where, essentially, I was offered the Kerry hurling job.

Nobody has ever known that until now.

But Mike McNamara was the new Clare manager, and though I felt a million miles away from hurling county again, he rang, asking me to call out to his pub.

I wasn't entirely sure what his relationship with Loughnane and Considine was at the time, but I suspect he just felt there had been too much division in Clare hurling and it was now time to start rebuilding fences.

And I was overjoyed when Mike asked me to rejoin the county panel. There were no promises, but we had a great conversation. 'All I'm looking for is the chance,' I told him.

'It's up to you to decide whether or not I take it.'

So I respectfully declined the Kerry offer and decided to give my Clare career one big effort at a final chapter.

Basically, Mike Mac was doing exactly what I believed Considine should have done. In my head I still believed I could get back as Clare number one, but I suspect Mike knew deep down that I just had too much ground to make up now.

I could feel it myself when I went back to county training. After a year out, the intensity almost caught me off guard.

Philip Brennan was especially aggressive in his attitude towards me, and I particularly remember doing a tackling drill one night in which I just felt he was a little over the top. It was as if he was trying to crease me, and, turning to him at one stage, I said, 'Fuck you, Philip, if you want it that bad you can have it …'

At that point I took myself over to the far side of the field and got someone else to do the drill with me, which, in retrospect, was maybe a telltale sign that my time here was almost over.

I could see that Brennan's attitude was 'I'm the number one here, you'd better keep out of my way!'

It bugged me at the time but, looking back, I have absolutely no problem with Philip. He was doing exactly what I would have done in the same circumstances. Marking his territory. Defending his patch.

I knew I needed games now because of the finger, but Mike Mac didn't give me one.

I was a sub through the early League games, and though I thought Philip lacked consistency in his performances, Mike Mac clearly didn't see enough to consider me a threat.

Listen, he didn't have to bring me back to the Clare squad, so I'll always be grateful to him for doing it.

And not everybody was exactly overjoyed at Mike's decision. I could feel that vibe from some in the panel. It was clear after all that had gone on in '07 that their attitude towards me had changed. There was a distance there.

So I was sitting on the line during those early League games, knowing deep down that I had no chance of getting a run. And I just felt I had too many years done to settle for that now. I wasn't bitter, though. Not remotely.

But by mid-March I knew in my heart of hearts that my race was run. And Mike did give me one last opportunity to hurl for Clare. It was for the official opening of our new field in Sixmilebridge, Kilkenny the visitors.

Mike started me that night in front of a big Bridge crowd, and it felt perfect. Playing my last game for Clare on my own club field.

I got a special jersey made for the evening and presented it afterwards to Olive O'Loughlin, a real stalwart of Clare Supporters' Club across the years and one of my most loyal fans. An unbelievable person.

Kilkenny came with most of their heavy-hitters that night, and I did okay against them, restricting them to just two goals. But I think most people knew at the finish that I'd just played my last game for Clare.

I was happy.

I'd hated everything about the year before, and now at least I was leaving on my own terms. Even if Mike Mac never did give me a League start, he'd treated me with respect.

He'd been civil to me from start to finish. I'll never forget that.

6

THE BRIDGE

I've carried many regrets in my life, and one of the biggest brought me to the Oakwood Hotel in Shannon a few years ago for an attempted reconciliation that, sadly, would get nowhere.

It was Father Harry Bohan who asked me to meet Seán Stack, suggesting it was high time that we put our differences behind us. Now, not everyone could sell the idea to me of a sit-down with somebody I was acutely aware probably despised me, but Father Harry is one of the most persuasive men I know.

He's also someone I tend to listen to on sensitive matters, and few fell deeper into that category within Sixmilebridge than the move I took against Stack in December of '04, replacing him as manager of our senior hurling team.

It was a move I deeply regretted in hindsight and one, I believe, for which others have never truly forgiven me.

If only I could get that time back again now I'd take it in an eye-blink. No matter how sincere my motives at the time, I was wrong to challenge Seán's position as Bridge manager. He was only a year into the job, and though there's always an annual review of the manager's position, my view now is that he was entitled to see his two years out.

Maybe it's taken my own experience in management to reach that conclusion, because I'd feel very strongly now that any man trying to put his own stamp on a dressing-room should, at the very least, be given time to do that. We all have different styles, different methods. Nobody's right or wrong.

Trouble is, you think you know it all as a player, but you never do.

A bad county quarter-final hammering by Kilmaley had set the wheels in motion and basically I think my ego obscured my judgement when a few people approached me, enquiring would I consider putting my name in the hat for manager.

What followed pretty much ripped the club apart, most older members absolutely opposed to the idea of cutting the legs from under Stack.

Within the dressing-room there was a definite feeling that we were in a spot of trouble though. The performance against Kilmaley felt like something that had been brewing, given that the few games we'd won leading up to it had all been on a bit of a knife-edge.

There was also a decision to have us do a long run just a couple of weeks before championship, something most of us felt at the time was crazy. On top of that, just the usual gripes. Maybe some players not being played in their best positions, and little outbursts of off-field indiscipline that we believed were being needlessly tolerated.

I doubt there's a GAA dressing-room in Ireland that doesn't resound to the very same noises.

And whether we considered the set-up to be good, bad or indifferent should really have been immaterial. We had no business doing what we did. I accept that 100 per cent now.

Anyway, Seán and his selectors, Martin Corry and Corey Downes, found themselves under aggressive challenge at the AGM this night, and as long as I live I'll never forget the expression on his face when a secret ballot vote confirmed me as the Bridge's new manager.

Seán got up, announced he wanted nothing more to do with the club, saying the decision had left him feeling 'betrayed'.

In one sense he'd been here before, given Ger Loughnane's change of heart about him as a future Clare manager in '99, effectively sacking Seán as a selector when he'd already intimated that he saw him, long-term, as his own successor.

I remember thinking at the time that what Loughnane did to him just wasn't right. Then I went and did pretty much the same.

Anyway, years later Father Harry proposed this reconciliation in the Oakwood, and I don't think I ever approached a meeting with less enthusiasm. Bottom line, Father Harry thought it was the right thing to do. I consider him one of my closest friends, but he's a man with massive regard for Seán Stack too.

And he just didn't like the idea of us being sworn enemies for life.

FATHER HARRY BOHAN : 'I'd have been very close to both of them long before I went to Sixmilebridge as parish priest. Stack was on my team in the '70s, and then I was a selector to Anthony Daly when Davy was still Clare goalkeeper.

'I saw them both as stand-out men in the world of hurling, and here, in this community, were these two great men not getting on.

'Seán Stack was very, very hurt. He felt betrayed. These two men were in a complete stand-off, and I just felt something needed to be done. So I went to both of them. Davy agreed quickly, but Seán was very reluctant for a while.'

So I walked into the hotel, found Seán sitting alone in a relatively private area to the right of reception, and the expression on his face told me instantly that his view of what happened in '04 hadn't softened across the years.

I remember thinking, 'This is not going to be good ...'

And it wasn't.

Basically, I tried to initiate a conversation by saying how I regretted what had happened and agreed with Father Harry's view that we should have this meeting and talk things over.

But Stack was completely blunt with me. Basically told me that my actions hadn't been good enough and – well, he'd never forgive me.

I repeated that I regretted those actions.

'Regretting it isn't good enough,' he said.

I kept trying to build some kind of bridge, kept repeating my sense of remorse, the fact that if I had that time back again I'd have handled things completely differently. But I was talking to a stone wall.

The meeting might have lasted fifteen minutes, but there wasn't an ounce of give from him. And eventually I realised I was now only talking for the sake of it. I'd given this man reason to hate my guts, and no matter what I said now that reason was always going to stand.

So there was no handshake, no reconciliation. I remember walking back out the door thinking, 'Father Harry, you're one of the people I'd trust with my life, but you got this one badly wrong!'

FATHER HARRY BOHAN: 'I was very disappointed. I know the GAA reeks with jealousies and bad feeling, but that's one that runs very deep. I still think Davy would prefer to have it resolved, but Seán wouldn't be as keen.'

Ironically, almost the exact same thing happened me a year later when I had a run-in with four of our best players over drinking.

It's a well-documented story that I've spoken about before, basically the players (including our captain) going on the beer despite my request not to after a Clarecastle defeat. We were playing a now crucial game against St Joseph's Doora-Barefield one week later and I needed everyone fully committed.

I felt I'd been getting a phenomenal commitment all year, given we had to train in LIT, because they were doing a job on the field in the Bridge. But the four didn't turn up to training the following night (they were still drinking), so we made the decision not to start them against Joseph's, a game we would lose 0-9 to 1-11.

I did bring all four on at half-time, a decision, in hindsight, that completely undermined whatever principle I'd been trying to communicate. To some extent, I lost my nerve.

There was still a lot of heat within the club over what we'd done to Stack, and I think some people were looking for any opportunity to put the boot into me. Had we beaten Joseph's, some of that heat would have receded. But now it was getting turned up higher.

Again people were taking sides, and, in fairness, the four lads got absolutely hammered within the club for making what I now regard as a small mistake. All four are good lads who I'd say regret the whole thing to this day. My regret is that I brought them on.

Because in doing so I lost all semblance of moral authority.

Not long after the Joseph's defeat I took a phone call warning me that if I didn't change my selectors, Syl O'Connor and Flann McInerney, chances were I wouldn't get a second year as manager. This now was a red rag to a bull for me. Syl and Flann were top-class people, fundamentally honest. And they'd shown a lot of gumption by agreeing to be my selectors in the first place, at a time when it would have been seen almost as taking sides against Seán Stack.

They never wanted to do that. But they did want to help the Bridge at a time the club badly needed help. Now I was being advised to toss them overboard.

That couldn't happen, and it didn't.

Yet in a sense I knew now too that I was a dead man walking in my second year. I don't think I was ever getting 100 per cent commitment, and half way through the season I remember thinking that I just wanted to make sure I could walk away from the job on my own terms. Something, in hindsight, Seán Stack should have been entitled to do too.

Again we got as far as the county quarter-final, losing to Shannon this time, after which I stepped down.

I hate the distance that's grown between me and different people who'd once have been huge figures in my life. Like, I played my first senior game for the Bridge in that year of '89 as an eighteen-year-old. I'd have started that year as number three choice goalkeeper, behind Paddy Collins and Brendan Flynn.

Paddy was the starting number one for Clare at the time and Brendan the starting keeper for the county under-21s. Then Paddy went off to Australia, and in Brendan's first senior championship game he tore his cruciate.

So I went from three to one almost overnight, and Tim Crowe would have been one of those investing a hell of a lot of trust in me.

My first game was against Tulla, and I remember they had Gerry Corry on stand-by for the second, against Ruan, just in case I didn't cut the mustard.

But I played well, let in no goal, and wouldn't miss a single championship game for the next twenty years.

If you asked me what was the happiest period of my hurling life I'd say it was playing for the Bridge seniors between '89 and '96. Playing with the likes of Gerry McInerney, one of Clare's best ever forwards and a man I idolised.

Playing behind men like Jamesie Keogh, John O'Connell and Kieran O'Shea, knowing that if anybody laid a finger on me they'd have flattened them. With the likes of the Chaplins, John, Danny, Christy and David. With Flan Quilligan, Pat Morey, Noel

Early. With John Lynch, my next-door neighbour when I lived in Thomond Terrace.

John captained the Clare minors in '81, and I'd have had him haunted any time he was out on the road pucking a ball. I'd be out with my hurl too, just hungry to have that connection with him. I could not overstate the influence he had on my career and he's someone who remains a great friend to this day.

These men literally took care of me. Often in those early days as a senior hurler with the Bridge I'd be inclined to actually sit in awe of them in the dressing-room. I almost couldn't believe I was hurling with these men, that I had their belief, their trust as goalkeeper.

DANNY CHAPLIN: 'The boys would take awful exception to Davy being targeted. They loved him. He was very vocal, but brave as a lion too.'

I look back on that now as such a simple time. Far simpler than my life seems to have become today.

I wasn't Davy Fitzgerald the Clare goalkeeper. I wasn't an inter-county manager with a national profile. I was simply Pat's son from Thomond Terrace. One of the lads. It felt so easy to play in that team, because everybody had my back. They were great people.

I'd still like to regard them all as friends, but there's no denying the dynamic between some of us has changed across the years. Obviously, the same thing has happened with some of my old Clare teammates too.

Why?

Maybe some of it is my own fault, in that I haven't actively tried to keep in touch. That's not deliberate, but I just seem constantly on the go these days. Like, I've pretty much been an inter-county manager non-stop since '08, and I always seem to be foot-to-the-floor, trying to get things done.

It means that whenever I get home I just like to close the gates behind me and savour the peace and privacy of my own space. On top of that I don't drink, so I don't frequent any local pubs.

And, on some level too, maybe I've fallen into the trap of trying to avoid meeting people locally.

It's nothing personal. I try to keep myself grounded by not socialising too much. I just feel I'm in the public eye enough – too much, maybe. And the moment I drive through those gates I feel different, calmer. When you're managing forty people, with maybe another twenty back-room staff, it feels as if the whole world is coming at you with different opinions. That's not easy.

Like, I honestly believe that, almost without thinking, a template I use for the type of person I like around me in a dressing-room is a man called Noel Murphy, who managed me in the Bridge all the way from under-15s up. He would have been in with me then when I managed the senior team too, one of the straightest people you could meet but someone who would never tell you what you wanted to hear.

I can honestly say that I loved that man. He passed away a few years ago, and to this day I miss seeing him around.

Keeping myself to myself around the Bridge now is something that's kind of crept up on me over the years. And the house is virtually in the parish of O'Callaghan's Mills, so I'm a long way out of the village. I suppose it's easy enough to become a bit of a recluse.

But since stepping down as Clare manager in 2016 I've gone down to the Greyhound Bar a lot more. I'd never have felt comfortable doing that while in charge of the county team, because I didn't really want to walk into that kind of blizzard of opinions about Clare hurling.

Father Harry sometimes scolded me about that. 'Jesus, Davy, there's so many people in the Bridge would love to see you …'

The pub, owned by Mike and Irene Gleeson, is run now by their son, Jack, and in 2018 I started going down for Monday-night card games with a few friends. I basically grew up maybe 30 yards down the street from it, and I feel very comfortable when I go in there to meet the likes of 'Kegs', Kevin Corry, Siobhan O'Gorman, Deirdre Gleeson, Jack Gleeson, Gazzy, Paddy Collins, Daragh Keogh, 'The Messer' Johnny Murphy, Deirdre Chaplin and Dessie, Phil and Ashling.

Nine times out of ten I'll end up talking to a rake of people, and I've actually come to love going in there. I'm proud to be one of theirs.

7

A NEW ALLEGIANCE

The call from Waterford arrived just as I was getting used to
the idea of a summer spent in the pundit's chair.

It came the Saturday after Justin McCarthy's departure,
the county chairman, Pat Flynn, looking to set up a meeting.
They'd been badly beaten the previous weekend by a Clare team
all but running riot on a day forever condensed into that single
image of Dan Shanahan resisting Justin's offer of a handshake as
he was called ashore.

I feigned a calm response as Flynn spoke, but my stomach was
already doing gymnastics.

I wanted the job. Waterford had looked good enough to win
the All-Ireland in '07, only to eventually run out of stamina after
being taken to an All-Ireland quarter-final replay by Cork. In my
view, their subsequent defeat to Limerick was down to fatigue
alone. They were better than Limerick. Streets better.

Pat, naturally, wanted our discussion kept private, as the names
of different candidates to replace Justin were now splashing
around media circles. Towards the end of the week my name had
crept into the speculation too. And now I had to tell him that I
was booked to make my *Sunday Game* debut the following day
in Dublin.

He knew, and I knew. It was almost inevitable that I'd be asked.

There was one other slightly complicating factor that I needed
to address as a matter of urgency. I'd been training Éire Óg,

Nenagh, for a couple of months and, if I'm honest, didn't believe I'd been getting the traction I needed. Just felt that some within the club weren't buying in to my way of doing things.

Nenagh had talent, but they'd won their only county title in '95, and I just got the impression that certain influential people there didn't quite understand the intensity now required to be competitive at senior level in a county like Tipperary.

My way was to drive the players maybe harder than some were comfortable with, and, soon enough, I could sense different lads pulling against me.

To this day I'm convinced we could have won a county title if they bought in to what I wanted to do. But I'd probably have needed a couple of years and it became clear to me I'd never get that. Just too many outside voices began to infect the dressing-room dynamic and, if I'm honest, I'd probably started considering an exit strategy even before Waterford came calling.

My decision to leave would eventually go down like a lead balloon, but I think all of us recognised that this just wasn't a happy marriage.

Waterford's interest in me, I imagine, came off the back of my management of LIT's two Fitzgibbon Cup victories in the previous three years, given that the college had never previously even made a final.

And on my way to Dublin for *The Sunday Game* now I took a surprise call from Paul Flynn. He'd clearly got wind that I was interested in taking over and was ringing, essentially, encouraging me to go for the job.

That was surreal. There'd never been much love lost between us, but then, in all honesty, I didn't exactly have the warmest of histories with any of Waterford's key men, like Flynn, Ken McGrath, Tony Browne, Big Dan, John Mullane or Eoin Kelly. I'd had heaps of run-ins with Paul especially, most notably in a Munster Club Championship game between Sixmilebridge and Ballygunner, when I gave him woeful grief after stopping a penalty and a 21-yard free from him.

My style was always to go to war in those games, no doubt giving the opposition every reason not to like me.

But that Waterford dressing-room had especially big characters and I'm sure, for some of them, the idea of me becoming their new manager wouldn't have been easy to digest. That's why I was so taken aback by Paul's call. In all my years competing against him, I don't think we'd ever exchanged a single, civil word.

Then again, I suppose that was always the setting I felt most comfortable at. Going to war. I wasn't a good player when relaxed. I'd be at my best only when on edge. I mean, I considered Flynn a genius, a hurler with unbelievable hands. But it had never been in my interests to engage with him on anything but a hostile level.

That's not especially grown-up type of behaviour, I fully recognise that.

But, if I'm honest, I never wanted to like an opponent. I always worried it would soften me. The flip side of that was I never particularly cared what they thought of me in return. Hatred is an almost comforting setting in these battles. Not real hatred, just the illusion of it. The lie that your opponent hasn't a redeeming fibre in their body.

In RTÉ there was no mention of the Waterford job before we went on air.

The Sunday Game was being presented at the time by Pat Spillane and, looking back, I suspect he was determined to catch me off guard while the red light was on in the studio. I could be wrong, but I got the feeling Pat might have seen his professional future in television at the time and reckoned it would do him no harm if he managed to have me squirming in front of the nation.

And that probably made for slightly awkward television.

Because I basically blanked the question when he asked it. 'I've nothing to say about that,' I told him, smiling. Then I repeated it. Over and over until the penny dropped for Pat that he might as well have been trying to interact with an answering-machine here.

I was determined not to say anything that might jeopardise my chances and was thrilled the following day when another call from the county chairman confirmed their interest in giving me the job. I agreed to meet him in Waterford and, before I knew it, he became my personal chauffeur for that week as the country's GAA writers were invited to the city for an introduction to Justin McCarthy's successor.

There'd been no agonising over the decision on my behalf, even though some close friends advised me strongly not to touch the job with a barge-pole. They reckoned I'd be walking into a minefield, a dressing-room of strong characters who – in some cases – had now gone over the hill.

Justin, they reckoned, had got just about everything there was to get out of the group, and the next man would be on a hiding to nothing.

Naturally, I spoke to my father too and he was wary of me taking over a dressing-room occupied by so many big characters. 'It's a big step, David,' he warned, 'you need to be sure it's the right one for you.'

He reckoned the optics of what those players had done now put them under extraordinary pressure, though I doubted he had much sympathy for the man they'd tossed overboard.

Personally, I'd always found Justin an aloof sort, inclined to advertise his own achievements a little too strongly. And I'd once witnessed that side of his personality at first hand. That said, nobody could deny he'd done a super job with Waterford, winning three Munster titles in seven seasons.

Trouble was, that perceived arrogance made him struggle in situations that called out for a little humility. And at a time when the Waterford players were desperate to take that next step, he seemed dismissive of their desire to work harder physically.

I wanted to bridge that gap between players and management. But I also wanted to make it crystal clear that I wasn't taking the job to earn new friends.

I could have thrown up on the footpath, turning in to my first meeting with the players in Walsh Park.

Maybe that's not something I should admit now, but I do have this vivid memory of walking in by a kit-van I would always previously have associated with enemy lines and realising that this was my side of the fence now. Slipping in the gate, I remember thinking, 'I'm only a few years older than some of these lads, and all they know me as is a mouthy opponent. Now I want them to listen to me as manager.

'I've got to carry myself right here!'

To be honest, I wanted to keep talk to a minimum and just get into the work. But I knew too that I had to communicate a strong message to them that evening and was confident in my ability to do that. Bottom line, everybody in the dressing-room now had one thing in common. We were all massively hungry to succeed.

I suppose more than anything I wanted to change the energy around them that evening. Justin would be a very technical trainer, so my high-tempo style was going to be a shock to the system. I told them that. 'If you're looking for higher intensity,' I said, 'that's exactly what you're going to get!'

I also told them that, from that night on, their gear would be laid out for them in the dressing-room before training. I went into my style of working, and I think some of them were a little taken aback by the amount of detail I included.

My opening line had been an effort to cut the ice. 'Trust me, lads, I'm as shocked as ye are that I'm standing here tonight.'

Then I told them that I was one of them now and would do everything in my power to deliver the success that they craved.

I remember making eye contact with Ken McGrath and I could see the surprise in his expression. Likewise Browne, Mullane and 'Brick' Walsh. They didn't know what to make of me there and then, and there was only one way that I could change that.

So, having spoken for maybe 20 minutes, I just said to the room, 'Right, let's go train!'

No player had volunteered an opinion in that time, and this didn't surprise me. They were in crisis mode here, having got rid of a man hugely revered within Waterford hurling circles. Basically, they were at the point of no return. The optics of what they'd done had been shocking from the outside, defined for many by Dan's refusal to shake Justin's hand in Limerick.

Given that everything was happening so quickly, the county board appointed Peter Queally and Maurice Geary as my selectors. I was more than happy with that. Both are good men, and I just reckoned immediately that – like me – they felt there was nothing for any of us to lose in this. That if Waterford just threw the kitchen sink at the coming weeks, anything was possible.

They were picked on the basis of being in charge of that year's two county finalists in Waterford, Maurice with Ballyduff and Peter with Passage.

I also made a point of bringing in a set of people to the back room who I knew I could trust implicitly, one of whom now was Liam Dowd. To begin with, my message to Liam was simple. I asked him to watch the players while I spoke, assess the individual body language.

Beyond that, I'd want him to be an extra eye in the stand during games, someone miked up for instant chat who'd dip down to the dressing-room then at half-time just to offer a few observations.

But what I needed, first up, was something simpler.

In nearly every dressing-room you'll find a few lads who want to be the smart alecs. Who'll say things under their breath while the manager is talking. Who'll basically pull the piss. Usually they'll be fellas who know they're not going to be in the starting fifteen and who feel they've little enough chance of having involvement off the bench.

Their poison can infect everything if you don't identify it quickly and stamp it out. So that was my message to Liam going into Walsh Park that evening.

'Just watch them while I'm talking, tell me if anyone's acting the bollocks.'

But Liam had a bluntness about him too that I felt wouldn't do me any harm to encounter every now and then. If he thought you were wrong about something, he wasn't afraid to give it to you between the eyes.

A couple of years later there'd be a National League game against Cork in which he just felt I didn't come across well in the dressing-room. He reckoned I had missed a few things and, maybe, been over the top on a few others. 'I thought you could have been better on that …' he said.

Of course, to begin with, I was furious. He'd been too blunt for my liking, and I suppose I did what a wounded animal will tend to do. I went with my natural instinct and attacked him. 'Fuck you …' sort of bullshit.

But later on that evening I got to thinking about what he said. And just about every hole he'd picked in me had been 100 per cent valid. So I rang him and apologised. 'You know what? I think you were absolutely right!'

It's for that kind of stuff I've come to value his opinion so much. He'll never just tell me what he thinks I want to hear. Sometimes what he says might even hurt me to the core. But that bluntness is something I feel I need.

And with Waterford now I needed it from the off.

That first training session set the template for how I intended to work. It was high tempo from first minute to last, and I think people generally were taken aback by how much we got through.

Immediately I sensed positivity from the group. They were anything but the mutinous bunch their removal of Justin might have implied. These guys were actually desperate for self-improvement. They never wanted to hurt their former manager but found themselves in a corner where it seemed they had no choice.

I think every dressing-room becomes tired over time if the dominant voice is unchanging. Kilkenny and Tyrone are maybe the exceptions to that rule, but then again you're not talking ordinary people when it comes to Brian Cody and Mickey Harte.

Waterford had been right up there under Justin, but his way of doing things didn't seem to change any with each new year. That was the players' argument. These guys wanted to win so badly they recognised the trap of doing the same thing over and over again while expecting different results.

From that first night in Walsh Park I could see the sincerity in men like Ken, Clinton Hennessy, Eoin Murphy, Brick and Tony Browne. These guys just wanted to work as hard as their bodies allowed.

I made it clear that first evening that I wouldn't entertain any derogatory talk about Justin McCarthy. That was the least he was entitled to. He'd done so much for these players, I wouldn't have been able to respect any of them picking holes in his time as manager.

That said, I was taken aback by the poor levels of fitness. The very concerns that had triggered their move for change had, in my opinion, been validated by what I now found.

But this was a problem too.

It was now June, remember, so I'd missed five months of training with these fellas. In my opinion they were way off where they needed to be. The flip side of that is that these guys were hurting. They'd come out so badly from how Justin's departure had been portrayed they were now willing to do anything it took to produce performances that might justify what they'd done.

The first thing I had to do was lift the pace of their training higher. After that it was up to me to channel the hurt into action. If I succeeded in doing that – well, who was to say where it might take us?

But I also had more immediate structural priorities.

Waterford had struggled for some time in the full-back position, and I decided to try a left-field solution, one that I knew wouldn't exactly be appreciated by supporters, who liked nothing better than to see Ken McGrath in full flow.

Ken was a magnificent hurler, a warrior, one of the best I'd ever seen. Over the years Waterford had used him as a prolific half-forward and centre-back. He had huge physical presence, was strong in the air and well capable of taking a score from anything inside 80 yards.

I knew everybody loved Ken in the number six jersey especially, but my view was there could be no point in having your best hurler at six if you're leaking goals in behind him.

'Look, Ken, naturally enough number three wouldn't be the first position I'd choose to play you in,' I said to him, outlining my idea. 'But we're leaking too much in behind.'

To be fair, he was open to it. He was always one of those natural hurlers who played off the cuff, but I just felt that if we didn't stop conceding goals, Waterford wouldn't be going much further.

But there was a second reason for the experiment.

I just wasn't happy with Ken's distribution from number six. That off-the-cuff quality meant that Ken was just inclined to leather the ball up-field when in possession, and I was adamant that we'd have to be smarter with possession against better teams. All well and good putting the onus on your forwards to win the ball if you had access to big, self-sufficient men, like Brian Cody could call on in Kilkenny. But if you didn't?

The game was changing. If you look at Kilkenny from 2006 to 2010, they were hugely aggressive front-to-back. It was really difficult to win 50/50 ball against them so, to have a chance, I always felt you had to deliver ball that favoured your forwards rather than going one-to-one with a defender who probably loved the sight of a high delivery coming in.

So I preferred the idea of Brick at six, because he seldom wasted possession. His way was always to lift the head and deliver short, maybe 20-yard deliveries to someone in a better position.

Deep down, I knew the Waterford supporters mightn't warm to this, that they'd probably prefer a freestyle approach, that notion of hurling with abandon almost. But the big-name players in the group weren't the athletes they'd been in their prime any more. In my view, we had to tailor a game plan designed to be smarter and less cavalier.

And I didn't need an astrologer to tell me that not everyone would be happy.

The group buy-in was immediate, and we had the good fortune then of a relatively gentle re-introduction to championship hurling.

We beat Antrim in a non-event at Walsh Park, winning by 21 points. After that it was Offaly in Thurles and we got home by a couple of goals. Then back to Semple Stadium again and an All-Ireland quarter-final against Wexford.

This was different. It was a day the players had to tap into some of that hurt and squeeze their way past a team that, on the day, was probably every bit as good as us. Wexford actually had a chance to win at the very end, Damien Fitzhenry blazing a penalty over Clinton Hennessy's crossbar.

It meant that we got home by a single point, and there was a real outpouring of emotion in the dressing-room after, the players massively relieved that, after everything they'd been through, Waterford were back in an All-Ireland semi-final.

We were in the semi-final against Tipperary and the panel was humming with positive vibes in just about every case, bar one. I knew that Paul Flynn wasn't happy, you see.

I hadn't been starting him for the simple reason that he wasn't working hard enough. That wasn't just my opinion. Some of the other players were genuinely pissed off with his lack of application in training. I knew that because they said it to me.

Now this was just weeks after the same man had been on the phone encouraging me to come to Waterford. I'd been told before we even started that he wasn't exactly the most enthusiastic trainer in the group. That's often the case with highly skilful players. They reason that their ability will make up the balance, but I've never bought in to that.

My thing has always been, I don't care whether or not you're a magician with the ball, you have to do the training. And Paul, quite simply, wasn't.

It's true he was carrying a bit of an injury at the time, but some of the players were saying that, injured or not, hard training simply wasn't Paul Flynn's thing. They told me how sometimes he'd just stand on the side of the field when they were doing the hardest stuff and, historically, tended to be let away with that.

I couldn't countenance that happening on my watch. My philosophy has always been that everybody must work hard for the unit to stay strong. One player I got some stick for starting ahead of Flynn was Ken McGrath's younger brother, Eoin.

But I made no apologies for it, because this guy would put his body on the line every single day he togged out, be it in training or a game. I'd hear all the grumbles that he wasn't skilful enough, didn't score enough. But, by God, the man gave us everything he had, and that's an attitude I've always cherished in the dressing-room.

I also had a big decision to make with Ken at this stage.

He'd shown massive character in the three games played at full-back, not conceding a single score to some of the most awkward full-forwards around, like Joe Bergin and Stephen Banville. But I could see from his body language that he was frustrated too. He felt massively restricted in the number three shirt, and that was increasingly plain for everyone to see.

Ken was also in big trouble with a knee injury, something that required a lot of treatment through the season. It wasn't his style to complain about it though. All Ken ever wanted to do was get out on the field and hurl, even if – sometimes – his body wasn't entirely ready for that.

Unfortunately, that defiance couldn't conceal the physical cracks beginning to appear now.

Before the semi-final against Tipp I took the squad away for a training camp in Clare, staying in two five-star venues, Doonbeg and Dromoland Castle. The group was bonding really well, and in Dromoland I remember taking them for a walk around the grounds in pitch darkness one night. I was trying to work a message into their heads that the key to the journey now was going to be belief.

'Lads, let's go for this …' I said. I wanted them to understand the scale of the opportunity now before them. And I was trying to read their readiness to take that opportunity on.

We had a practice match amongst ourselves in Ennis that weekend, and Ken pretty much got destroyed at number three by Eoin Kelly. In fairness, he'd been more or less just doing us a favour by playing there, but deep down I could see he wanted out.

My view was that, psychologically, he'd kind of thrown in the towel, and the way Kelly went to town on him really just emphasised that. In my head I'd already made the decision to abort the experiment anyway. It was obvious to everybody that Ken wasn't happy.

And an unhappy Ken McGrath was something I knew I couldn't afford from here on in.

There was a lot of hype following Tipp into that semi-final after their first Munster title win since their All-Ireland year of '01.

It was Liam Sheedy's inaugural year with them, and they were seen as a coming force now. There was also, naturally, a good deal of scepticism about Waterford's mental capacity to take the next step.

After all, they hadn't been in an All-Ireland final since '63 and, for all the provincial success achieved under Justin, they kept hitting a glass ceiling when it came to semi-finals.

Waterford had actually lost five in the previous ten years, and, coming up now against a Tipp team still unbeaten for the season, we could have no issue with the bookies making us outsiders. For me the key was how the players dealt with the weight of history now. Could they carry it?

I also wanted to make things as personal as possible.

One of my contacts got word to me that Tipp had already booked a Dublin hotel for the All-Ireland final weekend. Now, if I'm honest, this was no more than smart planning on behalf of their county board. No big deal if you lose a small deposit just by covering all your bases.

But this was grist to the mill for me now in painting a picture of Tipp arrogance, of them taking this Waterford team for granted. I was just pulling all the emotional threads I felt I needed to pull to get the players to the right intensity.

And I could honestly see them bristle the moment I told them about that hotel booking.

With Ken restored to six, we caught fire immediately from the start of that semi-final and were 0-6 to 0-0 up before Tipp realised what had hit them. It was exhilarating to see the work rate of everyone and the confidence flooding through the team. But I knew too that the hardest questions were to come. Sure enough, Tipp got back into things, and when we got the team back into the dressing-room at half-time I just felt I had to ask them an obvious question.

'Lads, straight up, do ye actually fucking believe ye will win this, or are ye only hoping?' I said. 'Because, trust me, there's a shower down the corridor that believes. And they don't fucking rate ye!'

'This is there for ye, but only if ye have a right go for it!'

Hand on heart, I wasn't 100 per cent sure what I was dealing with here. Waterford had such a history of coming up short at this stage, I couldn't be certain they believed that that was about to change. And I had to challenge them on it. I was like a man possessed in that dressing-room, almost goading them with the idea that hurling people in general would see only one winner here.

We needed a lot of small things to go right for us that day, and they did in the end. But that was down to more than luck. I firmly believe that a team with the right work ethic makes its own luck. And we made ours that day against Tipp.

I also believe Tipp took us a little for granted. Nothing reflected in their hotel booking, just the suspicion that they could see little in our form up to that point – not unreasonably – to make them fear us.

One key move I had to make was switching Brick to the forty to counteract the growing influence of their centre-back, Conor O'Mahony. He did it brilliantly, but that's a measure of Brick Walsh, in my opinion.

You could, quite literally, give him any role on a hurling field and he'll fulfil it without fuss. To this day I regard him as one of the most underrated hurlers in the country.

We did have to live on our nerves near the end, as you would expect, a last-minute line 'cut' from Eamonn Corcoran finding its way to our net, only for the goal to be overruled for a 'square' infringement.

But then the final whistle and an outpouring of emotion, the likes of which I'd never previously encountered as a manager.

Put simply, the whole of Waterford went nuts. Players, supporters, everybody celebrated as if they'd actually won the Liam MacCarthy Cup. It was lovely to see and, being honest, my first instinct was not to interfere, to let them all embrace the moment.

Everybody saw the tears on the field at the end, Eoin Kelly's especially. It was magical.

And I have a vivid memory of the train home, Bertie Sherlock doing master of ceremonies, the beer flowing, songs being sung, the players doing a conga line down the carriage. I watched it all from a little distance. Just sitting quietly at the end of the carriage, scribbling a few notes, preparing myself for the biggest challenge of my managerial life.

Watching the fun, I'll admit I could barely wipe the smile from my face.

These lads' reputations were on the floor when they got rid of Justin. Now, less than three months later, they had got Waterford to a first senior All-Ireland final in 45 years. To me, they deserved their celebrations.

When we got in to Waterford the station was absolutely thronged, and I was carried off the platform shoulder-high. I was mortified. And on some level, there and then, maybe I began to recognise the danger building in the hysteria.

It's been pretty much written into history that I sent Waterford out to rough up Kilkenny in the final. That I told them to bully the one team in hurling anybody with an ounce of sense knew full well couldn't be bullied.

Some of the players have said as much in their books. Dan said it. Ken said it. The picture they painted was one of me telling the likes of Eoin Murphy and Séamus Prendergast to hurl in a way that simply wasn't in their natural make-up.

The truth?

I suspect the hammering that came our way would ultimately colour everybody's recall of the build-up. But I also have to take responsibility for maybe not communicating my message with better clarity.

The truth is, I said very little before the Kilkenny game that was profoundly different from what I said before the defeat of Tipp. In fact I said very little that would have been streets removed from what I'd say before most games.

My message to Eoin and Séamus and one or two others would have been that I wanted them to be extremely physical with their markers. Now, that didn't mean I wanted Eoin to start wearing the hurley off Eddie Brennan. That would have been suicidal, given the probability of a red card.

But I did want him in Eddie's face for every last second. Above all, I wanted the players to avoid the danger of showing Kilkenny too much respect. I'd seen other teams come up against Brian Cody's men and stop just short of curtseying in front of them.

My fear was that Waterford would get swallowed up by the sense of occasion and, maybe unwittingly, stand off a team now going for three-in-a-row.

To me, Kilkenny had maybe three forwards that could be put off their game if marked with ferocious intensity. Probably a couple of defenders too. But do you honestly think I was sending out Prendergast to bully Tommy Walsh?

My message to Séamus was simply 'Front up here, don't you be bullied by that man!'

Of all the Kilkenny players, I think I had more respect for Walsh than anyone. He was an absolute terrier, but off the field I always found him hugely likeable and humble. Tommy would have been the last fella I'd be choosing to go to war with, because you had zero chance of bullying him. But I did feel that any player going in on Tommy Walsh would have to – as a minimum – stand up for themselves, which is essentially what I was trying to communicate to Séamus Prendergast.

That would have been the gist of my message in general. Stand up to these fellas, don't let them dictate to you physically. Never mind the colour of their jerseys. Take history out of this. You are every bit as much entitled to be on that field as they are.

Maybe I didn't get that message across as clearly as I had intended.

Did I target a few Kilkenny men? Trust me, every manager in the game will target members of the opposition. Do you think Cody wasn't going after one or two of ours? To me it's become a little too convenient to attribute what happened Waterford that day to the perception of a manager looking to get his players to do things out of character.

I'd have a different take on things.

Did I get stuff wrong? Absolutely. You have to remember I was barely three months into my first stint as an inter-county manager. I had no experience of leading a county into the biggest game of the year, let alone one contesting its first All-Ireland final in 45 summers.

It's fair to say that our build-up was swamped in general euphoria. Everybody seemed swept away on the emotion of it all, and I had this nagging thought throughout that, despite the win over Tipp, I still wasn't entirely sure as to how deep this team could dig in terms of character.

They didn't have the in-depth pre-season work done that I would have liked and, accordingly, I didn't have the level of information that I needed.

That said, I thought we had all the bases covered. I took the advice of county board people I trusted, trying to strike the balance of getting our preparation right without erecting a wall between the players and supporters. I just felt it was important to keep that connection now. To make sure that everybody felt they were part of this story.

Waterford people had been crying out for this, and I've always been a strong believer in players being approachable, to young kids particularly.

To that end, we had two supporters' nights. It was made clear to me that this would have to be the case, one in the city, the other in the west (Dungarvan). That's always how it is in Waterford hurling. There's this endless battle between Walsh Park and Fraher Field, a political battle almost. If one field gets a game, the other has to get the next one. Dungarvan was a nice field, but my personal preference was always Walsh Park, because I felt it had more of the feel of a fortress. We were hard to beat there, yet we were always dipping over and back between the two venues.

A lot of people questioned the logic of that second supporters' night, and I fully understand why. But, at the time, it was almost put to me that I really had no choice.

What I will say categorically, however, is that, contrary to the impression given, we didn't miss a single night's training. We set aside those two specific nights for the supporters. Hard as it was to damp down the euphoria, I was still happy that the work was getting done and – as far as I could judge – the players were fully focused.

Now hindsight, clearly, suggests otherwise, but I suspect too many have read too deeply into what we did or failed to do while neglecting to give Kilkenny due credit for what they produced.

I mean, Ken has suggested that the night before the final the players were 'as giddy as schoolchildren on Christmas Eve,' which meant they ended up knackered for the game. Again, I believe that's a convenient, but flawed, conclusion.

The truth is that we followed pretty much the same routine we had done for the semi-final, staying overnight in the Marriott in Ashbourne. I wanted the players to, above all, relax. We set up the team room theatre-style and started the evening with a 20-minute chat about the game. But, after that, I wanted to lighten the mood. The last thing we needed was a group so tight with tension they wouldn't get a night's sleep.

So we had a quiz, different games, and then a kind of an impromptu stage show where different people went up on stage, singing songs or mimicking someone in the room. Everybody had to do something, and it was absolutely hilarious. I loved it.

For an hour or more the room was just filled with laughter and I got a real sense that everyone was in a good place. We all went out for a 20 to 25-minute walk then before settling down for the night.

To me, it was perfect.

I can say with 100 per cent conviction that our arrangements in Ashbourne and the fun the squad had that Saturday night had absolutely nothing to do with the trauma coming. I do understand people trying to track down excuses for what followed, but they're wrong if they think players having fun the night before a big game had any input into the scale of the defeat.

Even the idea that a sleepless night can wreck a player's chances of playing well on the big day is, in my opinion, completely bogus. The danger is that some of this nonsense becomes self-perpetuating. People can almost talk themselves into underperforming.

Nerves always kick in with a vengeance on All-Ireland final morning, and there's very little you can do about that.

So we deliberately tried to keep things light on the bus to Croke Park, just to minimise the tension. Our sub goalie, Adrian Power, was a great character who did a bit of DJ work in his spare time, so, rather than have any heavy motivational video, we put him in charge of entertainment.

He was terrific, putting on songs appropriate to the day and a few sketches too, including a *Gift Grub* episode, mimicking yours truly. So the bus was reverberating with laughter as we arrived into the city – a good thing too, because the closer we got to Croke Park the more every single street seemed flooded with Waterford jerseys.

Then, just as the huge skeleton of the stadium came into view, the bus reverberated to 'It's a Long Way to Tipperary'. I was completely happy, hearing the laughter behind me. The last thing I wanted was the players to arrive in Croker like haunted men. I wanted them calm.

So what went wrong?

To me, the greatest team we've ever seen just happened to hit us that afternoon with the perfect performance. I've never seen anything like what Kilkenny produced. Everything they tried just seemed to come off almost without them even having to think about it.

A lot was made after about our warm-up looking frazzled, about one of our players reputedly dropping his hurley in the pre-match parade. What I do remember is a lot of balls being fumbled in that warm-up, and then, looking over as the players were lining up to meet the President and thinking, suddenly, that they looked incredibly nervous. Just something in the stiffness of their body language.

At that moment you could just see that the weight of being the first team to represent Waterford in an All-Ireland final since 1963 was coming to bear heavily on certain shoulders.

I remember thinking, 'We'll need a good start here to settle the nerves.'

And, of course, the complete opposite unfolded. We weren't even five minutes into the game when Henry Shefflin got a ball on the sideline about 70 yards out and, without even looking, put it straight over the bar. Kilkenny were like men possessed.

Hand on heart, I've never seen an entire team so perfectly primed in terms of touch, physicality, self-belief. They hit our players harder than they'd ever been hit before without ever needing to step outside the rules. I knew within five minutes that we were in deep trouble.

My honest opinion is that you could have picked the best of the rest in Ireland and they wouldn't have lived with Kilkenny that day.

They came to the occasion knowing exactly what to expect. The very formalities that had our players swallowing hard were almost invisible to a team now pushing on to three-in-a-row. Maybe that was inevitable. Kilkenny were playing their eighth final in the last ten years, Waterford their first in a lifetime.

That's not an excuse. I don't have an excuse.

But I will say that, looking back, it would have been very hard to expect both teams to be in the same head-space going into that final. And if you doubt yourself in the environment of an All-Ireland final against that calibre of opponent, well, there's really little chance of survival.

I've never seen a team more switched on than Kilkenny that day. It was irrelevant who we hit or what we tried. It was like coming up against a machine.

When Henry got that early point, my heart was already sinking. You could just see that ruthlessness in them. They were doing what nobody in hurling does better. Going straight for the jugular.

I look back now and suspect that, emotionally, our players were maybe gone over the top. I'm not entirely sure how we could have avoided that happening other than taking them out of the county after the Tipp win and sealing them away from the build-up.

That, of course, would have been impossible.

Instead we tried to embrace everything, and it's possible I got the balance wrong there too. Put it this way, when I was back in an All-Ireland final five years later with Clare I was able to use some of the harsher lessons learnt with Waterford to make sure the players were on a more even emotional keel.

But Waterford, even with the form they showed in '07 before losing to Limerick, wouldn't have lived with Kilkenny in '08. Tipp at their best? Wouldn't have come close.

There was an air of disbelief in the dressing-room at half-time. Everybody was in shock, me included. Like, it's just not in my nature to wave the white flag, but the only thing we could salvage now was pride. The game was over. We all understood that.

With about ten minutes to go to the break, I remember standing on the sideline, trying to figure out what, if anything, I could say that would be of value when we got into the dressing-room. These were proud men, great men. They'd won Munster Championships, they'd won a National League. They were in this final because, 100 per cent, they deserved to be in it.

But they were being humiliated here. We were already too far behind to even consider talk of salvaging the game.

'Look,' I said, 'I know this game is over, but ye owe it to yourselves to stand up and fight here ...'

They did what they could in the second half, but Kilkenny just kept on steaming away. By now I was hearing a bit of abuse come my way from the stands, and, being honest, I just started willing the game to be over. To, firstly, put the players out of their misery, secondly, to allow them the privacy to be found within the four walls of a dressing-room.

I also found myself paying more attention now to the opposition than my own team. Making mental notes, if you like, of what Kilkenny were doing and how they were doing it. How hard they were hitting. How far their wing-forwards were tracking back. Standing there, all I kept saying to myself was, 'I have to learn from this …'

Because what Kilkenny produced was the nearest thing I've ever seen to hurling perfection.

I honestly believe that nothing I said before or after really mattered now. It didn't matter what tackles we put in, how hard we ran, how willing was our work rate. It certainly didn't matter if I told a few of our team to horse into their opponents physically.

None of it was important.

I've no idea what words were exchanged between myself and Cody after. Nor what I said to the Kilkenny players when visiting their dressing-room. Like everyone associated with Waterford now, I was on automatic pilot. Just wanted the formalities over and done with, then to head home and disappear.

The players were inconsolable. Expectations had been so high, and now all anybody was inclined to talk about was an extraordinary All-Ireland final margin of 30 points. It was as if everybody had just been hit by a train.

Going down to the press conference, I felt it was important that the players were treated with proper respect.

'Maybe I got things wrong,' I told the assembled journalists. 'I did everything that I thought was possible, but maybe I will have to look at myself and ask myself questions. Maybe I didn't prepare right, or whatever. I am the manager, I have to accept some of the blame.'

I told them that it was important that Waterford people supported the players now.

I'll never forget walking out of that press conference and back up the corridor to our dressing-room. All the players were gone upstairs now, the only two people left in the room being Liam Dowd and my dad, Pat.

Seeing them, I just broke down. Started sobbing like a baby. It was as if at that moment the enormity of what had happened hit me with full force. I felt humiliated. Worse, I sensed the players upstairs felt humiliated too.

It was horrible. And I was glad to be out of general sight now as the tears came streaming down.

LIAM DOWD: 'I can tell you categorically that this thing about Davy sending out players to rough up Kilkenny is untrue. That script, unfortunately, has been written retrospectively. But trying to make sense of what happened Waterford that day, I suppose, invited all kinds of convenient theories.

'I shared a house for a couple of years with Cyril Farrell when we were in college, and I always remember him telling me about this fella who fucked him out of it as he was getting off the bus in Ballinasloe after Galway were beaten by Cork in the '86 All-Ireland final. The same fella was slapping him on the back a year later after they won against Kilkenny.

'When things go wrong, the numbers scatter. And the Waterford dressing-room emptied very fast that day. Davy was inconsolable, shell-shocked. I can still see him sitting in the corner, crying his eyes out.

'The way he saw it, he'd let the players down, let himself down. I'll never forget the emptiness of that room. What do you say? You're kind of just repeating yourself, "Listen, no point over-analysing …" But Davy's beating himself up now over things he should have done, things he shouldn't have done.

'But Kilkenny were near perfect on the day, while Waterford's players struggled to do things they'd normally do with their eyes closed. Just a freak day really.

'And Davy's just another human being at that moment, fragile like the rest of us.

'Everybody was in complete shock. I remember walking into the Burlington later alongside Brick Walsh and Tony Browne. Brick turns to Tony and asks, almost absent-mindedly, "Do you have any idea what exactly happened today?"

'"No, not a clue," says Tony.

'Back in the hotel, Davy asked me to come up to his room. Even though he's not a drinking man, I brought him up a bottle of beer. I just wanted him to stop beating himself up now. There was also the fact that he'd have to get into a suit now, go downstairs and face into the function. After a hammering like that, it wasn't going to be easy.'

By and large, people were decent, supportive, understanding.

Most people could see we'd just walked into the finest team of all time on their greatest day. Maybe we looked like rabbits caught in the headlights, but, honestly, it wouldn't have mattered what tackles we put in that day. Or how much we might have tried to 'rough' Kilkenny up.

My message to my defenders had been very simple. 'Make life fucking tough for these guys …' Hardly ground-breaking.

I had to make a speech at the function, and it's honestly one of the hardest things I ever did. I felt embarrassed. My only instinct was to apologise. 'We feel we let ye down, and that kills us,' I said.

The rain was tumbling down when we got back to Waterford that Monday night, the quays absolutely thronged with men, women and children welcoming their team home. Sitting at the front of the bus, I felt absolutely devastated for these people.

8

'TELL ME EXACTLY WHAT YOU LEARNT!'

had a small stone in my shoe now when it came to committing to another season with Waterford.

Not one sharp enough to tempt me into packing it in but one that I knew needed urgent addressing. During the course of the Kilkenny hammering one of our big-name players had taken it upon himself to switch positions without any consultation from the line. I couldn't have that. I wouldn't.

Maybe it had been how the team operated under the previous regime, but it couldn't be how business would be conducted on my watch.

Pat Flynn made clear the county board's desire for me to continue, and I agreed, but only with the proviso that I got an assurance from the player in question that that would never be repeated.

'Let me deal with this first …' I said to Pat.

When I rang the player he seemed quite taken aback. As if this was something that had never been an issue before.

I'd felt utterly helpless, watching him do it in the All-Ireland final. What could I do? Stop the game, run out on the field and hunt him back into position? Let me be clear: his decision had absolutely zero impact on the outcome of the game. That wasn't the important point here. The important point was that I couldn't be a lame-duck manager, allowing the bigger characters in the dressing-room to, effectively, do their own thing.

You've no authority in that scenario. And a manager with no authority is really only fooling himself.

Funny, within a week of the Kilkenny defeat Danny Chaplin had me helping him out with Broadford, who were trying to win an intermediate championship in Clare. Danny knew that the worst thing for me now would be to sit at home brooding on what had just happened.

So he'd phoned me the day after the homecoming. And that Thursday, I was down there.

DANNY CHAPLIN: 'Sure a week into it he was running the show. I was only going down filling water bottles! It was around that time he went to Australia to see Sharon. Took a session as normal, then said he wouldn't be around for the next one but would see us the following Saturday.

'That Saturday he arrives up to my house early, as usual, so we can go up and get the field ready for training. Cones everywhere. You'd nearly want to be a NASA student to know what's going on. So we're putting out the cones and I say, "So where did you go?"

'"Australia," he says.

'"On Tuesday?"

'"Yep!"

'We went on to win that intermediate championship, but, as luck would have it, didn't we play the Bridge in the final. Davy said he'd never train a team against the Bridge, so he comes into the dressing-room after the semi-final and says, "That's me gone, lads!"

'I don't think he even went to the final. And there's me, having hurled with the Bridge all my life, managing against my own. My own brother, "Rusty", their captain and centre-back! We were having a few pints the following Monday and a lot of the Bridge lads came over.

'Rusty comes into the pub and looks over at me. "Ya thunderin' bollocks, ya!" he says, grinning.'

I wanted to continue with Waterford, absolutely. I really liked the people. I liked the supporters. I liked the way the county board had remained so supportive immediately after the All-Ireland final.

They knew, and I knew, that Waterford's would be a tough dressing-room through the coming year. Why? Because, like it or not, some of the county's household names were coming towards the end of their careers. I can honestly say that I liked every single one of the players, but tough decisions would now have to be made that in all likelihood would mean some of them would end up not especially liking me.

My first real discussion about '09 with the county board centred on a need to begin the process of re-seeding the squad. It wasn't going to be easy.

But even before that we had to come to terms with what had happened us against Kilkenny. Ken McGrath said subsequently that he reckoned the group needed 'counselling' for the experience, something I considered to be a little over the top.

Bear in mind, the Clare team I'd been part of that became such a force of nature in the mid to late '90s took successive Munster final hammerings from Tipperary ('93) and Limerick ('94). Those experiences could have shattered the confidence of a group trying to win Clare's first provincial title since 1932.

But I can say with certainty that it would never have entered Ger Loughnane's head to bring in a psychiatrist to that group. The only way out of that predicament is to fight your way out. To take strength from the pain.

Easier said than done, I know, but people have to stand on their own two feet in those situations too. Maybe that's a slightly old-fashioned concept, but I do believe you can sometimes over-protect players when things go wrong for them. And in over-protecting them you diminish the very self-sufficiency that's now required.

One thing I did recognise was the fundamental decency of Waterford people, even in the face of such a harrowing hammering.

At the post-All-Ireland function in the Burlington Hotel I found myself instinctively apologising to some of them. I felt responsible. But nobody gave me a single second of abuse. The consensus seemed to be that they'd reckoned the team had been dead and buried after the Clare defeat in June, so the journey to the All-Ireland final had been a complete bonus.

Still, I couldn't wait to get out of the function.

The room I'd been given was absolutely tiny, but I suppose the only company I really wanted now was my own. You'd be running all kinds of stuff over in your head too.

Should I have seen this coming?

Could I have done things differently?

Had I been naïve to think we could ever take down Kilkenny?

I said very little to the players that night. Everybody felt so hurt by the day, the last thing they needed was me in their heads now. When you're that sick you want to talk about anything but the thing that's made you sick.

And I was amazed by the crowd welcoming us home that Monday night. A filthy evening in Waterford, yet maybe 15,000 people lining the quays. It was an extraordinary statement of support for the players.

And to me it was an image that all of us needed to keep inside our heads now. That of the Waterford people supporting these men at their lowest ebb. I'm not sure that turn-out for a hammered team would have been seen in many other counties.

I spoke to Maurice and Peter about staying on as selectors, and both were agreeable.

There was a team holiday organised to New York for the players, but I stayed at home, determined to hit the ground running for '09. I also wanted to keep a certain distance from the players, so that nothing felt too comfortable now. By all accounts, the holiday was a bit of a shambles. I didn't care.

The minute the players landed back I wanted to harvest every ounce of anger and hurt they had in their bodies and, hopefully, use it to our advantage. I had to make changes in personnel too, one of the key ones being the departure of Paul Flynn.

There was no discussion involved, he pretty much just removed himself from the equation, recognising – I suspect – that my desire to put out an even harder-working Waterford team in '09 mightn't exactly work out in his favour.

Look, I'd have liked nothing more than to have worked with Flynn in his prime. The guy was a phenomenal talent, someone who became one of the best forwards in the game during the early noughties. But the game was changing profoundly now and Paul seemed to be making clear a position that he personally didn't feel any need to change with it.

There was definitely another year in him, but only if he trained like everybody else. And Paul just wouldn't do that.

In January I sent the players running in St Molleran's on the Carrick-on-Suir side of Waterford. We also occasionally used a training circuit for horses near Kill. I just wanted to get it into their heads that we were training harder than any other teams around. To build them up mentally.

Dave Bennett had departed too, and I wasn't unhappy about that. I'd found himself and Flynn together formed an increasingly negative dressing-room presence once it became clear they weren't going to see much game time.

There was an edge of sarcasm to the pair of them, and I couldn't have any room for that in my dressing-room now.

One big thing for us in the National League was a victory recorded in our round three game against Kilkenny on a heavy pitch in a packed Walsh Park. That to me was a day they simply had to stand up and be counted. The win felt important, if only to reaffirm the fact that what had happened the previous September had been a freak of sorts.

There was proper heat in the game too, a few scuffles and sufficiently widespread deployment of the yellow-card rule to tell us that Kilkenny were taking the game seriously.

It meant something personal to me too, even if, naturally, I wasn't inclined to articulate that at the time. But this was my first win against Cody on the line. It felt a watershed.

Funny, towards the end of the year I would meet him at the Star awards in Croke Park. We were just chatting away casually and I said to him, 'Brian, I've learnt some amount from you.'

He grinned. 'Tell me exactly what you learnt,' he asked.

'Not a chance,' I said. 'But, trust me, I'll be back for more!'

I'd processed that All-Ireland final over and over in my mind, determined to learn everything I possibly could from the experience. And I was absolutely determined that if I ever came up against Cody in a big game again I'd – at the very least – hold my own.

I felt I'd learnt so much that day in terms of physicality, fitness, the importance of forwards understanding their obligation to track back. But there were other things I wasn't entirely sure about. Like, I couldn't get Kilkenny's work ethic out of my head. It had been incredible on the day, and I knew it wasn't a simple compute to get an entire group playing on that kind of selfless wavelength.

Cody absolutely fascinated me. It's well known now that I took myself to the 2010 All-Ireland final between Kilkenny and Tipp essentially to observe him in action at close quarters. Got a ticket to be seated right behind the Cats' dug-out so that I could monitor everything he did.

I wanted to see what made the guy tick. And I remember specifically a Kilkenny attack early in that game that he wasn't even looking at. His eyes were locked on his team's defensive structure, making sure they had their one-on-ones in place.

Beating his team in that '09 League game now was good for us psychologically but beyond that didn't signify a great deal. Because our campaign pretty much fizzled out after that, with three defeats on the bounce against Dublin, Galway and Limerick before a final-round victory over Cork gave us a mid-table finish.

It was almost inevitable that Justin McCarthy would come back into the Waterford story sooner rather than later and, with him now in charge of Limerick, he duly did in that year's Munster Championship.

Our first meeting was a shocking affair, producing just 20 scores over 70-plus turgid minutes, and it felt very much like an opportunity we'd left behind, eventually drawing a game we'd led 0-9 to 0-3 at half-time.

John Mullane would be our outstanding player that summer and had 0-4 from play scored against Stephen Walsh before Limerick responded by bringing Damien Reale across from the other corner.

People reckoned I was guilty of playing silly buggers with Justin when we were late out for the second half, leaving Limerick standing around in an absolute deluge. Some of their players eventually lost patience, running back into the tunnel, only to meet us coming the other way. It was a bit of an organisational mess in the end, with the referee, Diarmuid Kirwan, eventually having to send someone in to get the full complement of Limerick players back on the field.

The truth? I was worried that complacency might set in with that six-point lead and was simply too busy laying down the law to certain members of the team to hear the knocks on the dressing-room door.

Turned out I didn't succeed either, with Waterford failing to register a single score from play in what was a pretty putrid, admittedly rain-lashed second half.

One of the tougher decisions I had to make was replacing Ken at half-time. It was, I subsequently heard, the first time he'd ever been substituted in his Waterford career. But Ken was struggling big-time with his knee, hadn't been able to train 100 per cent, and I could see that lack of preparation was playing havoc with his head.

Trust me, he was the last player I wanted to take off. Ken had a unique place in the hearts of Waterford supporters, because of his physical courage and flamboyant style. Remember, I'd played against him for years in a Clare team that always recognised Ken McGrath as the key man to target if you wanted to beat Waterford.

But knee trouble or not, his legs were now going in my opinion. Ken himself didn't see that. In fact he would rail against that very idea over the next couple of seasons and, in doing so, make my management of the side a little trickier than I'd have liked.

Ken was inclined to sulk. And there was nothing remotely subtle about how he did that. I can say straight out that he was bad in the dressing-room when things weren't going his way. And I was going to have to deal with that now in the most sensitive way I could.

Six days after that drawn game with Limerick, Mullane was outstanding again in the replay, rattling home 0-6 from play in a Man of the Match performance as we won 0-25 to 0-17. I was more thrilled with the win than the performance.

The game was actually still on the line after an hour before we pulled away, out-scoring Limerick 0-7 to 0-1 from the 63rd minute to the finish.

Stephen Molumphy did an outstanding job on the forty against their Man of the Match from the previous weekend, Brian Geary, before being effectively taken out of the game by a ferocious late shoulder approaching half-time.

Being honest, we never really looked like winning the subsequent Munster final against Tipperary in Semple Stadium. The county board had been approached by Tipp to play it in Thurles, and when they sought my opinion I decided to canvass the players. The vibe I got was that they loved playing there but, in hindsight, I should probably have insisted upon a neutral venue, like the Gaelic Grounds.

Waterford didn't like playing in Limerick. I knew that. But Tipp didn't either. I knew they'd want to bury us after the previous year's All-Ireland semi-final, so handing them home advantage probably wasn't the smartest move.

We trailed by eleven points at one stage before a late rally brought the margin back to four and, again, if it wasn't for Mullane's superb 1-5 from play our attacking return would have been pretty underwhelming.

That said, of more concern to me was the concession of four goals, three in the first half. If I didn't sort things out defensively I knew there was zero possibility of this team winning silverware.

And that's, undeniably, where I found myself increasingly at odds with some of the bigger characters in the dressing-room.

They wanted a licence to hurl with more freedom, a freedom that I was adamant they couldn't now be given. I just felt we didn't have the legs to win shoot-outs against the best in the country, the Kilkennys and the Tipps, who simply had far more natural scoring power now as well as younger legs.

Big Dan was one of those now struggling most with my move away from freestyle hurling to a more tactical approach. He just hadn't the same gears any more and seemed to take particular umbrage at the fact that I wasn't going to entertain any sacred cows in the dressing-room.

He was furious with me when I didn't start him in the replay against Limerick, picking Gary Hurney at full-forward instead. He says in his book that I told him he was 'flying' after scoring

1-3 in a challenge against Dublin. I'm sure I did. I was desperately trying to humour Dan at this stage.

But if I picked Gary ahead of him it was because I believed Gary was moving better.

Dan didn't start then because he wasn't going well enough. This simply wasn't the Dan of '07, you see. That hurler was gone, finished, history. In his place was a man now just programmed to complain.

We argued the toss about that team selection, naturally. But his conviction that I was ever trying to humiliate him in front of the group would be miles adrift of the truth. I will admit, though, that the more I heard from Dan the less I now was listening to. He'd become self-absorbed and precious.

The departure of Flynn and Bennett had sent a message, and I will admit there were probably days in '09 when I referred to those two as 'whingers'.

They just seemed to be taking pot-shots at me at every opportunity, cutting the back off me now that they found themselves surplus to requirements for an environment in which they'd previously have seen themselves as big-shots.

And, now that Dan wasn't starting, I knew full well where his sympathies lay.

Trouble was, I was trying to handle a kind of civil war here. The younger lads in the dressing-room were buying in to the very work ethic that some of the older lads considered unreasonable.

And my issue with some of the older lads would have been that it was one thing not to particularly like the way I was doing things, quite another to be making your disgruntlement so plain.

So, to some extent, the dressing-room was a small bit split now, between those moving with the new imperatives of the modern game and those stuck in the complacency of thinking that every game should just be a shoot-out.

Needless to say, Justin didn't come to our dressing-room after the replay, and I was more than happy that he didn't. As individuals, there was no love lost between us, and deep down I suspect the players wouldn't have known where to look if he'd come in.

We had Galway next up in Thurles, an All-Ireland quarter-final that I reckon must have broken John McIntyre's heart.

John was a manager I always had a good bit of time for, a genuine hurling man who – with hindsight – couldn't buy a break during his time in charge of Galway. Twice during his three years as Galway manager we'd be the ones who knocked them out of the championship.

They looked to have us well beaten when six points up in '09 entering the final quarter, but of course we stole the game in the dying minutes. The key to our theft was a 68th-minute goal scored by Shane Walsh and set up brilliantly by Big Dan, both late substitutes.

That cut the margin down to one point, and, after Eoin Kelly levelled things, Mullane won the game for us in injury time with a phenomenal score from the left wing.

For Galway, it had to feel as if they'd just been mugged. They did a hell of a lot right that day but simply didn't get the breaks against us and must have been sickened by the defeat. For us it felt a real breakthrough win. A show of character from a position that many looking in from the outside might have considered hopeless.

I could see Dan was bulling at the end. He'd made that late goal with a phenomenal catch and offload and seemed to take this as proof that I'd been mistaken in not starting him. In his book he says he completely ignored my instructions to him as he was going in.

Maybe he did too.

But my attitude now was 'Dan, you won the fucking game for us, so I'm after getting something right here, whether you like it or not!'

A real team player, I reckoned, would have seen that.

There'd be no fairytale for us in the subsequent semi-final against Kilkenny, a game notable for Henry Shefflin having one of his best days ever, with a personal scoring return of 1-14.

They beat us by five points in the end, yet you felt all through that we were getting under their skin, rattling their cage. I found the game hugely frustrating, though, because I felt that a certain self-doubt never quite left Waterford's hurling that day.

Somewhere deep inside, the players were afraid of getting another hiding and it meant that, although they fought, they never seemed to believe that they could beat Kilkenny.

A couple of Shane Walsh goals put them under pressure, but we never pushed on. We never really went for the jugular.

I put Eoin McGrath on Tommy Walsh the same day, if only because I knew he wouldn't take a step backwards. Eoin was one of my favourite players for that very reason and he certainly didn't let me down that day.

Trouble was, when you're picking an unsung player like him ahead of big names you know you're going to get dog's abuse. And I did. Eoin's finishing could be questionable. He sometimes took wrong options. But the man was a tiger, whose stomach for battle could never be questioned.

I never regretted picking that man. If I was going to war in the morning, he's the type I'd like to have by my side.

Given where we'd come from eleven months earlier, I suppose losing to Kilkenny by just five points felt a victory of sorts. We could have crumbled, but didn't, you see. Six points down midway through, we 'won' the second half by a point.

I brought on both Ken and Dan – later, I suspected, than either of them thought reasonable. So be it, the dressing-room was changing.

And that was their problem now, not mine.

9

NO EASY GOODBYES

My legacy in Waterford is, naturally, open to opinion today. People are split on it, I understand that.

We lost six of eighteen championship games played on my watch, three each to Kilkenny and Tipperary. And we did take some horrible beatings, like that '08 All-Ireland final and, still to come, the '11 Munster final. I oversaw a changing of the guard that, essentially, ended the inter-county careers of Paul Flynn, Ken McGrath and Dan Shanahan, three of the biggest names in hurling.

I binned the swashbuckling, freestyle hurling so beloved of supporters for a more considered, tactical approach that demanded levels of concentration and discipline that were never going to be to everybody's taste.

And I believed in a concept of building from the back, of humility, of selflessness, of a real sense of the collective being more important than worship of individual brilliance.

To some, that seemed to make me some kind of anti-hurling monster. The ignorant conclusion drawn was that I didn't trust flair players. This was bullshit, but it stuck.

Some of those players took serious umbrage at me, and by the time I finished with Waterford I was left under no illusions about what was coming. After the '11 All-Ireland semi-final defeat to Kilkenny we were walking down the platform in Connolly Station to catch the train home when Big Dan sidled over to me.

It was clearly the end of the line for him as an inter-county hurler, and he had an autobiography on the way.

'Davy,' he said, 'my book is nearly done, and I just want you to know there's nothing personal in this. But I have a family to support …'

My response was a shrug and 'Whatever you have to do, Dan, you have to do.'

More visible to the general public, of course, would be that moment in Thurles one year later when both Mullane and Eoin Kelly celebrated so wildly in front of me after Waterford had overcome Clare in my first championship game as Banner manager.

The two of them went absolutely ballistic, right in front of the dug-out at the final whistle, in a gesture, it seemed, designed to humiliate me. I found the moment extremely hurtful, and it took everything in my power not to react.

Standing there, all I could think was 'Where the fuck is this after coming from?'

I'd had small issues with both, yet nothing that could ever have prepared me for that kind of behaviour. In my time with Waterford I always felt that Kelly was one of the most misunderstood players in the country. He had exceptional ability, incredible hands. Sometimes you'd see him get a score and be left wondering, 'How in the name of God did he actually do that?'

But I did give out to him occasionally about his work rate, and that was especially the case in the 2010 All-Ireland semi-final against Tipperary, when he made clear his displeasure at being substituted in Croke Park.

As manager I've never had a huge issue with a player being angry in those circumstances. He should be unhappy at being taken off. If he's not, there's something radically wrong.

Before I took charge of Waterford, certain people warned me that he could be 'trouble'. But personally, I never found that to be the case.

Eoin had a great ability to see the funny side of things. He could laugh at himself, and that laughter would, in a second, take the sting out of an awkward situation. I always found that side of him hugely likeable. He was a fundamentally good guy who just needed to be handled right.

As for John Mullane, I felt we'd had a decent enough relationship too, but that day in Thurles his eyes were practically jumping out of their sockets.

And I didn't shy away from addressing that behaviour when I went to the Waterford dressing-room afterwards to congratulate them on the win. 'Lads, for the life of me I honestly can't understand what the fuck that was all about at the end,' I said, my eyes now glued to Mullane in particular.

'You said stuff about us ...' he replied.

Turns out, word had come from another Waterford player's father that I had declared Mullane 'finished'. This was 100 per cent untrue, incidentally. But someone within the Waterford camp clearly believed it might be beneficial to have Mullane completely wound up. And, by Jesus, they succeeded.

Anyway, there and then he made it clear that he had no interest in hearing my side of things and pretty much confirmed as much the following week when questioned about his behaviour by Marty Morrissey on RTÉ television.

To this day I believe it was a deliberate ploy by someone on Waterford's management team to make the game some kind of personal crusade against me in particular. I actually spoke to Mullane a couple of months after about it on the phone, but he had no interest in apologising. To me, he'd been completely out of line that day. I still believe that.

But I chose the diplomatic route when asked about it by the media that day in Thurles. I told them there was still 'great stuff' in Mullane and there'd be 'no fear' of him. He'd been one of Waterford's real stand-out players during my time there, and

I wasn't now about to start some kind of public squabble with him, no matter the journalists' appetite for me to do so.

I always considered John a unique character, absolutely brilliant in many ways, hugely frustrating in others. You could be trying to make a very serious point at a team meeting and he'd just come out with this one-liner that would have lads almost falling around the place in hysterics. I'd be in pieces myself.

Someone else could be talking about nutrition to the players and he'd say something completely random about sausages and chips. He wouldn't be doing it out of badness and, sometimes, he mightn't even be trying to be funny.

He was brilliant for team spirit in that respect. Everybody loved him. He could lighten the load off the field, but everyone knew he'd always step up to the plate on it too.

Sometimes I might be explaining something a little intricate tactically, have gone over it four or five times with great deliberation and, just at that moment that I'd think everyone's happy, Mullane would have his hand up. 'Can you explain that again, Davy?'

If John was over a team now I suspect he might see things differently in terms of how I was trying to manage. You just had to accept sometimes that he wasn't really taking on board the tactical message.

He'd have us pulling our hair out too trying to get a message across about the importance of hydration. To be fair, John could be in the car all day and so it mightn't exactly have been convenient in those circumstances to be drinking two litres of water as he travelled.

We were doing the tests one night and John arrived in after a long day on the road, knowing he hadn't a hope in hell of passing. Next thing he's looking at all the samples already taken and spots a jar with Jamie Nagle's name on it, the urine clear as mineral water. Jamie, you will gather, did things by the book.

So Mullane filled a jar with his own sample, which was, as he put it himself, something the colour of Lucozade. Switched his name with Jamie's and went bouncing out to training, thinking he had us fooled.

The colour alone was the giveaway. Soon as we saw it we knew it wasn't Jamie's sample.

'Whose the fuck is this?' I asked, holding it up after training. What could Mullane do but put up his hand?

John liked his hurling off-the-cuff. He was a natural and, on his good days, a great bit of stuff. But he had a wandering mind too, and that day in Thurles it was clear someone else had taken control of it.

In Kelly's case, I heard subsequently that one of the Clare players said something deeply personal to him on the field. Eoin, not unnaturally, automatically assumed that I had put this player up to it. The truth is I was disgusted that anyone in my dressing-room would stoop so low.

I'd had enough poison spat at me as a player and, while I'll go to war against anybody on a hurling field, that kind of stuff is honestly beyond the pale as far as I'm concerned. One hundred per cent I would not condone it.

I met Eoin subsequently, making clear to him my feelings, and we shook hands.

But I suppose there's always been a slight edge to my relationship with some of the players I managed in that Waterford dressing-room.

I mean, I've always found it hugely ironic that Big Dan took such umbrage at my attempts to bring more humility and structure to Waterford's play when he became such a key part of a Derek McGrath regime that placed such store on those very same virtues.

Would the Dan of today maybe have been more open to my style of management between '08 and '11?

Listen, I still have big time for all those Waterford players, Dan included. And I've actually had to smile in recent times at some of the sideline 'rows' the two of us got tangled up in. Like, there was a Munster League game between Waterford and Clare a couple of years ago, played in Waterford Institute of Technology, at which Dan told me to 'fuck off back to Clare,' claiming I'd 'cost Waterford an arm and a leg!'

MICHAEL HOGAN (former Waterford treasurer): 'That was one of the great myths. I was treasurer I'd say for most of the time that Davy was there, and that perception was there that he'd cost the county board a lot of money. But I don't think any of the years that Davy was there that we ever ran a loss. And if we were ever close to it, it wasn't anything to do with him.

'He brought in new methods and new people, and we would have had maybe more back-room staff than what we'd have had up to then. But I found him very easy to talk to. He was always full of ideas and you wouldn't be able to do everything that he'd have in mind.

'But we never had any issues at all. If you said to him, "Look, we can't afford this," he was very amenable to that. You'd never have a row with him about it, he'd just come back with another suggestion. Everybody knows that the effort he puts into things is unbelievable and he was the same with us. He would have died for Waterford when he was here.

'And you must remember Davy came in at a time when team expenses were on the increase anyway. There was more emphasis on nutritionists and dieticians and physios – people like that. Up to then a lot of that was kind of hit and miss in Waterford.

'I couldn't say a single bad word about him. Look, he'll admit himself that he got things wrong with the '08 All-Ireland final. But we got hammered in the first round of Munster that year, weren't at the races. I'd say we weren't in the top six in the country that year, but he got us to the final. As far as I'd be concerned, it was his coaching that got us to that final.

'I think it suited some people to put that word out there that he nearly broke the county board. I can say categorically that was not true.'

The same day Dan told me that I wasn't the big-shot I 'let on to be', that he'd sold more books than I had. It just started off over something innocuous, an argument over a free or something, and next thing he's giving it to me down the banks.

Hand on heart, I found it very funny. He was playing up to the crowd behind us, and I honestly had no problem with that. He loves doing that. Maybe there's a bit of that in me too.

And in the car on my way home that evening I found myself actually giggling at the thought of it. All it had been was harmless banter, to be fair.

Sometimes you can look furious with someone but inside you're actually smiling.

In their entire history, Waterford have won just nine Munster senior hurling crowns, yet to this day I honestly wonder if our win in 2010 really registered with their supporters. True, there were great scenes of jubilation in Thurles that Saturday evening we beat Cork in a replay under lights. The reason we won that Munster title was that we had a different spine to the team, a spine built around ferocious workers like Brick Walsh and Stephen Molumphy.

But just as the significance of getting to the county's first All-Ireland final in 45 years had been completely undone by the scale of the defeat to Kilkenny two years earlier, the 2010 Munster crown was soon forgotten as we subsequently came up short again in Croke Park.

We'd had a respectable National League, winning three and drawing two of seven games in Division 1A. Then we beat a young, inexperienced Clare in the Munster semi-final on a horrible, drizzly bank-holiday Monday afternoon that drew just 11,000 people to Semple Stadium.

That was a day I decided to start Dan in a two-man full-forward line alongside Mullane, but he barely got a sniff off Cian Dillon and I had to take him off.

Dan was subsequently critical of feeling too 'isolated' up there, but it was exactly my plan to leave him isolated, one-on-one with a single defender. Think about that. There was no such thing as a sweeper at the time. Dan was huge, strong in the air, and knew how to finish. Why would I want other players around him when he had that natural strength in a one-to-one battle?

If I could have Dan close to goal with nobody apart from goalkeeper and last defender within 40 yards of him, was I not entitled to believe we were playing perfectly to his strengths?

I didn't want other bodies in there. I wanted Dan to stand up and be counted.

There's a ludicrous story out there that I'd never forgiven him for scoring three goals against me in the '04 Munster quarter-final and was allegedly soured by players jokingly bringing up that day every now and then in training.

The truth is I absolutely loved that kind of slagging on the training field and, to be perfectly honest, anybody suggesting that six years later I was sore about what happened in '04 is, to put it bluntly, making things up.

And Dan said a few things in his book about me that were simply untrue.

One was that I always seemed to think maybe he was pretending to be injured. I never for a second thought that. He says I never actually sat down with him for a one-to-one. I regularly did, but he seldom had much to tell me.

And let's be clear about something; I genuinely liked him as a person – still do. He was always very courteous to my family when I first arrived into the Waterford dressing-room and my son, Colm, still has one of Dan's jerseys, given to him after a big championship game.

After '09 Peter Queally and Maurice Geary had both stepped away as selectors, my suspicion being that they believed we'd taken the group as far as we could take them. I had no problem with that. They'd both been honest, decent men who'd given the role everything they could.

In their place I opted for two former county men. Páraic Fanning and Pat Bennett remain very close to me today, Páraic as a Wexford selector and Pat as one of my right-hand men with LIT.

I knew Páraic as a feisty Fitzgibbon campaigner with Waterford IT who'd worked the line with Mount Sion too. It was obvious to me that he knew his stuff, and it seemed clear too that he'd never be anybody's yes-man. And I wanted that in my selectors. I wanted to be challenged.

We'd first squared up to one another on the line during an unbelievable Fitzgibbon Cup final between LIT and WIT in '07. He'd won a few Fitzgibbons previously as manager but was just their hurley-carrier this day.

Anyway, Páraic wasn't shy on the line and this day I'd sent one of our lads down to have a few words. It had no effect, so I went down myself and it's fair to say he gave me as good as he got.

So I wasn't entirely sure now how he'd react to my approach.

PÁRAIC FANNING: 'When the county chairman rang asking would I talk to Davy, I'll be honest, my first reaction was, "I don't think I could work with him." Because I'd be a fairly strong-willed person myself.

'But I said I'd meet him, and Davy drove down to WIT that day, which immediately said to me that he was serious about this. I'd say within three hours of me agreeing to meet he was there. We were both grinning when we shook hands. I said to him, "The last time I saw you, you were telling me where to go!"

'We chatted for a long time, but I'd say within half an hour I'd made up my mind.'

Pat I knew from different places, and what I really liked about him was his way with players. He just had this way of getting their trust, a straight-talker who didn't bullshit.

Both Páraic and Pat will tell you that I communicated with Dan the whole time through all that period, but he'd give very little back. He was never a confrontational fella, you see, letting on to be a lot harder than he actually is. For sure, I could tell he was increasingly unhappy, but when I'd try to talk it out with him he just internalised everything. Bottled it all up.

That's what surprised me about some of the stuff in his book. Whereas I felt Ken was massively honest, taking real responsibility for his negativity in the dressing-room as things unravelled for him, Dan seemed inclined to blame me for the slow decline of his inter-county career.

He made it out as if I wanted him to fail. Nothing could have been further from the truth.

Bizarrely, he even took issue with me putting on a DVD before that Clare game, showing him scoring goals for fun in '07. I did that specifically to make him feel good about himself, to remind him of just how unplayable he could be on the good days.

It always struck me that Dan's biggest problem was a lack of self-belief. He doubted himself constantly. And when he did, you could see it in him from miles away. The flip side was that when his confidence was up he could do almost anything. He'd become a virtual force of nature.

What I did want now was the more established stars to increase their work rate. I'd have been harping on about that, talking about the need for All-Stars and Hurler of the Year awards to be parked at the dressing-room door. Now, given that Dan was the only Hurler of the Year we had, I suppose it was clear he was one of my intended targets. And one big issue I had with him was that his tackle rate was never good. In fact, let me blunt here. Dan just would not tackle.

He was a great man to catch a ball and score, but I wanted more out of my forwards now. I wanted them doing what the Kilkenny forwards did. I wanted them leaving their egos in the dressing-room and working like they'd never worked in their lives before.

Free-flowing hurling was fine in '02, '03, '04 and '05, but the game had changed now and I wasn't the one who changed it. I was, though, the one who had a responsibility to help Waterford respond to that change.

That Munster Championship opener against Clare was, as you might expect, a hugely difficult personal experience for me. Just think about it. The opposing manager was Ger 'Sparrow' O'Loughlin, Sharon's brother and a man I hurled with in Clare colours for so many years.

We'd been involved in two pubs together at one stage, renting the Usual Place in Ennis and owning Joe McHugh's in Liscannor. Some of my happiest memories reach back to those days, especially Liscannor and the personalities that became regulars. One particularly was a man – sadly now deceased – called Chris Scales, nicknamed 'Foggy', after the character in *Last of the Summer Wine.*

Foggy was a farmer who'd come in every morning, have his few pints, head away to work, back in for a few more, away again, then back in in the evening. His way was to be always giving out about something, but never without a glint in his eyes.

He could drink a pint in two mouthfuls and, holding court, gave off the air of almost owning the pub. Everybody loved him. Sometimes we'd head up to another pub in the village, Murty's, or out to Ennistymon, Doolin or Kilfenora to play cards as a team in these pre-Christmas gambles: Foggy, myself and another local, Denis Leyden.

There'd be big crowds wired into this game called 'Combs and Outs', a North Clare version of '45', and, Lord Jesus, the speed with which the cards hit the table would have my head in a spin. Basically, the counting worked differently in what they liked to call 'the old game', and half the time I wouldn't have a notion what I was doing.

Foggy would be reading me the riot act for being so clueless. One second … 'Fitzy, what's the score?' The next … 'Ah, for fuck's sake …'

'Locksy' Tyne was another great character, always looking to have a few bets and catch you out.

Other nights a few of us would head over to a disco in Lahinch, the Claremont, before they'd settle back in the pub for a session.

I absolutely loved those people and Dinny Cullinane, one of my great friends since, actually got me involved with Liscannor footballers when they won the Intermediate League and Championship as well as senior B. The team was sponsored by our pub, so he'd get me to tog out and have me listed as a substitute.

There was never any realistic chance of me seeing serious game time. I suspect Dinny just wanted me at the heart of it.

DINNY CULLINANE: 'We used train on this pitch in Lahinch near the golf club and Davy would often come in to have a look at what we were doing. This Tuesday night I said to him, "Davy, we're training tomorrow, would you take the session?"

"'I'd be happy to, Dinny," he says. "What time?"

'"Six o'clock."

'"Ah, that's grand."

'"Now, Davy, that's six in the morning!"

'Well, he never blinked. I came into the pitch at half past five the following morning, this beautiful, misty June day, dew rising off the field. There was one car in the car park and, looking down to the end of the field, I could see this vague shadow in the mist. Davy putting out cones.

'I went down. "Davy, what time were you here at?"

'"Ah, I came in around ten past five, just wanted to get myself organised."

That was something I quickly learnt from him. If he told you he was going to do something, you could consider it done.

'To be honest, I should have known. We're a very small club, and I remember first asking him to tog out for us in a challenge game against Kilrush. The game was on a Thursday evening, we were really struggling to get fifteen, so I asked him if he'd come along to make up the numbers. Remember, now, he'd have been at the height of his fame as Clare's hurling goalkeeper at the time.

'"No problem, I'll see you there," he said.

'And I remember thinking, "Sure you will, a man with two All-Ireland hurling medals in his back pocket …"

'But, pulled into the car park that Thursday and the first car I saw? Davy's!'

Liscannor then got to the Clare senior final in '02 and, the day of the big game against Kilmurry-Ibrickane, we erected a marquee on this wide footpath in front of the pub. I'll never forget it. Even though they lost the final 0-6 to 1-5 on a horrible day in Ennis, the place was absolutely jammers afterwards for nearly three days, drink being handed out the window it took so long to get in or out of the pub.

Eventually I remember ringing a garda I was friendly with at about 5 a.m. on the Wednesday and asking him, 'Any chance you'd clear this place for me?' We'd still be there today if I hadn't.

It was around that time I actually bought Sparrow out of Joe McHugh's, before selling it on myself in '04. So we had a long history together that, come that Munster Championship game in 2010, would have to be put to one side.

On top of that, one of his selectors, Danny Chaplin, to this day remains one of my closest friends. And, maybe the biggest one of all, my dad was due to be on the line in his role as Clare county secretary.

So I was deeply uncomfortable coming up to that game, just willing the whole thing over. No matter what your circumstance, you never forget where you come from and how it shapes your identity.

I have a picture from that day up on the wall at home showing Sparrow and me, no more than twenty feet apart, staring out into the field looking for completely different things. There were never going to be many words between us, before or after. He's a very calm, calculated fella who's a smart reader of the game. But he doesn't wear his heart on his sleeve like me.

I suspect that quietness ultimately made him underrated at county level, because his record with clubs is outstanding.

DANNY CHAPLIN: 'Back then, Davy and I would have been talking every single day. He'd ring me or I'd ring him. And he was worried coming up to that game that it might affect our friendship. He just found it awkward, but there was never anything there for him to feel awkward about.

'I remember we walked out the tunnel together and I just said to him, "Lookit, I'm going away over to the far side …" I was going to be miked up to Sparrow. So he went left, I went right, and that was it.

'I could tell he was uncomfortable coming into the Clare dressing-room after. It hurt him to be beating his own. But there wouldn't have been a bad word said against him in there.'

We both badly wanted to win that day, and it made for an edgy 70-plus minutes before we got through on a score of 0-22 to 1-15. We shook hands after, but there was no lingering conversation. I knew there wouldn't be.

And it felt absolutely weird walking into the Clare dressing-room after, commiserating with players, some of whom I'd played alongside, commiserating with Sparrow, with Danny and with my father. I could see everybody in the room was devastated, and that genuinely bothered me. I was still a Clareman. That jersey still meant a hell of a lot to me.

So I wished them all the best. Kept things very short. Got back out as quick as I could.

And, to be fair, I did not experience a single nasty comment from a Clare voice that day – unlike the year before, when I'd attended the Munster under-21 final between Waterford and Clare in Dungarvan. I was obviously there in my capacity as Waterford's senior manager but was genuinely happy to see Clare coming away with the win.

Walking out of the ground after, this fella I recognised from the Broadford-Clonlara direction began jawing at me, just being a smart-arse, acting the clown.

'You're some fuckin' Clareman!' he roared.

I think I'd probably hurled more times for Clare than any man at this stage, yet this flute thought it reasonable to start abusing me as some kind of turncoat now. I never opened my mouth, just glared over at him, turned around and walked away.

He just wasn't worth the energy of a response.

Anyway, that 2010 victory against Clare pretty much encapsulated the awkward position I now found myself in with this Waterford team. Because if I took Dan off that day, three of those I brought on as subs – Declan and Séamus Prendergast and Ken McGrath – were all hugely pumped to prove a point.

After scoring 0-3 from wing-back, Declan talked to journalists about feeling 'written off', while Ken went absolutely ballistic after nailing a monster score from half way, beating the hurley off the ground and roaring pointedly in my direction.

Even in the dressing-room afterwards he was like a man possessed. We'd won the game, but Ken was so preoccupied now with his own predicament that that just didn't seem to register. Páraic Fanning had to go over at one point and tell him to calm down.

The next night at training I made a point of calling Ken across to explain himself. To be fair to the man, he was apologetic, admitting his reaction had been 'over the top'. Basically, he said that he'd lost the head and that it wouldn't happen again.

If I hadn't known it before, I knew now I was fighting for my life here.

Put it this way. Ken McGrath is one of the most decent men you could meet, as well as one of the greatest hurlers of his generation. But the dying of the light can be a horrible process for anybody and the truth is he didn't handle it well.

What I admire hugely about him is that he admitted as much afterwards in his book.

At the time, Ken couldn't possibly have seen it from my position. It was maybe human nature to be paranoid and looking inward when his status as the main man in that dressing-room was now, effectively, collapsing.

We had a good, open chat about things after that Clare game, but I knew that that could only resolve so much. My view, and the view of the selectors, was that Ken's legs were going. His view was that this was a myth now blinding people to honest assessment of how he was playing.

We made our peace, but the truth was we'd never fully resolve our differences.

What I will say about Ken is that he was an open book. He hid nothing. There was nothing devious or underhand about him. You couldn't mistake the fact that he was in bad form, because he'd be like a dog in the dressing-room.

He admitted this himself after.

I just knew that Waterford would win nothing now playing off-the-cuff hurling and, for men like Dan and Ken, this was bad news. In the old game, Ken at number six could be an absolute colossus. Trouble was, his use of the ball was too wild, too random for what I needed.

To begin with, I would be pilloried for preferring Brick Walsh at centre-half-back, but Brick was perfect for a game in which protecting possession had become so important. And I take personal pride in the fact that two of his four All-Star awards would be won from that position.

It was in our interests that the two Munster finals against Cork in 2010 became massively tactical battles. Because Cork liked nothing better than a shoot-out. They always had a ready-made supply of skilful, wristy forwards who'd score for fun if you gave them space. My absolute priority was denying them that space.

And we did it brilliantly.

Cork, remember, were coming off the back of a big defeat of the '09 All-Ireland finalists Tipp, in which Aisake Ó hAilpín looked unplayable. My idea was to press their space in the middle third, crowding the puck-out zone and thus making life difficult for Dónal Óg Cusack fulfilling that quarter-back role he now did better than anyone.

PÁRAIC FANNING: 'Davy came up with a way of taking Dónal Óg's puck-outs out of the equation, which was the key to beating Cork. He did so much prep on that in advance, and I don't think there were too many teams who got into that kind of detail at the time.

'In fairness, the players nailed everything Davy had gone through with them too. And that wasn't easy, because it was maybe the first time people began to see a more strategic Waterford.'

I'd hoped the game would be low-scoring, and when we got to half-time in the first game, leading 0-7 to 0-6, that plan was working to perfection. But then Cork got two goals in as many minutes from, first, Aisake and then Ben O'Connor.

We responded with an absolute pile-driver from Eoin Kelly, and then, three minutes into injury time, Tony Browne rattled in a dramatic equalising goal after Kelly's 20-metre free had been saved.

My memory of Tony's goal is probably framed differently from most people's. It's of John Mullane breaking his hurley and this girl, Una Maher, running onto the field with a replacement. She was a friend of our kit man Roger Casey's and a schoolteacher who'd just recently lost her sister in a car crash. So Una, a passionate Waterford fan, wasn't in a great place at the time and we just thought it might be a little release for her to be in charge of the hurleys for the day.

Anyway, Una goes haring right into the middle of everything with a new hurley for Mullane and, watching her go, I remember thinking, 'Jesus Christ, Una, you could get killed out there!'

Next thing a swinging hurley almost makes contact with her and, to this day, I'm convinced it's the reason we were awarded that 20-metre free. I'm always on to my players to follow everything in, just in case the ball rebounds from the keeper or a post. And fair play to Browne, that's exactly what he did.

The Cork manager, Denis Walsh, described their first-half tally of 0-6 that day as a 'disaster' afterwards, but we did even better in the replay.

Pulling off one of the saves of my life against Cork in 2006. My days in a Clare jersey were numbered, but I didn't feel ready to go. (Brendan Moran/SPORTSFILE)

By the time I took over at Waterford, hurling had changed, and the free-flowing style that had defined Waterford for so long would have to change too. It wasn't going to be easy. (©INPHO/James Crombie)

We were well beaten by Kilkenny in the 2008 All-Ireland, and it came as a shock – to me, the players and the fans. As I began to push some of the senior players harder, tensions began to mount. (©INPHO/Cathal Noonan)

People can debate my legacy in Waterford, and that's fair. But while there were definitely lows, it's easy to forget we shared highs as well. (Stephen McCarthy/ SPORTSFILE)

Like our march to the final in
2008, and winning the Munster
Championship in 2010. (*above:*
Pat Murphy/SPORTSFILE; *right:*
©INPHO/Cathal Noonan)

By the morning of the final replay, the energy in the group was phenomenal. Training, tactics, belief. Almost three seasons of hard work and sacrifice had brought us to this point. We were ready. (Daire Brennan/SPORTSFILE)

Picking Shane O'Donnell for the replay against Cork caught a lot of people off guard; he was so young. His selection almost reduced us both to tears, but it wasn't until the final whistle that the emotions came pouring out. (©INPHO/James Crombie)

Disbelief. (Paul Mohan/SPORTSFILE)

Release. (©INPHO/Morgan Treacy)

My son, Colm, hadn't been around for my wins with Clare in the '90s, so it meant a lot to have a victory we could share. (Ray McManus/SPORTSFILE)

Bringing the Liam McCarthy home to Sixmilebridge. What a feeling. (©INPHO/ James Crombie)

The year 2014 was a washout. We were All-Ireland champions, but trouble was brewing behind the scenes. (John Kelly)

It's a measure of Dónal Óg Cusack as a hurling man
that in 2016 he so quickly gave up the 'glamour' of
the pundit's chair for a back-room role with Clare.
We really gelled as a team. (Stephen McCarthy/
SPORTSFILE)

The All-Ireland quarter-final against Galway in Semple Stadium on 24 July 2016, and
what would turn out to be my last game in charge of Clare. I'd had heart surgery a
couple of days beforehand. (©INPHO/Donall Farmer)

Dad's seen me at my lowest ebb and during my greatest highs. He's always had my back, just never at the cost of fairness. He lives for Clare GAA. It hurt to see him portrayed by some as a partisan. (John Kelly)

After resigning from Clare, my health was poor. Living with that ill feeling for so long, the weight of it, had aggravated my heart problems, and I was beginning to suffer from sleep apnoea. (©INPHO/ Lorraine O'Sullivan)

I hadn't expected to return to management so quickly – and I was probably mad to do so – but Wexford had so much potential and were ready to throw their weight behind the project. I couldn't say no. (©INPHO/Ken Sutton)

Going to war. Within ten yards of the touchline I knew I was in serious trouble. (©INPHO/Ryan Byrne)

Playing Clare in 2018 was a surreal experience. To be standing in front of the other dugout, looking over at players I'd known so well a couple of years previous. Times change, but when you've shared a journey like 2013, it never leaves you entirely. (Brendan Moran/SPORTSFILE)

People pay the most attention to the inter-county game, but I'm really proud of all we've accomplished at LIT. We've built a great system there, and it's been the basis of so much I've learned and achieved in management. (©INPHO/Morgan Treacy)

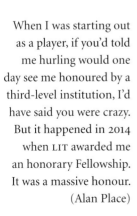

When I was starting out as a player, if you'd told me hurling would one day see me honoured by a third-level institution, I'd have said you were crazy. But it happened in 2014 when LIT awarded me an honorary Fellowship. It was a massive honour. (Alan Place)

You can't coach without support, and over the years, I've been able to count on incredible people, like Seoirse Bulfin, Louis Mulqueen and Mike Deegan. (*Left:* ©INPHO/Morgan Treacy; *centre:* ©INPHO/James Crombie; *bottom:* ©INPHO/Cathal Noonan)

For all the drama on and around the pitch, life at home has never been better. (Pawel Novak)

Talking tactics with two of the most underrated members of my backroom team. (Sharon O'Laughlin)

Who knows what the future holds. For now, it's Wexford and, hopefully, more match days and Croke Park. (©INPHO/Morgan Treacy)

At half-time we led 0-8 to 0-4, Cork restricted to a solitary point from play. I know neutrals wouldn't have seen much beauty in that statistic, but for me it was a massive plus. Still, Cork were always likely to come back at us and, when a 46th-minute Patrick Horgan free flew all the way to Clinton Hennessy's net, their tails were really up.

With the sides still level after 70 minutes, I was calm in the dressing-room, telling the players, 'I know we're going to win.' I could just see their energy levels were still high and the added 20 minutes of extra time would be no bother to them physically.

And we needed every ounce of that energy. The game eventually settled when Big Dan fizzed an 83rd-minute shot past Dónal Óg in the Killinan goal, the ball barely crawling over the goal line. Even then we needed Browne to make a miraculous block from Cathal Naughton in added time to make sure the Cup was coming home with us.

The scenes afterwards were phenomenal and we got stuck in desperate traffic leaving Thurles, the bus driver taking some kind of crazy route that made no sense. Sitting at the front, I remember turning to someone behind me and saying, 'I don't give a shite if it takes us a week to get out of here, I'm feeling no pain!'

We ended up back in Dungarvan, took over this big room in the Park Hotel and everyone stayed up chatting until six the following morning.

It was a beautiful feeling, but I knew I was still dealing with a complicated dressing-room. Ken admitted some time later that he had to shake himself out of a personal sulk on the bus home, realising what the win meant to the younger players around him. And those complications would come to bear when we met Tipp in the All-Ireland semi-final.

PÁRAIC FANNING: 'I found this difficult on a personal level, because some of the lads who were coming to the end were club-mates of mine and even former teammates. You could see they were on the wane a little bit. But these fellas were from a golden era for Waterford hurling, big personalities. There was never any intent to hurt anyone, we just felt they weren't quite where we needed them to be.

'What people didn't realise is that we were building a new team in Waterford. Bear in mind, that's the last Munster title we've won and, day of the game apart, there wasn't that much of a fuss.

'I remember when Waterford won their previous Munster title ('07) they ended up getting a holiday to South Africa. After this one we ended up paying for our own breakfast after an overnight on a weekend in Liverpool.

'So it was never really recognised or valued as the achievement that it was.'

I knew that semi-final was going to be a big ask, given that Tipp were beginning to find their true rhythm now. They'd suffered that heavy defeat to Cork in the Munster Championship, after which I took a call from their captain and my old friend from LIT, Mullinahone's Eoin Kelly.

We spoke for more than 40 minutes on the phone, just shooting the breeze about where they might have got their preparations wrong. Eoin felt Tipp had been flying in training and just hadn't seen the Cork performance coming.

He's a man I have massive respect for, and I remember telling him not to panic, that Tipp had far too much class not to still have an impact in the championship.

Now, three months on, they'd won games against Wexford, Offaly and a nail-biter against Galway to ensure that this class was now coming our way in a semi-final.

And this would be the day I decided that Waterford needed to start deploying a sweeper. Why? Because two of our forwards chose in effect to do their own thing against Tipp, and in doing so, the team's entire defensive structure effectively broke down.

If I'm honest, I could see it coming. About two weeks after the Munster final win we had a team meeting in Walsh Park, at which these two players came to me with the message 'Davy, we like playing free-flowing hurling in Waterford.'

My response was that we'd tried it the previous two years and it was obvious that, if the All-Ireland was our target, free-flowing hurling just wouldn't get us there. I knew it suited the two boys to play that type of hurling, but it didn't suit the group.

When that meeting had finished, three or four other players approached me, telling me in no uncertain terms that the bulk of the group agreed 100 per cent with what I was trying to do. They told me to disregard what the two lads were saying.

Trouble was, I became largely helpless the day of the game and it wrecked my head standing on the line that day, watching two players completely ignore team instructions.

I'm not saying we'd have beaten Tipp if these two did what they'd been told, but I do believe our backs would have found it far easier to deal with the opposition's attacking threat if everybody had been singing off the one hymn sheet. Bottom line, you must defend as a team, and on this day we had only thirteen players doing that.

PAT BENNETT: 'Davy was trying to change the culture of the dressing-room, which is probably an awful lot easier to do now but, at that time, you just knew certain players would never change. Because for so long these lads had been doing their own thing.

'They'd do what you asked them to do in practice matches, not a bother. But soon as it came to a proper game, bang. Back doing their own thing, going where they wanted to go. Bottom line, these lads felt they needed to be scoring, unlike unselfish hurlers, like Brick Walsh or Séamus Prendergast, who wouldn't give a damn if they never scored themselves.'

One of the consequences was Noel McGrath having a field day as a kind of loose centre-forward, something that led to a lot of ill-informed criticism of Brick. The truth is that Brick hadn't a hope against McGrath when defensive lines further up the field had become so ragged.

Had everybody been doing their job that day, others could have intercepted the danger long before Brick had to make the impossible decision of knowing whether to step out of position or not.

Tipp's attack went to town on us the same day, McGrath, John O'Brien, Lar Corbett and Kelly accumulating a crushing 3-13 between them from play. Yet I'd honestly have ascribed less blame to individual backs for that concession than I would to two players further up the field simply not fulfilling their defensive obligations.

I basically wanted the Waterford forwards to track back in much the same way Kilkenny's forwards had been doing under Cody. There was no great science to that, other than an adjustment of attitude. All I was looking for was a mix of energy and humility.

The latter, especially, is the key. Players have to be willing to work like dogs for that system to work. For that to happen you need 100 per cent buy-in in the dressing-room, and I was getting maybe 95 per cent. It wouldn't be enough.

If two players refused to track back, the rest of the team were wasting their time.

Trouble was, I knew this problem wasn't going to go away for me now either. Some players were simply not willing to work hard enough on that side of the game, yet were considered indispensable by the Waterford public when it came to choosing a starting fifteen.

That said, I did make a fundamental error with my team selection too.

I decided to go with a young Brian O'Halloran at full-forward, on the basis that if we could hit decent low diagonal balls in to him on either side, he'd have the legs on the Tipp full-back Paul Curran. All well and good, if that kind of possession could be guaranteed.

But Brian spent the first 20 minutes of that game a sitting duck under these high, floated deliveries to the edge of the Tipp square that, needless to say, Curran found entirely to his liking.

Hand on heart, the plan for Brian was exactly the same one I'd have three years later for a certain Shane O'Donnell in the All-Ireland final replay. Only real difference was that every other Clare player executed their role to perfection.

Páraic Fanning actually texted me after that 2013 win with the single line, 'Think I saw that game-plan before!'

Brian was a smashing young lad with huge talent. I used to collect him from Mary Immaculate College in Limerick to go to training and, for my final year in Waterford, we'd then pick up my new goalkeeping coach, Seoirse Bulfin, in Tipperary town.

Seoirse would leave his van at the Amber filling-station and, deciding to get diesel there this one day, I asked Brian to fill the tank and Seoirse to go in and pay. We were only half a mile out of town then when the engine began chugging. I sensed immediately what the trouble was.

'Brian, what pump did you use?'

He thought I was kidding and just smiled from the back seat.

'Brian, I'm fucking serious, diesel or petrol?'

The penny began to drop. 'Petrol, Davy.'

'It's a fucking diesel car, Brian!'

We had to pull in immediately, swing back around to Tipp town and make the rest of the journey in Seoirse's Peugeot van, young Brian in the back, almost up against the roof on tackle bags and ladders.

Honestly, in different circumstances I believe O'Halloran could have been to Waterford what O'Donnell has become to Clare.

But by the end of the day against Tipp now I'd replaced five of my starting six forwards, all to no avail as Waterford fell to their seventh defeat in eight All-Ireland semi-finals since '98.

I could hear the grumbles, inside and outside the dressing-room now too. And those grumbles were only going to get louder.

The 2011 Munster final thrashing by Tipperary stands as probably my worst experience in hurling.

It was a seven-goal slaughter I genuinely never saw coming, one that had certain disgruntled individuals thumping the dressing-room door in Páirc Uí Chaoimh, demanding to be let in to take their frustrations out on yours truly. I could hear these lunatics from the showers, recognised their voices.

They'd been part of an extended back-room team during my first two years with Waterford, men I'd decided to cut loose, for the simple reason that they'd become a little too aggressive and overbearing with their advice. Put simply, they had a specific job to do but seemed to think they were somehow on a par now in terms of dressing-room authority with my selectors, Pat and Páraic.

I just found they'd lost the run of themselves, showed them the door, and now they were back at it, seeking retribution.

To be fair, the lads manning the door knew exactly what was happening and did a great job in holding them at bay. Lord knows we were low enough between those four walls in Cork without needing the pantomime of two clowns coming in looking for a fight.

I honestly believed we were ready for Tipp that day. We'd had a more than decent National League, finishing third in the top table with four wins and a draw from seven matches. But it was a campaign in which I ended up serving a month's suspension for a crime I didn't commit. I blame it on a challenge match against a Kilkenny development side we played in Carriganore just three nights before we played Tipp in the League.

One of our lads went down injured, having taken a bang to the head, and I was absolutely furious when the referee didn't even stop play for our player to get attention.

There and then, I marched straight out on the field, telling the ref what I thought of him.

As luck would have it, wasn't he doing fourth official for James Owens three nights later in Thurles. There was a bit of a scuffle right in front of the Waterford dug-out and, next thing, I heard this absolute litany of abuse being roared at Owens from directly behind me. Now, when I say abuse, I mean heavy-duty abuse. Unrepeatable stuff.

Anyway, this fourth official seemed to think it was me doing the roaring, and I got reported for abuse of an official. A three-month sideline ban was proposed by the Central Competitions Control Committee, which we appealed to the GAA's Central Hearings Committee.

I'd actually been quite controlled on the line that night, keeping my peace even when Shane O'Sullivan and Clinton Hennessy were both red-carded in the second half.

So I brought sworn affidavits from our entire back-room team into the subsequent hearing in Croke Park, categorically stating that at no point had I directed any abuse at James Owens.

The hearing dragged on for hours, and it was indicated to me that if I played 'grass' on who the real culprit was my suspension would be rescinded. I wouldn't do that. I couldn't. Nor would I allow any of my back-room staff to name the man responsible.

In the end they reduced my suspension to a single month, which meant that for virtually the whole of March I was calling shots from the stand. Basically, the fourth official got it wrong. I've been guilty as charged often enough, but not that time.

PAT BENNETT: 'Davy's suspension meant I was effectively manager on the line when we went to Wexford in the League. I was miked up to him, of course, and, approaching half-time, the referee, John Sexton, gives a free against us that sends Davy into overdrive.

'We feel we're getting nothing, and Davy's in my ear now, telling me I've got to "get into" him at half-time. The whistle goes, and Davy's "Go, Pat, go, Jesus Christ, tell him to cop on …"

'As it happens, I buy my cars off Sexton's brother. So I go to meet him now as he's walking off the pitch. I'm wagging my finger at him, but all I'm saying is "John, look, I'm supposed to give you a right bollocking here, will you please give us an odd oul' free in the second half or I'm going to be feckin' devoured here!"

'Sexton was laughing. We won the game by four points!'

This would be the National League that effectively ended Ken McGrath's inter-county career. We played him midfield against Cork, and Pa Cronin ran him all over Dungarvan. It was almost cruel to watch it. In his own book Ken wrote: 'I was useless … substituted in the second half!'

I didn't play him in midfield to show him up in any way, as his wife, Dawn, subsequently suggested. Do you think that we honestly wanted to humiliate Ken McGrath? The suggestion was ridiculous. His legs were gone, though, so what were we to do? Drop him off the panel completely?

The truth is that Ken actually asked us to play him in midfield that day. We were going to start him in full-forward, but his view was 'No, let me have a run at midfield and see how I go.'

And Cronin just won a pile of ball off him. In fairness to Ken, he rang Pat Bennett afterwards to say he just didn't have it any more, that he reckoned it was time to go.

Brick had made centre-back his own, and the forward line was going well enough. So where could I fit in Ken? I could see his logic in that maybe at midfield he could get onto loose ball. It's a position you can kind of operate at three-quarters pace all the time. You don't ever really have to be going flat out. So we said we'd give him a go there and if it didn't work out he'd know himself that he was in trouble.

And that's pretty much how things panned out. We gave him about 45 minutes, then replaced him with Eoin Kelly in a game Waterford won by a single point.

There was just a final between the top two teams for that year's League, so we bounced from our group games into a Munster Championship opener against Limerick.

It proved a poor game, in which we struggled to contain the threat of the full-forward, Kevin Downes. Donal O'Grady's tactic of pulling forwards out the field to leave space inside for Downes was a virtual mirror image of what I'd been trying to do with Big Dan.

Being honest, we were lucky to come through the game with a single-point victory, considering the trouble Downes gave our full-back, Liam Lawlor. And maybe, on some level, that made me over-think the challenge now facing us in a final against Tipp.

They were, after all, All-Ireland champions, a team armed with forwards who could really put you to the sword. Everywhere you looked you'd see danger.

I decided to move Brick back to full-back, because those three goals conceded against Limerick were still playing on my mind. If we'd looked a bit too open against them we could hardly expect to survive doing the same thing against, arguably, the best attack in the game.

I also decided to go with a championship debutant on Lar Corbett. It's a decision that would, of course, come back to haunt me given that Lar went to town that day, finishing the game with 4-4 to his name.

Despite his inexperience, Jerome Maher was one of our tightest man-markers and a lad armed with the pace to go with a real speed-merchant like Lar.

And, hand on heart, I couldn't have been happier with the way things were going in training. In fact I remember putting out a virtual second team for a challenge game against Wexford in Mount Sion and our victory pretty much confirmed my belief that we now had serious squad depth to call upon.

You see, if we'd lost the likes of Flynn, Ken and now Kelly over the previous few seasons, we also had a strong younger generation coming through, particularly in the likes of Noel Connors, Páraic Mahony and Dan Shanahan's younger brother, Maurice.

The week before we faced Tipp we were allowed a practice game in Páirc Uí Chaoimh and, with a concert blaring from the marina, the players looked absolutely on fire. Honestly, I couldn't have been happier.

I remember standing there in the middle of the field at one point and being overcome by this surreal sense that they were almost hurling in harmony with the music now rolling in over the back of the terrace.

Trouble was, we left our form behind us on the field that night.

Because, when it came to our big day against Tipp, we just never showed up. And let me be clear on one thing. Jerome wasn't the reason we fell asunder. Actually only one of Corbett's goals arrived while he was his marker. Every one of us had to put our hand up that day and openly admit that we simply weren't up to scratch.

And Tipp, to be fair, were absolutely sensational.

They were under new management now, in Declan Ryan and Tommy Dunne, and came at us with a strategy of getting high ball in around the D, where they'd have runners arriving from every angle. It worked to devastating effect, largely because our forwards allowed the Tipp midfield and half-backs especially to deliver armchair, diagonal ball to the likes of Kelly and Lar.

To this day I believe Jerome Maher fully earned his opportunity to play that day but just had the misfortune of making his debut in a team that bombed in every sector.

And the trouble with man-marking Corbett was that he simply did not play in a single position. He was Mr Perpetual Motion, constantly switching wings or even, on occasion, pitching tent on the edge of the square. That became the story with all Tipp's forwards. Their movement was absolutely ferocious and we just weren't ready for it.

I have to accept that it was my responsibility to have the team ready, but Tipp went for our throats and an explosive four-goal scoring burst inside six minutes approaching half-time left us 17 points adrift and, clearly, already beaten.

It was horrible.

PAT BENNETT: 'We were all shell-shocked. I was to do a sideline interview before I went in with RTÉ Radio's Pat McAuliffe. Sure what could I say? Anyway, Pat's asking me all these questions and I'm kind of answering him in a trance, desperate to get in.

'Then he says, "Are ye going to make changes?"

'And without even thinking, the words that came out of my mouth were "Pat, what do you f…g think?"

'When I went home that evening my mother-in-law gave out to me for cursing on national radio!'

In the dressing-room, my only message was 'Boys, for your own sake, ye have to go back out there and fight. The game might be gone, but your pride can't be!'

I'd taken Jerome out of the firing-line before the real collapse occurred and threw on three more subs at half-time now in a desperate attempt to stop the rot. If you consider we lost the second half by just four, maybe we – at least – achieved that much. But it felt a day absolutely without consolation.

Near the end, Tipp made a point of getting Brendan Cummins a standing ovation to mark his equalling of Christy Ring's championship appearances record of 65 games by replacing him with Darren Gleeson.

Now, I'm sure Declan Ryan didn't intend it to be insulting, but that's very much how it felt from our side of the fence. Declan probably thought it would be in his interests just to get a few championship minutes into Gleeson, but I remember at the time feeling that they were just rubbing our noses in it in front of 40,000 people. Tossing salt into a very deep wound.

The whole experience was a nightmare, just one of those days you'd quite like the ground to open up and swallow you.

And I took savage abuse at the final whistle, different people shouting the worst that came into their heads.

'You haven't a fucking clue …'

'You've wrecked that team, you stupid Clare prick …'

'You're some fucking clown …'

I was trying to be magnanimous, shaking hands with different Tipp players and management, when one lad came across, hitting me a sideways punch into the chest. The same fella was gone before I could turn to confront him. All I saw was the back of a Waterford jersey disappearing into the crowd.

Just another faceless hero.

The year before, they'd nearly been carrying me off the field in Thurles. Now people were taking shots.

So I was glad to reach the sanctuary of the dressing-room, even though I could hear the lunatics at the door, looking to 'sort out that little fucker'. And I had to think on my feet now. How in God's name could I rescue something from this wreckage?

I mean, one of the hardest things in the world is to talk to a team in those circumstances and get them to actually hear. It's in my DNA to come out fighting, to channel my anger into the next day, but that's not in everybody's, I know that. Whatever I said next I'd have to make it count.

So I called the players into the second dressing-room, asking them to squeeze tight. Given the size of the rooms, this meant some had to crowd the doorway to hear what was being said.

'Guys, there's no drink tonight, no fucking cop-out,' I said. 'And you'll be in Dungarvan at eight o'clock in the morning.' I knew that would go down like a lead balloon, but we all needed to know who was up for the fight here.

By the time we got back to the Imperial Hotel, some of the players had been in the ears of the selectors, Páraic Fanning now despatched as a go-between. 'Davy,' he said, 'they're not in a good place, you might be as well to let them out for a few drinks. Might be no harm for them to let their hair down.'

I said nothing. I just knew that, whatever I did now, I needed to be sure it was the right thing for the group.

So I told Páraic I was going out for some air, slipped out a side door, and just walked around for three or four minutes to clear my head. And those few minutes were all I needed. With every fibre in my body I just felt that, if any of those players wanted to go on the beer after a seven-goal hiding, then they'd be better off involved with somebody else.

I wasn't for budging.

My feeling was that you can hide behind drink. You can blame everything and everybody for something that, in this instance, needed everyone – first and foremost – to look in the mirror.

I knew the lads were sick to the stomach from what Tipp had just done to them, but I wanted them to stay that way. I wanted them to hate that feeling so much they'd never allow it happen them again.

So I went back in, called over Brick and Stephen Molumphy. 'Guys, it stands,' I said. 'Are ye going to back me?'

To be fair, I knew I was asking two of the most solid men I've known in hurling. They said they knew some wouldn't be happy but, if that was my instruction, that's what they'd be doing.

We'd had our pre-match meal in Castlemartyr that day and I was staying there that evening. Being honest, I could feel some of the players staring daggers at me as I prepared to get off the bus. So I stood at the front and told them they could go two ways now.

'You can go out feeling sorry for yourselves and drink the night away or go straight home, man up, and we'll meet in the morning to have this out. But, trust me, if ever there's a time in your lives to stand up and fight, that time is now!'

I got very emotional as I was speaking, I suppose the weight of everything beginning to catch up with me now.

It just felt to me that everything we had was hanging by a thread here. Hand on heart, I didn't know what the players would do when they got back to Waterford. They could have gone on the piss and, if they did, my position would have been untenable. That much was crystal-clear.

It was a massive call, but I felt I had to make it.

Liam Dowd came into the hotel with me, but I was completely in a trance. I tried to eat but couldn't. Different people were coming to me and saying largely kind and understanding things, but they might as well have been talking to a zombie.

Eventually everybody started drifting away and it was just Liam and me. He still had a drive back to Leixlip ahead of him but stayed sitting, most of the time in silence. It was about 3:30 a.m. when he finally left and he told me after that he had to pull in a couple of times because he was falling asleep behind the wheel.

I'll never forget his concern for me that evening, given how, just five months earlier, Liam had lost his wife, Teresa, to a brain tumour.

LIAM DOWD: 'We'd been playing a National League game against Tipp at Semple Stadium in late March of 2010 and I was on the pitch after when I took a call from my daughter, Sinéad, asking what time I expected to be home. Teresa had been in Clonmel the same day, playing in a bridge tournament, when she started to feel ill.

'A friend brought her home early and that night it was recommended that we bring her to the A&E in Blanchardstown. At this stage there was no question in any of our minds that it was anything serious, even though Teresa had been very disoriented. She'd been a little off-colour for the previous few weeks and we thought it might be something to do with a sinus issue.

'But they kept her in hospital that night and again on Monday. She was due to be discharged on the Tuesday but, as a brain scan had been booked, they decided to go ahead with that, even though everyone seemed pretty confident that nothing untoward would show up.

'That lunchtime a nurse said to me that the consultant "would like a word." And it was then I started to feel a little uneasy.

'Maybe nine that night myself and Sinéad were finally called down to meet him, only to be met by a complete bombshell.

'"I'm afraid your wife has an inoperable grade 4 brain tumour, and there's nothing much we can do," he said. After that his mouth was moving but I was hearing nothing. Bear in mind, Teresa is outside sitting on a bed, waiting to be discharged.

'It'll go down as the worst moment of my life.'

So this man was dealing with his own issues, yet he stayed with me for hours. I've often thought about that since, about how – if anything – I should have been the one paying attention to him that night in Castlemartyr.

Naturally we'd talked a lot about Teresa through that awful time and, after her death, Liam often said that the hurling was a welcome distraction. He spent a good bit of time down in Sixmilebridge with myself and Sharon.

I could see what he meant in how the game sometimes grew so big in our lives it almost squeezed everything else into oblivion. And I'll say it against myself, that evening the only thing in my head now was how on earth I could get this Waterford team to recover from an absolute mauling.

Liam was a vital sounding-board.

I'd called that session for 8 a.m. in Dungarvan the following morning and, if I'm honest, I wasn't 100 per cent sure if that was a good idea now.

LIAM DOWD: 'The reason I stayed with him that night in Castlemartyr was I was genuinely worried about him. I'd never seen him so low. Not even after the '08 All-Ireland. He was completely rattled, completely down.

'And I knew, deep down, he was wondering now about the call he'd made on lads going for a pint. About calling the morning session in Dungarvan. Was he right? Was he wrong?

'He was trying to second-guess everything, and, if I'm honest, I'd probably have gone the other way with the drink call. I just thought the players were in such a bad place, maybe a blow-out was what they needed now. But not a chance was I going to say it to him now.

'He was a fairly battered man and I just knew he was too fragile at that moment.'

I didn't sleep at all, got up at 6 a.m., drove to Dungarvan and sat looking out at the water.

This, I knew, could go either way now. I began questioning why I put myself through this kind of torture, the uncertainty of not knowing if the players would even show. And, if they did, would they be pulling against me?

But, to my relief, the cars began arriving and soon enough the entire panel was circled in the dressing-room, picking through the wreckage of a horrible day. It was a candid and often edgy meeting that lasted about 90 minutes, a lot of the subs now getting stuff off their chests about not being given the opportunities they felt they deserved.

I got abuse, gave some abuse. Some elder statesmen, who weren't getting their game, let me know in no uncertain terms that they believed nobody to be more culpable for the Tipp slaughter than me. By and large, the people asking questions of me were the people who weren't playing. I had no issue with that. They were entitled to that bit of bitterness. But when you have a panel of, say, 40, deep down you know in your heart and soul that you're going to struggle psychologically to hold on to the last fifteen. They're going to be against every move you make, no matter what that move is.

Put it this way: if there's ever a dressing-room vote taken about your management, they're fifteen votes you can write off straight away.

It got fairly heated at times but, if tempers weren't raised on this day of all days, then we were dead in the water. So I just let things take a natural course. After that we did maybe a 20-minute stretch, got into the cars and drove to Clonea Strand for a stroll in the water.

SEOIRSE BULFIN: 'I didn't have to go to the meeting so was playing golf that morning with a friend in Dundrum. There was a delay on the first tee and these four Tipp lads were playing in front of us. They wouldn't have known me from Adam and were just having the craic.

'So it was all "What time did you get home last night?"

"'Ah, I think it was around 7:19!"
'Falling around the place they were, and me standing there
fit to be tied!'

Before we left, a group of maybe fifteen supporters that'd
gathered on the bank applauded the players off the field. It was
an incredibly powerful and important moment for the group.
Instinctively, everyone who was there walked across to these
people, shaking their hands, thanking them for their support.

It was brilliant. Every single player had turned up fully togged
out and had now had their say, with no subject off the table. I
just felt it was a great statement by a group of people who were
hurting.

And yet I was carrying massive demons of my own now.

If I'm honest, my confidence was on the floor. Local radio
crucified us that Monday, Stephen Frampton especially having a
real go. I thought, as a former player, he'd have known that we were
low enough already without needing someone of his stature putting
the boot in. He's a bright guy and someone I always had good time
for. That day I felt he could have been a bit more understanding.

WLR were hounding Pat on the phone, telling him we had to
speak, that we were getting a desperate slating. Pat told them we'd
talk after the Galway game, not before.

And I remember especially this chap Dave Walsh from the
Supporters' Club giving it to me in the neck. Just two years later,
when I won the All-Ireland with Clare, the same man wrote me
a beautiful letter, actually apologising for what he'd said that day.
It's my deep regret today that I didn't send him a reply.

I've just never been good with letters and then time goes by
and, I suppose, the opportunity seems to pass.

Everything still felt raw driving home to Clare that morning,
and I was hoping that's how the players felt too. Because I was
thinking that hurt might just be our one and only friend here.

Once home I just wanted my own space, didn't want to talk to anyone. Sharon knows exactly what to do on days like that. She leaves me to myself. Gives me the time to sort things out in my head.

My father came up to the house, but I just told him to go away. I have this swivel chair in my office and I just sat on it in silence, running things over and over in my head. The television was flickering away, but I saw nothing. Hadn't a clue what was on and just sat there into the early hours.

We went training the following Wednesday in Walsh Park, and instantly the hurt of Páirc Uí Chaoimh was written across everything I could see.

Without me having to say anything, they just went at one another, hammer and tongs. For half an hour I let this practice match run and the sound was of timber splintering everywhere. Every last one of them was like a briar.

I was delighted. The day before, I'd given a fair few hours on the phone, chatting to every single squad member individually, just picking their brains to see if they'd any fresh perspective on what had happened us against Tipp.

And all I could hear in them was an absolute desperation to put things right again. To win back some honour.

That practice match was exactly what we needed.

PAT BENNETT: 'The lads were breaking hurleys off one another, going at it hammer and tongs. I remember Richie Foley in the middle of the field pulling a bad slap against someone and Davy pulling him off.

'Richie walks off, flings his hurley out over the wall and sits on the ground with a head like a bear. Davy's driving his team now, I'm driving mine, and about ten minutes later he roars, "Richie, get up!"

'Richie gets up, pulls on his helmet again, then remembers his hurley is out over the wall. And he has to climb out over it to get it back.

'They took chunks out of each other that night and you just knew we were back on track.'

So I had an inkling of what was coming against Galway. There'd been so much misinformation about this group of Waterford players – how they rolled, what things mattered to them – that a lot of people seemed blind to the fact that they were incredibly proud people.

They would also go to Thurles for that All-Ireland quarter-final knowing that, in nine previous championship meetings, Galway had never beaten Waterford.

I brought Brick back out to a happier perch in the half-back line, giving Liam Lawlor the start at number three. And it's probably fair to say that Galway never stood a chance.

An early Joe Canning penalty put them a point ahead, but we absolutely devoured them through the middle third, out-scoring them 0-14 to 0-3 between the 17th and 50th minutes. Kevin Moran had an absolute stormer at midfield, Shane Walsh scored 1-4 from play and, when Aidan Harte hit a late consolation goal for Galway, we responded instantly with one of our own from Thomas Ryan.

Hand on heart, I felt sorry for John McIntyre after. He saw fit to make a public apology for Galway's performance, but the truth is they came up against wounded animals that day. Me included.

I'd been taking some smart-arse phone calls in the dead of night, getting stick from people who should have known better. I suppose that's the nature of the beast when you take a fall. There's always someone only too happy to give you a kicking.

That would be McIntyre's last day as Galway manager and, as we shook hands, he and I both knew the storm of bullshit coming his way. Another good man about to be thrown under the bus.

Two weeks later Kilkenny did to us what they did to most teams. They showed us the door with a minimum of fuss.

It was our fourth consecutive year reaching an All-Ireland semi-final, but we went under a little more gently than I'd have liked. True, it was nothing like the '08 massacre, and, given that Richie Hogan opened the scoring with a third-minute goal, that ghost was circling for a while that day.

But the truth is that game turned on a great 33rd-minute save by David Herity from John Mullane, from which Kilkenny counter-attacked and scored a second goal through Hogan. That killed us in our shoes.

Instead of going in front 2-7 to 1-9 we now trailed 1-7 to 2-9, Kilkenny taking a six-point lead to the dressing-room that, if I'm honest, we never really looked like reining in.

We did all we could to rouse the players at half-time, but we were fighting a losing battle. You could just see it in certain faces. Key guys now visibly resigned to their fate against a team they didn't believe we could beat. As Pat, Páraic and I walked back down the dressing-room tunnel for the start of the second half we turned to one another and, almost in unison, agreed, 'We're fucked!'

With fifteen minutes to go, Kilkenny would be ten points to the good and, although the lads rallied and kept their heads up, there was a sense of just going through the motions over those closing minutes.

I was gutted. Clinton Hennessy fired his hurley across the dressing-room in frustration when it was over, roaring, 'When are we ever going to learn to win these fucking games?' He was frustrated, I suspect, because he'd seen exactly what I'd seen again. Too many lads just leaving the plan once the pressure came on. Doing their own thing. Mullane had scored 1-6 from centre-forward but, if I'm honest, I don't think we ever truly worried Kilkenny that day. Yes, we'd kept our dignity. Yes, we'd avoided a collapse when at times it looked possible.

But we'd shown none of the anger and, yes, lack of respect for them that we'd shown against Galway. On some level, they'd managed to get into our heads again. We'd been too nice, too compliant.

And I couldn't stand that.

10

'MOUNTAINS ARE FOR SHEEP ...'

After the Kilkenny defeat I'd asked the Waterford chairman, Tom Cunningham, to give me a few weeks to figure out what I wanted to do next.

During that time Clare suffered an unmerciful All-Ireland qualifier hammering against Galway in Salthill. I went to the game with Louis Mulqueen and it's fair to say that what unfolded in Pearse Stadium was ugly. Clare were beaten off the park and coming away after I remember saying to Louis that it was high time Clare hurling started to become respectable again.

One of the people we bumped into on the way out was Mike Deegan. Mike had been involved for years with Cratloe and, though we didn't know one another that well, everything I heard about him always suggested he was a straight-shooter, someone who was black-and-white in his opinions. That day in Galway, almost as one, the two of us came out with the exact same line. 'Jesus, there has to be more in Clare than that!'

In many ways, Sparrow O'Loughlin had taken on an impossible job, the players having got rid of Mike Mac in '09. Sparrow won three back-to-back Limerick county titles managing Adare and had now started a process with Clare that needed to be started. But it seemed to me that expectation had begun out-stretching reality in the county now because of two successive Munster Minor Championship wins and awareness of a booming young talent base about to spawn three All-Ireland under-21 wins in a row.

It was a long drive home to Sixmilebridge that day, but the chat with Mike had already got me thinking that he was a man I wouldn't mind working with in the future.

I'm a creature of instinct when it comes to people and just some of his observations about how Clare set up in Salthill struck me as coming from a sharp hurling brain. Had I thought about the possibility of managing Clare at this stage? Hand on heart, I'd been thinking about it since I first got involved as a coach.

There'd been a bit of slagging over the years from close friends like Kevin Corry and Alan Murphy too, just banter about it being time for me to 'come home.'

And I'd say I really had my mind made up to walk away from Waterford within three or four days of the Kilkenny defeat. The performance had been respectable, but I just got a feeling from the players that they never genuinely believed it was a game that they could ever win. That frustrated me deeply. If that belief wasn't there, it represented a fundamental failure on my part.

PAT BENNETT: 'He could have gone another year in Waterford, but I remember saying to Davy, "The best thing for Waterford is for you to stay, but the best thing for you is probably to go."'

I'd now had four throws of the dice with Waterford and just felt the players might be better off listening to a different voice in 2012.

I'd also begun to find the travelling tough so, when I met Cunningham at the subsequent Tony Forristal tournament in Mount Sion's grounds (my son, Colm, was playing for Clare), I told him of my intentions. I knew Tom would have supported me if I wanted to continue, but he could see the logic too of exposing the dressing-room to someone with different ideas. People might imagine the wheels were already in motion for me to get the Clare job, especially given that Sparrow had indicated by now that he'd be stepping down, but that simply wasn't the case.

DINNY CULLINANE: 'Around the time he got an inkling that the Clare job was available there was also talk that the Galway job might be up for grabs. We met for lunch in the Shamrock in Lahinch one day, and I said to him that I thought he'd be perfect for Galway.

'"What about Clare?" he asked.

'My view was that Galway were further down the road to a potential All-Ireland, that the Clare job would take a lot of time and patience. And his reply to me I'll never forget. "That's true," he said, "but there's a right bunch of young players coming through.

'"And when might I ever get the chance again to win an All-Ireland with my father?"'

The truth is I had absolutely zero contact with the Clare County Board for a good three weeks after my parting of the ways with Waterford. Only then did the chairman, Michael O'Neill, ask me to meet him in Clare Abbey.

My father, Pat, was certainly staying out of things and I've no doubt that Michael had plenty of people telling him not to touch me with a barge pole, that the involvement of one Fitzgerald was more than enough for Clare GAA. That said, my record was there for anyone to see. It would have been strange if Clare didn't at least enquire about my availability.

When we met I told Michael of my belief that, with the profile of players available to Clare, we needed to do something different. That if I got the job, my plan for the first twelve months would be to completely redraft the senior panel, to integrate a lot of the under-21s and give them a season of experience at senior level.

This process had been problematic for me in Waterford four years earlier, where recent successes meant certain people felt untouchable in the dressing-room. With Clare, that wasn't going to be an issue. We'd done nothing in recent times. Nobody could argue if the new manager came in with a fresh broom.

Michael took my proposals back to the executive and, pretty soon, I was outlining plans to the next county board meeting in the West County Hotel.

When I said that my immediate target would be promotion from Division 1B in the National League, I could almost sense some delegates snigger at such naïveté. Clare had been stuck in the lower division for years, with little indication that an escape would be coming any time soon.

That said, I think the feeling at the time was that Clare had nothing to lose, that things were at such a low ebb any attempt at doing things differently might be worth the gamble. Our recent record in the Munster Championship was abysmal, three victories in twelve seasons. I was aware that certain people in the county weren't exactly thrilled to have me as manager, but the only way I could win them over was through making Clare competitive again.

To that end I wanted to assemble a serious back-room team, but that didn't prove quite as simple as I'd hoped.

The first man on my list was the one who'd travelled with me to that slaughter against Galway in Salthill. Louis Mulqueen and I went back a long way. He'd trained me both as an under-21 and senior with Clare and had been involved with Cyril Lyons in '02 when we got to the All-Ireland final. He'd been an impressive back-room figure during the Ger Loughnane years, a period during which we'd always sit together at the front of the Clare bus and room together on overnight trips.

He'd also been in charge of St Joseph's Doora-Barefield when they won three county titles, two Munsters and an All-Ireland in a remarkable stretch of seven years.

Louis and I just had very similar views on hurling and how to make the best of a team. We'd come together the year before to help Killanena, an East Clare side, win their first ever county intermediate title.

> LOUIS MULQUEEN: 'I was cutting the lawn one day and Davy appeared at the gate. "We've a job to do, bud, come on with me," he said. "Where?" I asked. "You'll see now," he says. "Sure you're at nothing there!"
>
> 'He was after getting involved with Killanena casually as they were still battling to make this famous breakthrough. So up we go to this challenge match, Davy saying, "I want you to watch these for me." I'm watching away, and he says to me, "I'm away to the States for four weeks now, but I want you to train them!"'

Killanena would finally make the breakthrough that year, beating Ruan (who had Cyril Lyons in their corner) in the final. The place went mad afterwards – bonfires for days. Promotion to senior status was huge for the club, and they celebrated accordingly. To be fair, I didn't need that experience to know I wanted Louis in my corner now. He'd been involved in one way or another with maybe a dozen Clare managers at different grades now, stretching all the way back to Seán Hehir in 1980.

My only concern was that, as principal of Rice College in Ennis, a school with maybe 50 staff and over 700 pupils, he might baulk at the idea of coming on board. I knew too that a lot of fairly influential people in the county would have been advising him against the idea. To me, it's a measure of Louis's strength of character that he went his own way in the end, weighed things up himself and decided that I wasn't some kind of Lucifer.

Mike Deegan was next man on my list, and after a day or two he too agreed to come on board. I sensed he'd be a hugely valuable addition but – if I'm honest – had no idea yet just how smart a reader of the game he'd prove.

Then I rang Brian Lohan.

He'd been such a warrior directly in front of me during my time as Clare goalkeeper, I knew first hand the courage and character he could bring to a hurling dressing-room. He'd worked with Patrickswell and Clare minors by now and I'd have considered us close at the time too, with both of us holding what I believed were similar views on how to put a team together.

But Brian spoke to precisely the same people who'd counselled Louis against joining me and, to my disappointment, chose to follow their advice. His explanation was something along the lines of being too busy with work and now not being 'the time'. I think it shows how much I thought of Brian Lohan that I asked him to come on board and I suppose his response suggested the feeling wasn't entirely mutual, although – to be fair – he did have four young kids at home to consider.

I also brought Paul Kinnerk on board, someone who'd built up such a good rapport with the Clare minors and whose work I'd also seen at close quarters with the Bridge under-21s. With those minors he worked really well alongside the joint managers, Donal Moloney and Gerry O'Connor, two men who shared my conviction that a game plan needed to suit the specific players at your disposal.

Paul had studied PE at the University of Limerick and I really liked the way he worked with the young players through structured games, always played at manic intensity. His training drills were brilliant and it was clear he had the absolute trust of a group coming through that, famously, would win those three under-21 All-Irelands in a row.

Paul and I met one day in the Radisson Hotel, where I explained how I thought he'd be well suited to working with me, given his Gaelic football background (he played for Limerick) and an understanding of the relationship between movement and the protection of possession.

My view was that, as good as the minors had been in that department through his coaching, they could have been even better – that simply moving a player into the defensive pocket wasn't enough for what I'd be trying to achieve.

Now Paul's a really sharp guy and, within seconds, he understood what I was getting at. And one thing he said to me that day I really liked. 'I know you're good at training teams,' he told me, 'but you're about to find out that I'm even better!'

Kinnerk related hugely to some of the younger players, most notably guys like Tony Kelly and Podge Collins. He had a real bond with the forwards, was very intelligent in terms of movement, but his way with the under-age players was all pace and energy, forwards dancing around their markers. I'd have to get it across to him that this was a different world now, that it mightn't be quite as easy if you were getting a shoulder from a Tipperary or Kilkenny senior. It probably took us that first year to get those young forwards to acclimatise to their new surroundings. But Paul and I would have some craic slagging one another every night at training. He'd be looking to do an attacking drill.

'Fuck's sake, Davy, how many forwards am I getting tonight?'

And I'm, 'I'll give you three today, I need sweepers.'

Over the next three years we'd split the training pretty evenly between us, with Louis stepping in on occasion too. It worked perfectly. They're both strong enough characters to challenge me when they thought I needed to be challenged, but the principles we believed in always overlapped.

There were other holes to fill too, and I knew precisely the people I wanted to fill them. I'd first come across Seoirse Bulfin in LIT around '04, where he was sports development officer. A brilliant man with infectious enthusiasm, he came on board in my final year with Waterford and has been with me ever since.

Joe O'Connor, who'd also worked with me in Waterford, would be my strength and conditioning man in name, a dozen times more than that in reality. Joe believes a team should integrate hurling into almost every single training-ground drill and I share that view.

After that?

I wanted Gazzy Collins for certain, a man who would serve seven different Clare managers before coming with me to Wexford. Gazzy is just one of those people who make players feel good about themselves. What does he actually do? The short answer is 'everything'.

Then I needed men to take control of the dressing-room environment, by which I mean ensuring that everything that needed to be in place, be it gear laid out or whatever, was in place. And that's not as simple as it sounds.

For this I got Seánie McMahon, the former inter-county referee, from Newmarket, two other referees, Fergie McDonagh and Tom Stackpoole, as well as Hego, Tommy Hegarty from Clarecastle. They'd work a roster between them, ensuring that two would be on duty every evening.

There'd be a small squadron of others too, people I absolutely trusted, like Mike Corry, Dinny Cullinane and Mike Deasy, all on stats. They made for a brilliant stats team, though I'd say I broke their hearts over the next few years, asking them to pull out video segments, not just of games but of training sessions.

I know people are reading this thinking such a big back room must have cost Clare County Board a fortune across the years. But most of these men wouldn't even get diesel money for their involvement. Over an entire season I doubt the expenses total for the whole lot of them would have exceeded €2,000. That's the absolute truth.

Pure and simple, they put in the hours because of their love for Clare hurling.

The Supporters' Club (since disbanded) became a huge help too, people like Michael O'Neill, Olive O'Loughlin, Emmet Moloney, PJ Kelly, Michael Maher, Orla O'Donnell, Amanda Hogan and her mother, Kathleen. I mention these people now because, trust me, there wasn't much glory to be had by association with Clare hurlers in 2012. But these were people willing to put the hours in through a belief that, working together, we could make things better.

Every single cent raised was accounted for, every detail presented to the audit committee. And that's what makes my blood boil when, even to this day, some smart-arses toss out that lazy question 'Where did all the money go?' about the Supporters' Club in Clare. Open your eyes. Ask the audit committee. Ask the county board.

The truth is that we made Clare a hell of a lot of money in my time as manager, when the focus seemed forever on what we cost them. People just looked at the expenditure without factoring in the increased revenue brought in. I mean, the year we'd win the All-Ireland the cost of training the team was something in the region of €500,000. But we brought in well in excess of €400,000 through the combination of gates and grants.

Put it this way, in my final year as manager there would be €258,625 spent on Clare's senior hurlers, €159,777 spent on the senior footballers. One key difference, though: the hurlers netted €202,552 for Clare GAA without even factoring in what money we'd raised in the US. The footballers netted €28,554.

They're not my figures, incidentally. They're the figures that the treasurer, Bernard Keane, brought to the Clare county convention.

So a huge amount of what we did was actually self-financing. People who imply otherwise really haven't got a clue. I was so conscious in Clare because of my father being county secretary that I'd make that trip to America every year to raise money for the team. If we were going away to a training camp the rule was always that we'd pay half ourselves, the county board the other half.

And a lot of the money we raised went into the under-age structures too, something I'm very proud of to this day. But people really have no idea of the work those people on the Supporters' Club put in. Mike Corry and a former county board treasurer at the time, PJ Kelly, were in charge of the finances, and I've never met men with more integrity. If I asked for a tenner Mike would need an explanation as to exactly where the tenner would be going. He was meticulous, he'd have to hear the reason.

You know, if I was setting up a company in the morning I'd want someone like Mike Corry at the top of it. We got huge help and support too from Keane, the county board treasurer. They all understood the extra energy I put into raising money, because I didn't want to put my father under pressure. And I don't doubt that Dad felt he had to be tougher on me for the same reason.

Bottom line, Clare would not have had the success that was now coming our way without the trojan work of the Supporters' Club and the people behind it. Without our sponsor, Pat O'Donnell. Every single cent that was raised went to supporting the senior and under-age teams, be it through contributing to the strength and conditioning bill or giving players who might have been struggling without work a small financial dig-out. In some instances I even did this out of my own pocket.

And, for the record, I never took a single cent for myself from the Supporters' Club.

Probably the abiding image people have of my first National League campaign as Clare manager is Limerick's James Ryan barrelling into me in the Gaelic Grounds.

It was no more than I deserved, to be honest. We'd hammered Limerick in our first game under lights, so when it came to the two teams meeting again in the 1B final (why a final was necessary when we'd already won promotion I could never understand) they launched themselves at us like men possessed. I could see it coming, because we'd absolutely blitzed them in that first meeting and there was simply no way they could let that happen a second time.

So I fully appreciated their reasons for hitting us so hard. I just couldn't tolerate the sight of my team accepting it.

The game was going against us, because we wouldn't match their aggression and naturally, when that happens, you go looking for an edge. How? I suppose I began shouting my mouth off at a couple of the Limerick players, stuff like 'Get stuck into him, hard as you can! He's not able for it!'

Needless to say, this was a red rag to some Limerick bulls, and James Ryan came over at one point, shunting me hard in the chest. The biggest mistake he'd make all day.

I didn't react, just went down on my hunkers, genuinely winded. As I did so I remember thinking, 'If there's anything in our lads now, this'll surely find it!'

True enough, from that moment on Clare horsed into the game and it felt a big statement to pull away to win in the end. Because there'd been a proper edge to it, even the gentlemanly John Allen squaring up to me on the line at one point. Again, I couldn't entirely blame him. He had to be seen to stand up for his players too.

I didn't get any apology afterwards for the Ryan incident and I didn't want one. Our League campaign would end with a 0-14 to 1-20 loss to Kilkenny at the semi-final stage, but we'd got precisely what we wanted from that National League. Taking on Kilkenny on anything close to equal terms was something we might aspire to further down the road.

About two weeks before that Kilkenny game we took the players to Carrauntoohil for a bonding weekend. It would be our second time up there, the first having almost ended in disaster.

In a sense, this was unfinished business for the players. When we'd gone there the previous December we got our timing slightly wrong, the mountain freezing over and so turning the notorious Devil's Ladder route into a virtual death trap. Aborting our efforts to get to the top of Ireland's highest mountain, we all quickly realised that getting back down would be just as daunting a challenge.

There'd been a light powdering of snow on the way up but, once the frost slipped down, the whole personality of the mountain changed.

Suddenly, the Ladder was really dangerous, an icy nightmare of razor-sharp boulders and treacherous scree. One patch of it was particularly bad, a big fall to our left, a massive drop to our right. So we literally slid down the mountain on our backsides, clinging to one another for support, Joe O'Connor at the front in constant touch with an increasingly concerned mountain rescue unit.

One of the players let a hurley slip and to hear it bouncing down into the coal-black gully just made the blood run cold.

It was madness. Devil's Ladder has become increasingly destabilised in recent years by the sheer weight of traffic, but try coming down it in darkness when every rock-face is glazed with ice! There's no question, what we did was extremely ropey. Our first real team-building exercise, almost a fucking disaster.

But it left an itch the players now wanted to scratch and a few of them came to me some time after, saying, 'Davy, we want to do that again, only get to the top this time.'

So this time we went back in the middle of the night, getting back down around 4 a.m., then sleeping in tents at the foot of the mountain. And if it told me any single thing about the group, it was that they didn't much like being defeated.

Waterford: it was always going to be Waterford. Just felt it in my bones, knew it in my heart.

The championship draw simply confirmed what I could always see coming. Clare hadn't won a Munster Championship game since '08 and now we'd be trying to end that record against the players I'd been managing in that very time-frame. Their new manager, Michael Ryan, decided to poke some fun at us in the build-up. Having heard of our Carrauntoohil adventures, he declared that mountains were 'for sheep'.

Good man, Michael, taking the piss out of us. Funny man.

We could have won the game, but Stephen O'Keeffe made two great saves near the end to deny us. And of course that would be the day when John Mullane and Eoin Kelly came barrelling across at the final whistle to make a point of celebrating in my face.

Mullane's explanation – as outlined in a subsequent TV interview with Marty Morrissey – would be that my alleged comments about him being finished were 'in my head all week.' Comments somebody, somewhere within the Waterford camp had conveniently manufactured. John admitted in the same interview, 'It takes a small thing to set me off,' and there's no doubt that certain Waterford people took advantage of that fact. They knew how to trigger his temper. To this day, I'm sure they feel they fully achieved their goal.

What I couldn't deny, admittedly, were certain comments I'd made to Kelly during the game itself.

A boom mike had been placed right beside me, picking up the exchange. I considered this deeply unfair, given that I'd never, ever heard another manager's comments picked up on television. Are you honestly telling me I'm the only GAA manager who's ever cut loose in a big championship game like that?

That mike simply shouldn't have been there. What's said on the line shouldn't be for public consumption in my view and, for the record, Kelly and I were absolutely fine about it once we got the chance to sit down and talk things through some time later.

I made a point of complaining to RTÉ about the intrusion, my comments to Eoin even having been debated on that night's *Sunday Game,* as if managers being miked was a commonplace thing.

Anthony Daly then brought Dublin to Ennis for an All-Ireland qualifier game, marching his players right down through the town, as if to say, 'We're taking over this town now!' Dublin were a serious team at the time, having won the National League in 2011, and I suspect he wanted them to stick their chests out and savour a special atmosphere.

MIKE CORRY: 'I remember standing outside the dressing-room when Dublin came in, Daly at the front of them, just staring straight ahead. They were like gladiators. I think they'd been in the Temple Gate and marched down through the town. It was actually a great play, but they didn't back it up. But I do remember looking at them, thinking how much they looked up for the game and wondering, "Are we ready for this?"'

It was a smart thing to do. Dalo didn't want them cowed in any way. I understood that. But it gave me precious ammunition for my own team talk too. 'This is *our town!*' I roared before sending Clare out that day. 'And they think they're coming down here to shit all over us?

'Go out there now and give them their answer!'

We were slow to start the same day, trailed by four points at half-time, then had Nicky O'Connell sent off. It was a big challenge to the team but one they met full on, digging their way out of a big hole to win. I thought it was a massive statement.

After that we came up against the opponents I suppose we least wanted: Limerick. When you've beaten a team twice already in one season, chances are they're going to be coming after you on a mission, and Limerick were no different. Maybe there was a little bit of complacency on our part too, because we gave up a couple of sloppy early goals to run out of road eventually.

I wasn't exactly devastated.

We were never going to be All-Ireland contenders that year and, having been given a three-year term, we'd achieved our first goal of gaining promotion to 1A. Anyway, the real Clare story unfolding that year was the under-21s, heading for All-Ireland glory under the management of Moloney, O'Connor and, of course, Kinnerk. Fair play, they'd given us full access to their players and sixteen or seventeen of that under-21 group trained with us all year, Paul being a natural link between the two set-ups.

It meant that we could educate the younger players on how we wanted Clare to hurl now, that philosophy of short-passing and movement. I always believe if you train under-age hurlers night in, night out with seniors it has to help them massively when they return to age-grade stuff. So it was a huge boost seeing those under-21s take what we'd schooled them in on the training-ground all the way to emphatic All-Ireland victory over a Kilkenny team that included men like John Power, Walter Walsh, Pádraig Walsh, Ger Aylward and Kevin Kelly.

I made a point of hiring a minibus from PK Travel to bring our senior back-room team to all the under-21 games that year. Just felt it was important that we gave the lads our full support while at the same time strengthening the bonds between us as a group.

And, one year into the Clare project, I could tell we were on the right road.

11

A HURT TEAM IS A DANGEROUS TEAM

Just two games into our 2013 National League campaign I felt it important to pick a fight I knew I couldn't win.

Johnny Crowley is a good foot taller than me and, clearly, packing a little more weight. He's a good hurling man too, maybe best remembered for mopping up against a two-man Galway full-forward line in the '86 All-Ireland final. Cyril Farrell's strategy of pulling one of his inside forwards out the field had completely unsettled Kilkenny in the semi-final.

But for the final the Cork manager, Johnny Clifford, decided Crowley should hold his position rather than follow any wandering Galway forwards and his number four ended up with a Man of the Match award.

That day would be Jimmy Barry-Murphy's last in a Cork jersey and, of course, he was the Rebels' manager now as we pitched up in Páirc Uí Rinn looking for our first win of the League.

We'd lost our opening game by a point to Waterford in Ennis, a hugely frustrating experience that ended with me almost breaking my toe by drawing a kick at the box I was in on the roof of the Cusack Park stand. Just reckoned I could read a game better from that height, so myself and Mike Deegan spent the game up there, communicating by walkie-talkie with Louis Mulqueen on the line.

Poor Louis must have had earache by the end, listening to Mike and me lose the plot as Clare lost a game we categorically should have won.

We'd gone into that League feeling good about ourselves, having won the Munster League, absolutely blitzing Tipperary under lights in a Thurles final. Our movement that night was devastating and I remember thinking, 'We could be on to something here!'

But now doubts were setting in again. Almost half way through against Cork we were five points down and, clearly, getting bullied. I was the recipient of dog's abuse from outside the wire, and when Patrick Horgan caught Domhnall O'Donovan with a nasty enough belt approaching half time it infuriated me that, as a team, we seemed to have no response.

Soon as the half-time whistle went I made a bee-line straight for Domhnall.

'Dunny!' I roared, determined to make myself heard by some Cork ears, 'were you hit there off the ball?'

'I was!' he answered.

'Well, Dunny,' I said, 'I'm giving you licence now to cut the fucking hand off that man. And I don't give a shit if you get red!'

Not the most diplomatic approach, I know, but I needed a spark of something here. Dunny, I recognised, incidentally, wouldn't hit a fly. If anything, he was probably more shocked by my behaviour now than any of the Cork players. There was no way he'd be taking the law into his own hands – I knew that. The only important thing to me was that other people heard. And, sure enough, Barry-Murphy came straight over, announcing what he thought of me.

Now, Jimmy's one of the finest gentlemen I know in sport, so for him to get involved will give you an idea of how tempers began to flare. He arrived with plenty of back-up too, Crowley pitching in by suggesting that I was 'just all fucking talk!'

Taking a quick glance around me to make sure there were some Clare bodies in the general vicinity (I might be mad, but not *that* mad), I made a sudden lunge at Johnny, knocking him backwards. At which point, just as I figured, the whole place went bananas. From my experience, Cork would normally just shrug off these kinds of verbals as being beneath them, but now fuses were blowing everywhere, lads having to be pulled apart.

And I will admit that, walking to the dressing-room, I grabbed a hold of my polo shirt, ripping a hole in the front.

Once inside I made sure the lads could see the torn fabric as I berated them for being too passive in the game. It looked as if I'd just been mauled by a pit-bull. 'I'll fight them if I have to!' I roared, giving the impression that I'd just been attacked outside. 'I don't give a fuck, I've fought them all my life. But what are ye going to do? Stand up for yourselves or just let them bully us all the time?'

LOUIS MULQUEEN: 'I'd never see a reason to row with anyone in my life, but because you were standing beside Davy you were in the trenches. And that's fine. Because that's what you've chosen to do. He always had people around him who'd be loyal to the end, who'd come out swinging.

'But Davy plays a madman only when he wants to play a madman. Some of it is theatrics. Sometimes he just knows he has to do something. Then other times you'll see this emotional side of him, the capacity for love. It means that most people don't tend to know the real Davy.'

Well, it was like I was flicking a light-switch.

The lads went back out, scored ten unanswered points in a twelve-minute spell and we won the game by six. If I was trying to find out what character lay inside the group, that night delivered my answer. Yes, I know I probably came across as slightly demented, but Clare just couldn't afford to be in any way casual against these teams.

That's what I was trying to get across. If, psychologically, we weren't on some kind of war footing we'd get blown away. I will admit I did feel a little uncomfortable afterwards about having had that shouting match with Barry-Murphy, a voice in my head on the way home asking, 'Why did you get sucked in to that?'

Deep down I knew the answer, though. I wasn't in this job to be keeping or making friends. I was in it to change Clare hurling.

That would be a strange League for us, one in which we collected just two more points, ending up in a relegation play-off against – God help us – Cork. That sounds worse than it was, though. Tipp were the only team to give us a bit of a trimming and that was an obvious pay-back for what we'd done to them in the Munster League final.

Playing Cork again would, in time, become the story of our year and this one turned into an absolute epic in the Gaelic Grounds, stretching into extra time. If I'm honest, we were barely hanging in at times during the opening 70 minutes but then took control in added time.

And you could see that Cork were absolutely gutted to be relegated. It really went against the grain for them, particularly in a shoot-out against Clare. If I'm honest, I felt just a little uneasy watching our supporters celebrate wildly at the end, as if we'd won the All-Ireland. Because I just had an inkling that we might be seeing those red jerseys again sooner rather than later.

One thing I did regret that day was taking Jonathan Clancy off just before the end of extra time. He wasn't long on the field as a substitute and there was absolutely nothing tactical in the decision. I was simply trying to kill time and, maybe, wasn't paying enough attention to how I did it. Like, I would have played with Jonathan in '05 and '06, and the last thing I wanted to do was embarrass him.

He picked me up on it in the dressing-room afterwards. 'Jesus, Davy, you put me on and more or less take me straight off again …'

He was right. I shouldn't have done that. All I could do was apologise.

The steel we showed that day in Limerick went a long way towards reassuring me that this group was now growing in front of our eyes.

We'd done a lot of different things in pre-season designed to test their spirit. On our end-of-year DVD there'd be that famous shot of Tony Kelly running alone in Cratloe Woods at around 5 a.m., me following in a jeep, the headlights showing him the way forward. It probably looked extreme, but the whole group had been due to assemble there at 8 a.m., and, with Tony having to go to work at that time, I just felt it important that we were seen to make no exceptions.

That would have been 23 December 2012.

Every last one of the players hated those runs, I understood that. I could actually sense them questioning the logic of what could be two hours of torture in the woods at a time so far removed from the start of the hurling season. But, to me, it was a way of getting them mentally stronger. Of forcing them to answer questions that, deep down, they didn't want asked.

Before that we'd also spent a weekend at Kilworth army camp, something I managed to organise with the help of Kieran 'Fraggy' Murphy, who was involved with these former Army Rangers.

I knew Joe O'Connor had mixed feelings about this kind of stuff, but I kept stressing to Joe how I just wanted to keep exposing the players to experiences that would really test them. In this instance we met the Rangers at Mother Hubbard's in Fermoy, everybody changing into camouflage gear.

And, from the moment we arrived, the energy around the group stiffened.

A jeep screeched to a halt beside us and Rangers came charging out, screaming *'Get off the bus!'* I knew exactly what was coming but didn't let on, even suggesting to Joe that it might be valuable from his perspective to participate fully. Next thing, everybody was being blindfolded and getting hands strapped behind their backs before the short drive to Kilworth.

Once there they were brought straight into the woods, Rangers roaring in their faces, jostling them, physically bullying them. If I'm honest, I even threw a few sly digs myself. The object of the exercise? Nothing should bother you when you're on the field of play. If a knock can make you lose your focus, well, chances are your opponent will come to realise that and hit you a clip.

Then the blindfolds temporarily came off and the real punishment began, with these gruelling runs, complicated by having heavy equipment on your back. After that, blindfolds back in place, they were marched into this river for a so-called 'trust exercise'.

Now, for some of the lads I knew this was terrifying. Basically, they were beckoned forward in the water on the understanding that there was a twenty-foot fall ahead, with the promise 'Don't worry if you can't swim. There's fellas down there to pull you out.'

The drop was actually only a solitary foot and, at its deepest point, the river never got deeper than three feet. But the lads weren't to know that. They were completely out of their comfort zones now, which was the point of the whole thing. How would they react under pressure?

There was a bend in the river where the water was quite swollen, and one of the exercises was for groups of four to cross from one side to the other, ferrying an injured man on a stretcher. Next thing, I see one of the stretchers spinning off downstream, Podge on board and nobody holding it.

And I'm thinking, 'Aw, Jesus, lads ...'

It was a massive day that left everybody wrecked physically. But it put real glue between the players too. I'd done it a few years earlier in Portumna as a player – when Dalo was in charge of Clare – and remember the penny dropping fairly quick for me that the more this kind of thing challenged you the more rewarding it could be.

The key was in being ready for anything. I remember getting into the sleeping-bag one night with the tracksuit on, knowing deep down that there'd be no way they'd leave us have a peaceful night's sleep. It couldn't possibly be that straightforward. And, sure enough, around 4 a.m. in they came with this bagpipe blaring.

Soon as they did I was out of the bag, ready for the road. Everything in my body language telling them, 'You won't fucking break me!'

Another place we used that winter was an equine sand-track in Broadford Hills, owned by the Ryan family. Now, this was really brutal. There's a small track to begin with that we'd use for a gentle warm-up. But then I'd direct them towards the hill. And, soon enough, the vomiting would start.

I'd say it's close to 600 metres long, the sand is deep, and the gradient that of a ski slope. It was a great team exercise, because people had to do it in groups of five, the rule being that you couldn't leave any one of your group behind. We might get them to face the hill six times, and I have a vivid memory of a gasping Darach Honan being literally dragged up that hill by his group, like a horse being dragged towards a burning barn.

Darach was probably the poorest trainer we had in my time with Clare, albeit I do accept that he was struggling a lot of the time with injury.

But we weren't doing stuff like Kilworth and Broadford Hills for fitness purposes. It was about character-building, growing team spirit. You'd see pretty quickly during those two weekends the guys who'd want to take a short-cut, who'd turn away from work. And that would stay at the back of my mind when it came to a game. If that was in their DNA one day, chances were it would still be there the next.

Because, believe me, it's the same principle. If you wanted to hide on those runs, you'd probably hide when the going got tough in a game.

In many ways I suppose I was replicating what Mike Mac had done with Clare in the '90s with that hill in Shannon and those famously gruelling sessions in Crusheen. Shining a light inside men. Building them up for the hard road ahead.

Getting them to believe that nobody was being worked harder.

Hand on heart, I couldn't say I saw what was coming next.

There'd been flashes from the team that told me we wouldn't be a million miles away (Munster League final; second half of that Cork game in Páirc Uí Rinn), but was I thinking we'd win the All-Ireland? No. To me, this was a project still in its infancy.

I suppose the story of the MiWadi and biscuits has gone down in history as a kind of loaves-and-fishes moment. A transformation of people. The truth is I felt I was fighting for my life that evening I brought the entire Clare squad up to my house in Sixmilebridge. In some respects it had always been on the cards that Cork would avenge their two League defeats against us if we collided in championship.

A hurt team is a dangerous team.

By now we'd already been on the other side of that argument, opening our Munster Championship campaign with a relatively comfortable defeat of a Waterford side that had beaten us narrowly in our two most recent meetings. So the Cork loss was almost predictable and I considered the fall-out a long way over the top.

It's well known that Louis had a programme thrown at him leaving Limerick that day, some disgruntled punter roaring stick at him about our short-game.

> LOUIS MULQUEEN: 'I was coming down out of the stand and a woman ran down towards me, calling me over. I thought it was someone wanting to say something along the lines of "Keep the chin up!" But she told me that we were "useless", threw the programme in my face and told me, "That's what ye can do with your short fucking passing!"'

I got plenty of it myself. Cork had been hugely up for the match, but their eight-point winning margin camouflaged the fact that we'd had five clear-cut goal chances and taken none of them.

We'd also suffered a sickening blow in the first half, with John Conlon taking an awful bang to the head from William Egan that necessitated his substitution. It happened directly in front of me and, while I'm sure Egan didn't intentionally hit him in the head, he was clearly determined to make serious physical contact. I couldn't believe it when Barry Kelly didn't even award us a free.

It certainly wasn't the reason we lost, but it was another little asterisk I felt that needed to be placed under the final outcome.

In the immediate aftermath I was in turmoil. I could lie here and say I still had the absolute courage of my convictions about the system I wanted Clare to play, but the truth is, I really hadn't.

I remember going down home, my stomach in knots, and – for the first time ever – my father took aim at the style of hurling I was insisting on with Clare. 'David,' he said, 'you're going to have to stop that short-ball shit and get back to traditional hurling!' I was furious. Staring him in the eye, I barked back, 'So you're one of those fuckers now as well, wilting under the pressure?'

Before he could answer I walked back out the door, slamming it hard behind me.

I was hugely rattled. I still have this vivid memory of driving past the Purcells' house just up the road, thinking to myself, 'Is he right?'

Now, I'm not exaggerating when I say that that thought lingered for no more than maybe five seconds, but the very fact that it materialised at all began to worry me. Deep down I knew we hadn't the players to go 'traditional' with the likes of a Kilkenny or Tipperary. To me, a refusal so see that reality right in front of our noses was the reason Clare had won nothing in fifteen years.

Bad enough to have the rest of Clare losing faith in what I was trying to do now, but my own father!

In time, to be fair, I could see that he'd probably taken dog's abuse that day too. The county secretary and father of the team manager, he was a sitting duck. He was probably upset for me too, knowing the torment I was now experiencing. But something told me that if ever I needed to hang tough, now had to be the time.

I never normally watch a game back the same day, but that evening I broke the habit. And the DVD lifted my spirits immediately. I realised if we'd taken even two of those five clear-cut goal chances it would have been a very different game. That's when I sent out the group text for everyone to come to my house at 4 p.m. the following day.

And I rang Mike Corry, telling him I wanted all the key information in front of me before I met them.

MIKE CORRY: 'When you lose a big championship game, normally you wouldn't hear from Davy for three or four days after, maybe the full week even. He'll just go into a dark place, his whole world on the floor. But he rang me that Monday, looking for the stats, and I was delighted, because Dinny and I had them all done.

'"No problem, Davy," I said, "and I can tell you there's a lot of good stuff in it."

'"I know that," he said.

'Everyone was on the bandwagon at that stage, picking holes in Clare's tactics. I'd never seen Davy the day after being beaten in a big game, but the way he was talking having watched the game back it was obvious he saw what we saw. I knew nothing about the meeting planned in his house, and he didn't tell me. That was for players only.

'He didn't tell me what he was doing. Just said he wanted twenty copies of the stats.'

I couldn't be sure what kind of psychological place the players were in now, given the negativity assailing them about our style of hurling. But I did know I needed to get a very definite message to them, specifically about those five goal chances. 'Lads, if we take even two of those …'

I collected the stats off Mike outside John Crowe's Centra the following day and despatched Colm and Sharon to get an industrial quantity of MiWadi and biscuits. The neighbours must have wondered if there'd been a bereavement in the house when they saw all these cars lining the lane up to the house, but I knew I couldn't do what I wanted to do now in a hotel. This had to be strictly private. People had to feel absolutely free to speak their minds.

So we squeezed everyone into the living-room, I put on a video of the game and started by showing them those five goal chances we'd missed. Then I handed around the stats sheets, and we broke into group chats, everybody invited to offer an opinion on what they imagined we might be able to do better. And I just kept beating this drum that we'd been a lot closer to Cork than the impression given by the scoreline and now faithfully reported in the media.

'Don't for a single second think that we were beaten well yesterday,' I stressed. 'We weren't beaten well. Guys, I'm telling ye, if we learn from this we can achieve anything. Ye might think I'm fucking mad, but I fervently believe that!'

I put absolutely no focus on what had happened to Conlon. To me, this wasn't an environment for the introduction of negatives now. I knew it was something I might return to in the future, but not at that moment. Not when it could serve no worthwhile purpose.

And I could feel the energy in the house lifting as we wound things up. This didn't feel like a defeated group to me. If anything, they were angry over the blown chances and the general distortion of what had happened to them. As everyone prepared to leave, my parting message was 'Right, we'll get back down to business this week and work even harder.

'And God help the poor fuckers who get us next!'

If we needed time and patience, we knew we wouldn't be afforded those luxuries now.

We had anger, though. And I knew that could carry us a long way while we kept to our process of bedding down the system. I had identified Pat Donnellan as our best candidate to play sweeper and it's fair to say it wasn't until we reached the All-Ireland quarter-final against Galway that that role was sufficiently stress-tested for me to be completely happy we were on the right track.

As I suspected, we pulverised Laois in our first qualifier after the Cork defeat (every outfield player bar Domhnall O'Donovan getting on the scoresheet). Yet the same day I was getting abuse through the wire from some clown, telling me I hadn't a clue and that I'd 'ruined' Clare hurling.

Then carelessness was to blame as we got taken to extra time next day out by Wexford.

That was ridiculous. We'd been in total control, coasting in a game that never even closely resembled a contest, without quite putting Wexford away. Then, slowly, they began nibbling into our lead, until it was down to four points and I could just feel our lads begin to tighten. Jack Guiney struck a late Wexford goal to tie it up and next thing, to my disbelief, we found ourselves lurching back down the dressing-room tunnel with 20 minutes of extra time to play.

I was furious. We'd brought this entirely upon ourselves and I told the lads as much. But I also took a leap of faith that, to this day, I'm not entirely sure where it came from.

'You know what, lads?' I said. 'This will define us. We've just allowed a team get momentum against us that had no business getting that momentum. But trust me on this.

'If we dig ourselves out of this mess, we'll win the All-Ireland!'

It's all on tape, so this isn't me being clever with hindsight now. Why did I say it? Honestly, I just felt there was massive potential in this group if they held their nerve and focused. 'Keep coming back' was my mantra. 'Because that's what defines people. Character.' I absolutely believed that too. If they learnt to ship whatever blows came their way and bounced back stronger, they could achieve anything. In other words, if the group just got their stuff together, there was no limit to where this could take us.

They went back out, of course, and won extra time by ten points.

And against Galway, then, we really began to fly. They were beaten All-Ireland finalists from the previous September, but we absolutely destroyed them. The truth is they just didn't know how to cope with our use of sweeper, Donnellan proving absolutely outstanding in providing an extra layer of protection to the Clare square. But this was about more than tactics. In fact the very idea that playing a sweeper system represented a negative strategy should have been categorically put to bed that day.

Because our hurling was full of imagination and a sense of freedom, maybe best encapsulated by a reverse hand-pass from Podge Collins under the Kinane Stand that drew something close to a great 'Olé' roar from the Clare supporters.

Bugs did a great job on marshalling Joe Canning too and we had nine points to spare at the finish.

Soon as the final whistle went I shook Anthony Cunningham's hand and rushed straight down the tunnel. I just had no interest in back-slaps now from the very people who'd been hammering us over our short-ball game. Jesus wept, we'd stayed up in Division 1A using that style, our under-21s had won the All-Ireland, yet it felt as if every step we took had to involve yet another defence of the system. I was sick of it.

Maybe a bit of siege mentality was kicking in with me.

But it was lovely too to step in out of the maelstrom and have those few minutes of absolute peace in a deserted dressing-room. I could hear the bedlam outside and, yes, loved the fact that – finally – it represented vindication of the course I was trying to chart for the group. We were in the final four with what I believed to be better than a puncher's chance now of going all the way.

Limerick had won the Munster Championship amidst great scenes of euphoria in the Gaelic Grounds two weeks earlier – beating Cork by nine points – and we'd now be facing them in an all-southern All-Ireland semi-final. I believed fervently that we'd beat them, but there was a small mountain of planning ahead of me for the challenge.

I waited until everybody was in before getting to my feet and delivering a short and simple message. 'Lads, tell me anyone in this championship that's better than ye! Ye have no prima donnas, and I love that. This was great today, but remember, if we don't win the next day in Dublin, this'll mean fuck all!'

◄◊►

Our plan for Limerick initially brought me into conflict with Paul Kinnerk.

I wanted Podge Collins to play out the field, leaving their centre-back, Wayne MacNamara, loose. Now, an unmarked number six could do untold damage to us if he got enough ball – I understood that. I'd had Wayne at LIT and knew his qualities better than anyone. He was a serious operator, almost unplayable under a high ball.

But one thing I knew about him too was that he wouldn't stray from his patch. Wayne's style was to hold his ground, to mind the house, if you like. My plan was to play around him and, to that end, for the two weeks leading into that semi-final we roped off a 20-metre-square area where the centre-back would usually be, nobody allowed hit ball into that space.

The idea was that Wayne would, effectively, be taken out of the game by keeping the ball away from him.

Because of their first Munster Championship success since '96, most people expected Limerick to beat us. They had the momentum and the hype. I'd been doing co-commentary on the Munster final for RTÉ with Marty Morrissey and the scenes afterwards were extraordinary.

That night I'd put up a message on the group WhatsApp reading, 'Lads, the atmosphere in Limerick today was unreal, do we want some of that for ourselves?'

SEOIRSE BULFIN: 'We weren't being given a prayer really. The first night going training for that semi-final, I remember pulling out of Bruff and I counted something like 26 or 27 Limerick flags in my estate alone. And, from the border in Cratloe to Ennis, I think I counted six Clare flags. You could see the usual hype had taken hold in Limerick.

'They had a song out. They thought they were already in the final. One of my buddies rang me, saying his uncles wanted to know if I could get them tickets for the final, because they were going to come home from London. He didn't say, "If Limerick win …" I remember telling Brendan Bugler, sure that kind of thing was perfect.

'I was up in the field in Kilmallock on a Saturday morning with my brother-in-law, Andrew O'Shaughnessy. He says to me, "How do you think it'll go?"

'And I said, "If we play to our potential we'll win, because we have better hurlers!" And Andrew says, "You're right!"'

Now we had the chance to take a massive step towards our own piece of history. But I was adamant that we needed to do something that Limerick wouldn't be expecting. To take the game away from a conventional fifteen-on-fifteen, 'may the best man win' sort of contest.

Mike and Louis were instantly agreeable to my plan, but, like I say, Paul became a harder sell. I understood his reservations. If the lads didn't stick to plan and loose ball began raining down on MacNamara, he could end up bossing the game rather than becoming a frustrated bystander. We had to play everything down the flanks or this could turn out to be a disaster.

I suspect it was only when he saw the plan in practice during our training games that Paul finally saw sense in what I was trying to do. Some of the sessions were electrifying.

The week of the game I showed the players clips of the 2012 championship game in which they beat us, the sloppy goals conceded, the celebrations afterwards. Mike Corry also did up a video of them going ballistic after their Munster final win. I just wanted the players to feel they were being completely written off here. To start storing up some hurt.

And I'd say for the first ten minutes of that semi-final nobody in Croke Park could quite figure out who was Limerick's loose man, their management included. Donnellan was again absolutely brilliant as sweeper, settling in to the role now better than I could have hoped. But our hurling was unreal too.

This was the day that Tony Kelly stepped onto the national stage big-time and I remember one point of his from out near the sideline especially, Tony feinting to score off one side, then just flicking the ball over his marker's head, catching it and absolutely nailing his shot towards Hill 16. It was a score symptomatic of how we played that day.

The players might have been adhering to a system, but nobody on this Clare team was going to be enslaved by it.

Coming away from Croke Park, we left Podge Collins and Aaron Cunningham behind us to give urine samples. It meant they missed the post-match meal and arrived just as our train was about to pull out of Heuston Station.

They'd grabbed two Supermacs meals on the way, but Joe O'Connor went straight over, took the paper bags off them, and put them in a bin. He'd kept two proper dinners for them. I remember someone saying, 'Ah, Jesus, Joe …'

It might have seemed a little harsh, but Joe's attitude was 'No, little things will make the difference here.' The lads weren't going to go hungry but, even if they were, that'd have been Joe's preference ahead of them getting a bellyful of chips.

That's how professional our set-up was now. We'd be leaving absolutely nothing to chance.

12

PROMISED LAND

I t was important that I led from the front now, showed no emotion. I knew that if the players considered me over the top on anything, chances were they'd drift in that direction themselves.

That simply couldn't be allowed happen.

So I used visualisation a lot, imagining every conceivable scenario, working out what my appropriate reaction should be. This was a time for the right body language. For communicating to the players that I had absolute trust in them.

I suppose it was only human to have '08 at the back of my mind. Had I misread any obvious signals with Waterford? Could I have done anything differently that might have averted that collapse? Being honest, I didn't sleep a whole pile in the weeks leading up to the final. Too many worries, too many questions.

I'd wake up in the middle of the night, brain in overload, and begin writing down a few notes about whatever had come into my head. It could be anything. A tactical issue or something to do with the logistics of the weekend. I wanted us to perform, which Waterford simply hadn't done five years earlier. I wanted us to play with freedom against Cork now, but I also wanted us to be smart.

Pretty quickly, we decided not to play a sweeper. Just felt we couldn't afford to accommodate Anthony Nash's ability to laser a puck-out by leaving any Cork defenders unmarked. I can categorically say that we wouldn't have beaten Galway or Limerick without a sweeper, but this was a different challenge now.

It was also in my head that Cork would presume we'd stick with a system that had been working so well and would, accordingly, train to that end for three weeks. No harm if I we could surprise them then, put them on the back foot.

Everybody on the management side had an input into the decision-making. I personally took great strength from that, the fact that Louis, Mike and Paul were so pro-active every step of the way, always happy to argue and question. Without those strong characters around me the job simply wouldn't have been doable.

We decided that Conor Ryan's strength in the air made him the right man to mark Séamus Harnedy and I spoke to Patrick Kelly, our goalkeeper, about the possibility of having to face one of Nash's ferocious 20-metre frees. This had become a running story in the media now, the fact that his lift would take him almost in to the fourteen-yard line before he'd hit an Exocet that, literally, could have killed someone.

It was evident to everybody that this had become dangerous. Not Nash's fault. He was simply doing what everybody else had done historically, except hitting the sliotar at a velocity that was probably unprecedented.

It might have been a one-in-a-million chance that the ball would hit a defender in the Adam's apple, but imagine if it did? The ball was coming at them so fast they'd little enough chance of even seeing it, let alone stopping it. A decision was subsequently taken, decreeing that the ball-striker could not step inside the 20-metre line.

But in 2013 Nash had the freedom to come in as close as his jab-lift could bring him. It meant a 20-metre for Cork was an almost certain goal.

That said, Patrick was a bould enough character, maybe cut from the same cloth as me. He wanted nothing more than the opportunity to face down Nash. To charge down the puck if at all possible. I told him to go with his gut on it. A man willing to put his body on the line was never going to get an argument from me.

To that end, I also brought up the hit John Conlon had taken when they'd beaten us in the Munster semi-final, reminded the players how physical Cork had been against us that day. How, essentially, they'd bullied us. 'Are we going to let them do that again?' I kept asking.

I wasn't doing it so much in the team environment as going from individual to individual, planting seeds, pulling strings. I didn't want to burn their brains with long meetings now. This game had to become personal for us because, if we didn't hurl with an edge, Cork would always expect to beat us. So I made it about them and them only. I made it about the sight of John being helped off the field that day in Limerick. I made it about the arrogance of tradition and people in certain counties thinking themselves superior.

The thing I was determined not to make it about was winning an All-Ireland. As much as I could, I kept trying to rinse that idea out of every discussion. This had to be about simply winning a game, not chasing history.

All the way up to the night before my stomach was in a knot. And then, miraculously, all that anxiety left me. How? I think as a manager you come to a certain acceptance at that point that, really, your work is done now. That the players effectively have ownership and you've either got it right or got it wrong.

I prefer my own company the night before a big game and slipped away with the dogs for a walk in Cratloe Woods before settling in for a night that I knew would bring little sleep. Then, first thing Sunday morning I did what I always do on these big days, taking myself away up to Tulla, to Sheila Considine's grave.

Funny, hurling people exist sometimes in a massively aggressive, macho environment, but one of the toughest people I've met in my entire life was a tiny, wheelchair-bound girl, condemned to a slow death through spina bifida. Sheila died in October '98, but her presence is still all around me on those big days. I can't explain it. From the time I first met her – she was positioned by the dressing-room tunnel at a pre-All-Ireland final training session in Ennis in '95 – to her death, the illusion was that I was helping her.

I began visiting her a lot, encouraging her in a horrible fight that it was clear she couldn't win. That girl came through so many scrapes with her health just when it seemed she might be fading, you couldn't but be inspired by her resilience. I made Sheila a guest of honour at my first wedding in the summer of '97, and the view of Pete (RIP) and Biddy, her parents, would have been that she got a great lift from my friendship.

But the truth was I'd come away feeling inspired any time I called to their house. We have an idea in sport that we understand what courage means, but this small girl put the hardest men I've ever met into the shade.

So this has become a ritual for me now. Up to her grave at maybe 7 a.m. and just a quiet chat between us. I know people might read that and think I'm off with the fairies and, to be honest, I'm not even entirely sure what constitutes religious faith. But I know the strength I take from going up to that graveyard.

My fervent belief is that people close to you can pass on to the next world and still remain a part of life. Kevin 'Trixie' Twomey is another example. I still talk to them both, still ask them for help. I still believe, absolutely, that they can hear me.

We all met up then in our usual spot, Setrights, a pub in Cratloe. Just parked the cars in the back car park, no room organised, nothing fancy. The more informal I could keep things the more likely I felt the players would be to take things in their stride. And watching them circle around one another, playing keepy-uppy in the car park with a sliotar that morning, I remember thinking, 'This feels exactly as I want it to feel.'

You're guessing, of course. Every inch of the way is some kind of guess.

For me, the key was keeping everything relaxed yet still moving like clockwork. To that end, I was my own logistics manager. I'd taken the decision to go to Dublin the week before, Liam Dowd picking me up off the train. Together we did a recce of the journey to St Patrick's College in Drumcondra from Heuston Station, then on to Croke Park, working out the likely travel times we'd have with a Garda escort.

We'd had the same arrangements for the semi-final against Limerick, but it's a huge thing to me that our timings are spot on. If not, you can end up either flustered or with too much time on your hands. That even extends to my team-talks, incidentally. If the meeting starts dragging on any longer than, say, twelve minutes, I'll get a signal from Mike Corry. And there and then I'll call it to a halt.

On match day, twelve minutes is more than time enough to get your message across. If you need longer, you're just not well enough prepared.

I can't speak highly enough of how well the Supporters' Club organised the train from Limerick, one carriage for the squad, the other two for players' families and our most loyal supporters. As ever, Jim Gavin was a joy to deal with in the station. Two great friends of mine, Darren Ward and John Fall, manned the doors of our carriage to make sure only ticketed people got on.

I've always loved that freedom the train gives people to get up, walk about and, basically, stay loose. It's not claustrophobic. We even used it for games in Thurles.

Over a hundred rooms had been booked in the Clyde Court Hotel and, believe it or not, I'd discussed the possibility of a draw with my father. I had to. There was a banquet organised and we had to know what we'd be doing if there was still a game to play three weeks later. Our decision was to go ahead with it, win, lose or draw.

Three weeks would be long enough to rinse a blow-out from our systems.

My relentless message to the team that morning was not to overreact to setbacks. I remember telling them in St Pat's, 'Listen, if you make a mistake, get over it. Nobody's died. It's just a game of hurling.'

The danger with an All-Ireland final is it's so easy to forget that. To feel suffocated by the occasion. Cork, I knew, would probably hit us with a sucker-punch at some stage. It was important that we understood how to stay on our feet when that happened.

What I hadn't, couldn't really have legislated for was a team that had scored a solitary goal all season hitting us with three in a single half. Which, of course, they did after we'd dominated the first 35 minutes, actually dominated it to the extent that Cork managed just a single point from play in the opening 32 minutes. It took them ages to come to terms with the fact that we weren't set up as they expected us to be but, once they did, they opened us up.

A lot of that was down to self-harm and, if I'm honest, my own fingerprints were on that story too. I knew that playing orthodox could leave us vulnerable, and there were times in that second half I had reason to question myself. That said, there's absolutely no doubt that Cork should have been down to fourteen men less than half way through the first half when Shane O'Neill caught Darach Honan with a terrible blow across the head.

Still, we were coasting with just thirteen minutes to go, 0-21 to 1-13 ahead, twenty-one scores to fourteen. I couldn't see us losing. Then two more Cork goals rattled us to the core, albeit those last 35 minutes would tell me a hell of a lot about the character of my players too. Conceding three goals in the second half of an All-Ireland final would kill most teams. But we were still level with them beyond the 70th minute.

I'm not sure I've ever felt sicker than when Patrick Horgan then put over what looked a winning score at the Hill end. I actually couldn't believe what I was seeing. We'd been the better team and Cork were about to steal the Liam MacCarthy from under our noses. If Brian Gavin blew up there and then, I think it's possible I'd have been physically ill on the line. 'Stay calm, don't react,' I remember saying to myself.

'Please, God, just give us one more chance ...'

Were Sheila and Trixie listening?

Who can honestly say? All I do know is that, to this day, I've no clue what switch flicked inside Dunny for him not alone to push forward but to go so high up the opposite side of the field to his normal station. What was even better was that Patrick Kelly, whether by accident or not, chose to drive his puck-out up the left too.

I like to think that Patrick saw we had an extra man up that side, but even then, so many things had to go right for us now if we were to rescue this.

And Dunny? He's a hugely intelligent guy, but he'd taken an unmerciful slagging after our hammering of Laois in the qualifiers when someone pointed out that he'd been our only outfield player that day who didn't raise a flag. If you asked anyone in that Clare dressing-room to draw up a list from numbers 1 to 30 of the most likely people to dig Clare out of trouble with an important score, Dunny himself would tell you that he'd be number 30.

The great thing was that we didn't panic on Patrick's puck-out, we didn't take a shot from too far out. That said, when I saw Dunny get it into his hand, my immediate reaction was, 'Oh, no, Dunny, don't!'

And, of course, he went and nailed an equaliser that'll never be forgotten.

MIKE CORRY: 'When the final whistle goes, myself, Dinny and Mike Deasy are just sitting there in the box, still numb with the tension. Next thing, the door opens behind us and a fella in a suit, one of the stewards, comes in with this beautiful, shiny Liam MacCarthy Cup.

'He leans in over Deasy's shoulder and shoves it under the shelf. Says nothing and goes back out again. We're sitting there, looking at this. Nobody says anything. We're afraid to touch it in case it's bad luck, but thinking too how close we'd been to taking it home and how close it had been to being lost too.

'We didn't touch it!'

Soon as we got back into the dressing-room I could sense some of our lads were very down. So I took them into the warm-up room and got straight to work on them. 'Don't be down, this is fucking great!' I smiled.

'We get to play another All-Ireland final. Bring it on. We'll go again!'

Then I took myself away from everyone, into the manager's room, just for a couple of minutes to gather my thoughts. People wanted to know were we sticking with the decision about the banquet. We'd provisionally agreed to, but did we really honestly imagine we'd be faced by this predicament?

I suspect Louis and Mike and the other back-room boys reckoned I'd change my mind. But the more I thought about it the more I felt the players needed to wind down now. They needed to let off steam.

So I went back out and announced, 'The banquet goes ahead, go and have your few drinks and enjoy it!'

SEOIRSE BULFIN: 'It's like going to a wedding and someone's been left at the altar. What do you do now? The band had to play, the meal was paid for. Sure it ended up in a hooley, but there had been such a build-up of tension, the lads needed a release.'

Cork went the opposite way and I'd imagine most people expected me to do likewise. I'm not a drinker myself and sometimes that can be interpreted as being anti-drink. I'm not. I just know the trouble it can cause if lads aren't careful and one of the safeguards I took that night was I told Darren if they headed to Coppers, he was to go with them.

I didn't do that to have him watching what they drank. I did it so he'd look out for them in case anyone started to get messy and threatened to start letting themselves or the group down. Darren's job in that situation was to put them in a taxi, send them straight back to the hotel, where we'd make sure to put them to bed. If you haven't drunk in a while, the effects of alcohol can be more aggressive.

We just needed to be looking out for one another now.

On the train home the following day I knew I was shattered. Just physically hit a wall. When I got back to the house I had to ring Doc Quinn. I honestly felt absolutely wretched. He came out and quickly diagnosed that I was just physically and mentally exhausted. I hadn't slept in days.

My mind had been racing relentlessly. Everything was just 'next day, next day, next day ...' Now I was paying the price.

He gave me a Xanax and I went upstairs, quickly slipping away into the sleep of the dead. I needed it. My head was like Spaghetti Junction now and I needed something to shut it down for a few hours. Without the doc's help I'm not sure that would have been possible. I've never liked taking tranquillisers or sleeping tablets, but in this instance I felt I had no choice.

And I woke the following morning ready to drive at Cork with a new plan.

Let me tell you a story about our build-up to the All-Ireland final replay that, to this day, makes me wonder if Sheila and Trixie were pulling strings.

I'd already decided that our attack had been too predictable in the drawn game, that Darach had been too easily blackguarded and, with him struggling, Cork believed we had no secrets to our attacking game. Basically, if Darach wasn't winning primary possession and taking defenders on, his threat was neutralised.

You only have to look at the number of appearances Darach made for Clare during my time as manager to know how highly I rated him. A bright guy with strong beliefs, he was never the hardest trainer, though. I saw Darach winning an under-12 final for Clonlara against Sixmilebridge almost on his own and, from that day on, he was seen as a bit of a prodigy.

Having eventually grown to 6'7", I felt he could become a unique weapon for Clare hurling, because he had all the skill in the world too. But sometimes it was almost as if Darach was too much of a gentleman in battle. And he began to have continuous trouble with his hip that would eventually reach the point of no return when he took a bad belt on it early in 2016 against Laois in Cusack Park.

Anyway, I felt now that Darach wasn't giving us what we needed him to give us. At the post-game banquet I got talking to Shane O'Donnell and told him that he'd definitely have some involvement the next day.

In my heart of hearts I'd already decided that he would start. With his pace and his nose for a goal he just carried the kind of threat that I suspected Cork now imagined we couldn't muster.

At the start of the year some people told me I was off my head bringing this young chap with a mop of curls into our squad. But he'd made an instant impression when brought in for a challenge game against Limerick the previous November. I was actually in the States at the time, but Louis was raving about this young lad from Ennis.

LOUIS MULQUEEN: 'Davy had phoned from the States to say we had this challenge match arranged in UL, and I was protesting that we wouldn't have enough players.

'"Pull in a few lads from Éire Óg," he said.

'So we pulled in David Reidy and Shane O'Donnell – the best two I could think of – and that night on the UL Astroturf, didn't Shane get a hat trick of goals. Afterwards I said to Davy, "This young lad is worth keeping an eye on."'

Shane didn't really fit in to any conventional moulds. He had yet to develop physically and, at the start of 2013, nobody really saw him as a Clare senior hurler. But from the get-go I could see he had brilliant hands and a serious hurling brain.

He also had blinding pace and a hunger for goals that I'm not sure I've ever seen in another hurler. It was as if Shane had zero interest in taking points if he believed there was even a 10 per cent chance of getting inside his marker. True enough, that could be frustrating at times, when he'd opt not to do the simple thing. But then, at other times, he'd look unplayable.

Trouble was, the physical jump from senior club to county is massive, and I suspect Shane found the intensity of our training a little crazy to begin with. Actually it took him a couple of months to come to terms with it, but once he did he'd be a stand-out figure in almost every training game we played.

We'd got a glimpse of what he might bring to us in that League game against Cork at Páirc Uí Rinn too, when he just kept running at defenders whose minds you could instantly read saying, 'Who the fuck is this?'

My suspicion now was that Cork just assumed he didn't figure in my plans. But that night in the Clyde Court I told Shane, 'Listen, I maybe made a mistake in not using you today, but you'll definitely play some part the next day.'

What I certainly didn't do was tell this nineteen-year-old, just setting out on his senior career, that he'd be starting an All-Ireland final three weeks later.

Anyway, that story?

The weekend before the replay Sharon was playing a camogie match for Clarecastle in Ennis and I sat behind one of the goals, hidden behind a pole holding up the big net, trying to stay as inconspicuous as possible. Next thing, this stranger approaches, says hello and we have the following exchange.

'Ah, Davy, all set for Saturday? I can't wait!'

'Yeah, good now, thanks. Hoping for the best.'

'Lord Jesus, I'm sick with nerves already!'

'You are?'

'I am, even though I have it on good authority that ye'll win ...'

So, I'm sitting there with a polite smile on my face, hoping this chap won't linger. I like to be nice in these situations, but I suppose my instinct is to draw the conversation to a close as politely as possible too. And that was when he told me he'd just been to a psychic in Galway.

'You were?'

'And she told me that a fella with S in his initials will play well, score a few goals, and that the big fella will come on then and win it for ye at the end. So, Davy, I know ye're going to do it!'

Now, I'm not exaggerating when I say I nearly fell off my seat. At this stage only the management group knew our plans for the replay. I'd be breaking the news to Darach after training the following Tuesday and planned on asking him, at a moment of what I recognised would be massive personal hurt, not to tell anyone outside close family. As for Shane, I knew I'd have to leave it as late as absolutely possible to avoid him becoming smothered by the nerves.

But now this complete stranger had more or less read our intentions.

Naturally, I shrugged away his psychic's message with a chuckle, telling him I hoped she'd be right and pretending to make a call on my phone. But I couldn't believe what he'd just said to me. The moment he was out of earshot I put through two calls to Louis and Mike. 'You won't fucking believe what I'm after being told ...'

Our physical preparation for the replay was deliberately minimal. For me the priority was keeping the players fresh now. To have them mad for road. We'd put in a huge amount of physical work already and didn't need to dog them any more. Some of the training had been brutal, but they'd had their light moments too.

The first weekend after the drawn game we'd gone to Doonbeg where, at most, we did half an hour of hurling training. We had a golf scramble on the Saturday and my abiding memory is Podge's tee shot on the first swinging a good 150 yards off line and ending up in the thatch on the old clubhouse.

It would be fair to say he was trying!

We talked tactics a small bit too, believing that Cork's preoccupation with marking Tony Kelly would spell opportunity for others. Paddy Donnellan was encouraged to come bombing forward into the space Tony would vacate, because we knew the further he got through the middle the more Cork's defensive structure would be corrupted.

I also had a plan for Anthony Nash's Exocets. If Cork got a 20-metre free I wanted a dozen players back on the Clare goal-line. I went to the hurley-maker John Torpey and got him to make half a dozen hurleys with a huge bas, which Pa Kelly was only too happy to take away for his own use after.

My idea was that we'd have, say, our usual five stoppers standing out front, with another seven standing behind. In other words, Nash would have to pick a spot, as distinct from just opting for raw power.

There was a fair degree of speculation that we might revert to the sweeper system again, my old teammate Anthony Daly suggesting as much in the *Irish Independent*. But I was never going to do that against Cork. Not with Nash's puck-outs to consider.

On the Friday week before the replay we tried putting our plans into practice with a 40-minute practice game. And what followed almost set the grass on fire. You know they always speak in Kilkenny about these great A v. B matches in Nowlan Park, as if they're somehow unique. In 2013 our training matches were absolutely do-or-die in Clare. The competition for places with the likes of 'Bruiser' (Fergal Lynch), Conor Cooney and a couple of other seasoned guys who were going to cut your throat to get on the team made for fiercely competitive games.

Even Louis and I would be at each other's throats during those games, him in charge of one team, me the other.

LOUIS MULQUEEN: 'One day I remember Pa Kelly pucking the ball out in one of these practice games. Davy and I were both in the VIP box in Cusack Park. My team was winning, and oh, holy Christ, Davy jumps down into the tunnel to get to Pa, because he's pucked the ball out wrong. There'd be that edge. Like, he was fun to work with, but it was intense. And there comes a stage where it affects your work, family – everything else. Because it's 24/7 with Davy.

'That's the perfection he seeks. You have to give it 100 per cent.'

Looking back, I'm not sure we'd ever quite have that edge again after 2013. Because it made for phenomenal training nights. Games that would leave you buzzing.

On this particular evening I started Shane on the As and within ten minutes he'd scored 2-2. Donnellan got two goals too, scything through from a midfield position, just as we hoped he might do against Cork. The tempo of the game was extraordinary and I quickly came to the conclusion that I needed to rein back some of the energy. The As were running riot, posting 8-9 inside 21 minutes.

Actually, after that opening ten minutes I switched Shane to the Bs. Said something along the lines of wanting to 'look at something else,' and I could see he was frustrated. But I just couldn't allow him run amok any further, for fear it might become obvious to the group that we'd even consider starting him.

It wasn't just Shane, though. We'd done so little since the drawn game, the whole group was electric. Just over 20 minutes in I decided that that energy needed to be preserved. 'Guys, we've enough!' I shouted, calling things to a halt. And I knew the group was exactly where I wanted them now, every face around me registering with disgust.

MIKE CORRY: 'One thing Davy always did leading into a big game was he'd get the Bs to wear jerseys the same colour as the team we were due to play. So it'd be Doora-Barefield jerseys if we were playing Galway, Scariff if it was Limerick, and in this instance the red of Crusheen for Cork. That was the organisational level he went to.

'That night everybody was on fire. He kept swapping lads in and out, nobody really sure what was significant and what wasn't. But nobody saw Shane O'Donnell starting. He was only a kid, nineteen, doing his Leaving Cert. Incredible.'

The following Tuesday I called Darach aside in the Sherwood after grub and told him the hard truth. We'd be naming him in the team, but Shane would be starting.

'I'm doing that because I want to keep the pressure off him,' I said. 'I know you'll be hurting and that this is a rotten thing to be hearing, but you can still play a huge part for us next Saturday. I'm genuinely sorry to do this to you, but I have to do what I think is best for the team.

'And I'm asking you now not to tell anyone, apart from immediate family.'

Darach, naturally, didn't take the news well. But I had to be straight with him. I had to do this properly, and, to be fair, his conduct remained exemplary in the days that followed. Deep down I suspect he knew himself that he hadn't been performing – not that that made his ordeal now any easier. But he kept our secret to himself. As a group, we should be forever indebted to him for that.

Funny, the closer the game came the more soundly I started to sleep. I think my worries about suffering a repeat of '08, of seeing the team I was in charge of effectively freeze on the big day, had been put to bed now. If nothing else, I knew we were ready to go toe-to-toe with Cork again.

Our match-day arrangements were an exact replica of what we'd done for the semi-final and drawn final. And it was just after the players had eaten in St Pat's that I called Shane aside. 'Bit of news for you, Shane,' I said. 'I'm going to start you today.'

As I said it, I instantly got a lump in my throat. Just the expression on his face made me well up with emotion. And this lovely, honest young kid began thanking me, telling me how he wouldn't let me down. He hadn't been expecting this – I could see that. He'd been hoping, at best, for ten minutes near the end.

From the very first night we'd brought him for that trial game at UL in the winter of 2012 we could see that Shane had an incredible instinct for scoring goals. A hugely intelligent, well-mannered kid, he'd just taken time to adjust to the huge physicality required to be a senior county hurler.

Now, without warning, he'd been given the biggest news of his young life. He was still in mid-sentence when I patted him on the arm, told him to just be himself out there, and walked away. Honestly, if I'd stayed there a split second longer tears would have come streaming down my face. I couldn't let him see that. I couldn't let anyone.

You always look for sharp angles in a team-talk, some real, some imaginary. In this instance I went for something in between. I was convinced that Cork figured we had no real goal threat in us, and that they considered our bench weak. They were reading far too much into our recent history against them, into the fact that Clare had managed the grand total of three goals in the previous six League and Championship games against Cork over a stretch of five years.

So I said something along those lines, about them 'laughing the last day at our substitutes.'

About them thinking 'we can't score goals …'

I wanted lads bristling again at the idea of Cork looking down their noses at us. I wanted a little bitterness in our play, but I also wanted to get the message across that we had the better hurlers. That, contrary to the traditional assumption, Cork had inherited nothing from the womb that we didn't have too.

I have one absolutely vivid memory of the day that made me smile then and still makes me smile now. It is of us being out on the field about an hour before throw-in and I looked down to the far end where Cork, in these pristine white tracksuits, were doing this regimented drill in twos. Everything about them carrying an almost military air. And us? The lads were in a circle, playing keepy-uppy with a sliotar. Every time it went to ground the guy responsible was removed.

So an hour before an All-Ireland final and we were all grins and groans and hoots of laughter. 'Yeah, we're good here,' I remember thinking.

So history tells us that this tousle-haired kid from Ennis, a genetics student in UCC, went out and almost single-handedly murdered Cork.

Within nineteen minutes of the throw-in Shane O'Donnell had already scored 3-1. Fairytale stuff. But his first goal, scored in the sixth minute, actually encapsulated our day. Because it was a terrific team-goal. This story wasn't just about Shane, you see. It was about a team executing a plan to virtual perfection.

We wanted to go for the jugular and that's exactly what was communicated by Paddy Donnellan's charging run through the middle and the fact that, Cork's defence opening up in front of him, our captain resisted the temptation to tap over an easy point. Paddy knew Shane was in the team for a reason. And that reason was to score goals.

What largely went unrecognised in the fuss that blew up around Shane would be the hugely unselfish work of others, particularly the decoy running of men like Tony Kelly, Conor McGrath and Podge Collins. Don't get me wrong. Shane O'Donnell was a revelation, the quality of his finishing spectacular for a kid with so little experience.

But this was about the group. This was about the soul of Clare hurling finding expression in one of the best All-Ireland finals ever played.

Needless to say, that was down to Cork as much as us. As often as we ripped them open, they just kept coming back at us, refusing to give in. I mean, from a position of relative control (3-9 to 1-7 after 26 minutes) we went asleep as a group between the 30th and 53rd minutes, during which time Cork out-scored us 0-9 to 0-1.

Their goal had come in the sixteenth minute, despite our best efforts, from a Nash thunderbolt. Good luck to him, having a dozen bodies on the goal-line didn't faze him.

SEOIRSE BULFIN: 'Fitzy told me, "Go down and tell the boys to get someone off the line for the follow-up in case it's saved." So I went in around the back of the goal, and I was roaring at Pat Kelly, "Pat, Pat ..." and he just couldn't hear me.

'I remember looking up around me. The lights were on, it was getting dark, and even thinking about it now puts the hair up on the back of my neck. It was just, "Fuck me, take a mental picture of this moment, because if I never again get to a hurling match it won't matter."

'Johnny Ryan, a linesman on the day, was hunting me away. So I went about twenty yards left, and that's where I stayed. But you couldn't ask for a more perfect setting. The lighting, the noise, Nash coming up the field, I'm screaming at Pat Kelly, Johnny Ryan's screaming at me. Everything just building, building, building.'

Cork's scoring burst meant, effectively, that we had to go out and win the game again.

Three-quarters way through, the sides were level. Ten minutes from time – level again. Shane might actually have had a fourth goal, but Conor McGrath chose to go on his own this time and scored what I consider, to this day, maybe the best All-Ireland final goal I've ever seen. But if he hadn't nailed it with Shane standing unmarked inside?

I'd have been fit to be tied.

The game just kept on gusting wildly, endlessly jackknifing just when you thought it had found a settled rhythm. And with less than ten minutes to go I had a decision to make. I knew Darach was like a bear with a sore head behind me and, given that Shane had now scored 3-3, I couldn't help thinking of that psychic in Galway and what she'd prophesied would happen.

'... The big fella will come on then and win it for ye ...'

As I told Darach to warm up I was still in a quandary about which inside forward to take off. I'd already replaced Podge with Cathal McInerney and now had a straight choice to make between Conor McGrath and Shane. So, maybe six minutes to go, the game still in the balance, what to do?

In my gut I just reckoned Conor's experience could still be vital. He's one of the best forwards I've seen and a natural play-maker. As I called the switch, Mike Deegan leaned across me. 'You sure about this?' he asked.

I wasn't, but I lied.

So in Darach goes and, of course, scores the injury-time goal that settles it. I was thrilled for him on a personal level, given the way he'd conducted himself after losing his starting place. He deserved to be central to one of the greatest days in Clare's hurling history. A day most of us will never forget.

I've little real memory of the final whistle sounding, only the TV images of me collapsing to the ground, bringing home just how drained, physically and emotionally, I was at that moment. The rest is a blur. Paddy's speech, Bugs on the accordion in the dressing-room, everybody hugging, grinning, crying. My dad: just a short embrace between us that meant the world.

He'd write in his report to convention later that year about how 'taken aback' he'd been at the accusations of nepotism over my appointment in 2011. Feeling the need to defend himself as 'a fair and honest man', Dad would describe himself as 'fully vindicated' now. That meant the world to me.

Later my Mam, Helen, Sharon, Colm ... then thoughts drifting towards the skies. Sheila. Trixie. Thanks.

If I have a regret it's that I somehow found it a struggle to enjoy what followed. The banquet, the homecoming, the Cup on safari.

It's almost as if within seconds of us being crowned champions I was filled with apprehension for what was coming down the line. A lot had been made of the fact that our starting attack had an average age of just over 21.

They were kids now being pitched out into a world of totally different circumstances.

People would behave differently to them now, on and off the field. I knew that. It worried me. Something was tugging at me straight away before we even got to Heuston for the train home. Meeting journalists the morning after, I said as much, predicting 'a tough year' ahead for the group.

SEOIRSE BULFIN: 'I remember sitting beside Tony Kelly in St Pat's before the replay, the two of us watching Shane O'Donnell being called aside. And I said to him, "Well, TK, it's going to be over in a couple of hours now one way or the other. How're you feeling?"

'And he says to me, "Seoirse, I can't wait for a Supermacs and a can of Coke!" This young fella was going to end up Hurler of the Year and Young Hurler of the Year. But that was what he was looking forward to.'

When we got back to Ennis that Sunday night I went straight home. I wish I hadn't now, because the entire group went down to the Queens nightclub and, when I saw the pictures afterwards, it just struck me that they reflected a precious moment of togetherness that we couldn't be sure would ever be repeated.

The following Wednesday, before we played the GOAL match in Sixmilebridge, I got the lads into a room in my pub, the Belsfort Inn, and essentially begged them to be careful. 'How you carry yourselves over the coming weeks is something you'll never be able to change, remember that,' I said.

'Don't end up with regrets. Clare people are incredibly proud of ye now. Let's keep it that way.'

MIKE CORRY: 'Davy never really enjoyed winning that All-Ireland. I always thought that it was a strain on him … whether it was the responsibility of the young fellas or … Not too many understand that there's a softness about him that's frightening really. He doesn't show it too often, but it's there.

'He definitely was worried about some of the younger fellas, and that's what hurts me about the way some of them have let him down. That's the conflict for me with Clare, because I'm a Clareman. Proud. But there's some Clare fellas that I'm not proud of, given what he's done for them.

'And I'm not blinded by Davy. I know his weaknesses probably better than most. But, as Clare men go, there's very few that have given what he's given. I know a lot of it is personal for him now, but I saw things he did for people afterwards that no-one will ever know. He wouldn't want anyone to know about it and more's the pity.

'As Shakespeare said, what good men do is oft interred with their bones.'

I was trying to watch out for the players, because I knew people would be pulling and dragging out of them now. And I just had a sixth sense too that nothing coming down the line would be simple from now on. One of the things I'd commissioned was the printing of a special jersey for every member of the panel. I think we made 38 of them, with *All-Ireland Final* and the date printed under the badge. Once in the dressing-room, I made a point of those jerseys being handed out, starting with number 38.

I wanted everybody to feel a part of what we'd achieved, to feel special.

But coping with success can be a horribly difficult challenge. We'd seen Tipp storm to senior and under-21 All-Ireland wins within a week in 2010 with an incredibly talented bunch of hurlers, only to then take six years to get their hands on the Cup again. If that could happen Tipp, what were the dangers for us now with an even younger group?

I knew too that we'd a tendency in Clare to shoot ourselves in the foot. And, for certain, there were people within the county who wouldn't be happy that this victory had come on my watch. A small minority, admittedly, but one that could create big problems.

All of that was in the back of my mind now as the Cup was being paraded around the county. That all kinds of people would be sticking their oar in, getting involved in stuff they had no business getting involved in. Playing games with our success.

Some of them, I knew, already coveted my job. With the successes of the under-21s backing up this All-Ireland there was a lot of talk of Clare now having changed the game for everyone. Of how we'd begun building a dynasty. Believe it or not, that kind of talk can feed a lot of spite and envy. It nourishes self-interest.

Deep down I could sense that building even before we brought the Cup home. People calculating how they could pull us down a rung or two. It's something we've done in Clare over and over, press the self-destruct button the moment we have success.

And I had an overwhelming anxiety that that was about to happen again.

13

STORM BREWING

Maybe it was down to that worry about what was coming down the tracks, but probably the worst I've ever lost my temper in a dressing-room was in Limerick the following February.

The Waterford Crystal Cup final against Tipperary turned into a second-half slaughter that offended every fibre in my body. I'll forgive a lot of things in a team, but throwing in the towel isn't one of them. And that's what we did that evening. Leading by a point at half-time, we just rolled over afterwards, allowing Tipp to ease away to a fourteen-point win.

Watching on the line, I was apoplectic. Losing to Tipp in any circumstance will never sit easy with me, but almost bending the knee in front of them – when we were supposedly the best team in the country – Lord Christ, that sent me into a different orbit.

I'd started eight of our All-Ireland final team, but it seemed too many minds were elsewhere. There wasn't an ounce of fight in us, because there wasn't a shred of conspicuous pride.

I get on with most opposing managers, but Eamon O'Shea was never really one of them. I considered his attitude towards me a little arrogant. And that night, as Tipp began making mincemeat of us, he kept roaring for his forwards to go for goals. He wanted us absolutely buried.

I've never forgotten that and there's no doubt O'Shea's attitude just blackened my mood further as the digits on the scoreboard kept on rising. By the time I got back into the dressing-room I should probably have carried a Government health warning.

We were the All-Ireland champions and we'd just let Tipp walk all over us. Was this how we planned on defending our only other trophy?

I had a hurley in my hand as I came in the door and, if I'm honest, began swinging it at anything in front of me. I hit gear bags, boots, the clothes pegs on the wall. Honestly, I was vicious. If somebody said the wrong thing to me, God alone knows what I might have done. But the lads just stood there, frozen like headstones, watching me wear the timber off everything I could, the breeze of it keeping them silent.

I actually remember pushing the hurley towards the faces of a few, roaring at them, '*We never fucking throw in the towel! You hear that? Never!*'

They were shell-shocked, I could see that. But some of them had just been swanning around out there, going through the motions, as if to say, 'This stuff is beneath us now!' That worried me. Without fight, we were nobodies. Without fight, I knew we'd be swallowed up by the chasing pack.

Everything that had kept us honest through good and bad the previous summer was on the line here.

Kilkenny would be coming to Ennis just over a week later for our first League game and to show this kind of attitude against a Brian Cody team would condemn us to humiliation. If the very thought of that wasn't repugnant to everybody in the dressing-room now, we were in right trouble here.

I knew from my contacts that Cody had been working his players like dogs through October and November and that they'd be locked and loaded for this game, determined to pull us back down to size. He'd had to endure a lot of excitable media commentary since September about how Clare had completely rewritten hurling's rules of engagement now, and anyone who didn't follow could expect to be left in the past.

LOUIS MULQUEEN: 'One of the things that struck me after winning the All-Ireland was, you'd look around the dressing-room and it was like you were looking at boys. At a minor team or an under-21 team. Young and innocent.

'I remember talking to Davy a few days after and he was saying, "This will affect them!"

'Yet some newspapers were calling it the dawn of a new era. People talking of there being a few All-Irelands in the team. But deep down I think we knew that the brand of hurling we'd won the All-Ireland with … people would find a way of stopping it the following year. We'd suddenly become untouchable. Why?

'Because we'd beaten a team that tried to play hurling against you? Not one set up specifically to stop you hurling? So while you got the accolades you knew there were people already at work with the intention of stinging you. They were already in the gym, working to that target.'

I can't tell you what it felt like as a Clareman watching Kilkenny form a guard of honour for our arrival onto the Cusack Park pitch that day. The greatest team hurling has ever seen basically standing sentry as we made our entrance.

That's about as good as it gets for someone from a county like Clare, where we've spent so much of our history playing second fiddle to the so-called superpowers, the blue-bloods who – they'd like us to believe – inherit skills at birth that the rest of us could barely imagine.

Up to this point my own history with Cody had been very much in the category of student and master too, and I'll admit I really wanted to get one over on him here. More to the point, I wanted to do it with this Clare team, making a strong statement about how we intended to defend our All-Ireland crown.

To that end, I reiterated what I'd said after that Waterford Crystal final embarrassment. 'Today we fight,' I told the players. 'And we don't stop fucking fighting until we walk back into this dressing-room together!'

There was a crowd in excess of 10,000 in Cusack Park that day, and though we had nowhere near as much done as Kilkenny (having only gone on the team holiday in January), we played with the pride that our new status demanded.

And, make no mistake, Kilkenny wanted to beat us.

At one stage I was having words with the referee when Cody met me with dog's abuse on the line. I just turned away, smiling. The greatest compliment that man could ever pay me was to become agitated against my team. In doing so he made it crystal-clear just how much Kilkenny wanted to take our scalp.

And that day especially I wanted everything about Ennis to feel different. I wanted us to look like champions, behave like champions.

And the players were magnificent. The symbolism of the day just seemed to register with them and they never gave Kilkenny a moment's peace, even when it looked like we might be running out of legs. Henry Shefflin was playing his first League game in almost five years but was denied a goal on his return when Donal Tuohy saved his 45th-minute penalty. Kilkenny actually went in front with about twelve minutes to go, but the team knew exactly what this day meant to our people and they dug deep, to win by a single point.

Looking back, the effort pretty much drained the tank, because next day out Dublin beat us in Parnell Park. And that would become the story of our League.

Up one day, down the next. Flashes of brilliance followed by bouts of carelessness.

We went to Thurles, hitting four goals to devour Tipp, then nailed five the next day against Waterford in Ennis. That would be the game in which Derek McGrath was persuaded he could no longer go with an orthodox six defenders if he hoped to beat the serious teams. Because we cut them open almost at will.

Later that year, Derek would come to my house in Sixmilebridge, where we chatted for hours about our respective hurling philosophies. As it happened, we had very similar thoughts on how the game should be played, but only one of us seemed to be putting those thoughts into practice. That intrigued me.

Of course I knew from personal experience how the Waterford public liked their team to hurl with the abandon of Justin McCarthy's time, but they simply didn't have the players to do it now. And Derek seemed to be getting it in the ear from every side after another underwhelming year.

I remember asking him, 'Is that how you actually want your team to play?'

His response was, 'No, not really.'

'So why do it, then?'

'Because it's what the supporters want.'

'Well, what have you to lose?' I asked. 'If you're getting the abuse you're getting anyway, wouldn't it be better if you were getting it for doing something you believe in?'

Derek's a really smart man, much more tactically astute than most. He just needed to be true to himself, to play a game that suited the players at his disposal. Soon as he made that change, Waterford would win only the third National League title in their history.

And we would get early evidence of that change in a fairly saucy behind-closed-doors challenge match against them maybe a week and a half before the commencement of the 2015 National Hurling League. To say it was hard-core stuff would be an understatement. Waterford were absolutely psyched on the night, hitting really hard.

I've a lot of time for Barry Coughlan as a defender, but he sometimes lives not just on the edge but a little over it. And he gave Shane O'Donnell an awful time the same night. Shane's such a gentleman he was inclined to take it. But Barry tried it once then with Conor McGrath, and let's just say it didn't end well for him.

Conor's not a dirty player, but nobody takes liberties in his company.

It was that type of game, a real rough-house challenge with a few red cards and Waterford bedding in their new sweeper system in a contest that felt real. They beat us the same night too and there was no handshake, nothing between Derek and me after. He'd found his mojo and was driving on.

And I knew Waterford would be a different animal now.

Anyway, our own League petered out undramatically in that campaign of 2014, a flat performance nowhere near good enough in the semi-finals against a Tipp team now on a revenge mission of their own.

So how were we fixed for summer? I'm honestly not being wise after the event when I say that I knew things weren't anywhere near where I needed them to be.

There's a natural price to be paid for winning an All-Ireland, and the biggest part of that is an obligation to keep your people happy.

One of the things I felt really strongly about was that the Cup should go to every school in the county, that we'd make damn sure our All-Ireland win registered with the next generation. I got this card printed with a picture of the team on the front and messages about nutrition and practice and the value of sport printed on the back. In any school we went to, every kid there got a card.

It was my own idea. I just felt this was a priceless opportunity to help shape the younger generation in Co. Clare and that we'd regret it for the rest of our lives if we allowed it to slip by.

I also gave a speech to LIT students in the spring of that year, focusing largely on alcohol and bullying. It was a 30-minute presentation out of which maybe eight seconds was taken by a particular journalist and completely misrepresented. I basically said that there had been a small number of Clare players in the noughties who'd done things they shouldn't have done and, accordingly, wasted a portion of their careers.

The point of my address was to advise the students on stuff to steer clear of and the avenues to follow if they were ever feeling down. It was hugely well received too, so I was completely ill-prepared for the barrage of criticism that came my way afterwards, suggesting I'd tarred all Clare hurlers of that period with the one brush.

That really hurt me. I just felt my message was completely misconstrued. One prominent former colleague had a right go at me afterwards, something I found ironic given that he'd once gone to the county board to say he'd refuse to play with a couple of lads in the squad because they were acting the maggot.

The truth is I couldn't speak highly enough of 95 per cent of the players I hurled with for Clare. Yes, there were a few messers, but they're in every county. Just a pity that some had seen fit to twist my message. But then, those were the kinds of energies now brewing.

We tried to draw a line under the celebrations after Christmas, but it simply wasn't possible to finish it completely. There was just this seemingly endless flow of requests and, though I pretty much put a stop to any unnecessary functions, there was always a house call of one sort or another that, in conscience, we couldn't turn down.

DINNY CULLINANE: 'When we won the All-Ireland, I asked him a personal favour. I had a sister-in-law who'd been in a nursing-home in Liscannor for about fifteen years, left blind and in a wheelchair from MS. And I had an aunt who'd been paralysed in a crash. I wanted him to visit both, as well as the schools in Liscannor and Fanore.

'So this January Saturday we were to make that trip when, the night before, I got a call. It was from a family in Doolin where this 57-year-old husband and father, Pat Fitzpatrick, a hurling fanatic, was dying of cancer. They'd heard Davy would be in the area and was there any chance that he'd make a call?

'I said nothing until we were in the car, myself, Davy and Gazzy. "Do you mind if we take a little detour on the way to Fanore?" He was reluctant when I told him the story. "Sure I don't really even know the man. What am I going to say?" I gave him the only honest answer I could. "Davy, I haven't a clue, but will you do it?"

Anyway, we get to this house in Doolin, into the kitchen, everyone sitting around drinking tea. Next thing, Davy stands up. "Pat," he says, "why don't you and me slip out to the conservatory for a little chat." They must have been gone 20 minutes and, to this day, I've never asked him what they spoke about.

'But I'm in the undertaking business, and, sadly, I had to do Pat's funeral maybe two months later. And I'll never forget going up to the house where he was being waked and, there in the coffin, was a picture of him with Davy.

'That same day I got him to call in to two more people, both elderly women. And just the classy way he dealt with every one of them will never leave me. And, you know, every one of those people has passed away since. I saw the joy that he brought them that particular day. Nobody's going to tell me that doesn't matter.'

To be honest, none of that stuff bothered me in the slightest. On the contrary, I was touched to see the impact Clare's win could have on people often in really dire personal circumstances. I'd actually come away from those visits hugely emotional. Something I often say to my players is to remember that all we're actually trying to do here is win a game of hurling.

It's never life or death. If we don't succeed, we'll hopefully still have our health after, still have our families. Hard as we might take losing, we always get over it in time.

No, a few other things were needling me now, one especially. Just when you might have imagined we'd have the absolute good will of our own county, we came to realise this wasn't entirely the case. One club specifically began rallying others to get more internal championship games played in Clare just at the time we were gearing up for our Munster opener against Cork.

Listen, I could see their point. The problem I had was how they chose to go about it. Instead of engaging with the county board they began calling meetings without any board involvement, determined – essentially – to keep my father out of the dialogue. It was as if they'd already concluded, 'Sure Pat Fitz *is* the county board, and he's just going to be minding Davy.'

Now that really galled me.

I would honestly say my father was tougher on me as a Clare manager than he's been on any other during his time as county secretary. We'd fight like cats and dogs. People would see us, hear us and feel uncomfortable just to be in our proximity. I remember Seánie McMahon being in the office in Clare Abbey one day when Dad and I went at it hammer and tongs, after which I stormed out, slamming the door behind me. Seánie said afterwards that he never wanted to witness anything like that again.

My father was always adamant that the footballers should be treated exactly the same as the hurlers, even now, even when we were defending All-Ireland champions and they were still stuck in Division 4.

That, naturally, led to some blazing rows. I just didn't feel it was logical any more to treat us as equals when we were so far ahead of the footballers in terms of profile and commercial potential. 'Dad,' I'd argue, 'they're in Division 4, they're not bringing in the money we're bringing in!' But, in his head, Pat had to be seen to be scrupulously fair and, if that meant treating the All-Ireland champions the same as a team in Division 4, that was exactly what he intended to do.

'David, they will be treated the same as ye …' was all I'd hear.

You know, the man has been Clare's county secretary through the most successful period in our history. The work he does is absolutely incredible. He's an unbelievably fair man, and though we'd go to war, it really hurts me how certain people have treated him down the years.

Dad's seen me at my lowest ebb and also during my greatest highs. He's always had my back, just never at the cost of fairness. One of the greatest feelings I've had was getting back to the dressing-room after beating Cork in that 2013 final replay and just looking across at him, seeing the expression on his face.

He'd never be over-demonstrative at those moments, but I knew exactly what he was feeling, and it meant the world to me. We didn't need to speak.

You know, me getting the Clare job would have added massively to the pressure he felt as county secretary. He did the job for 20-odd years without taking a single cent, but now that he's a paid official people resent him for it. Yet he's up at 7 a.m. every day and seldom home before 8 p.m. I'd say the furthest he ever brought my mother on holiday is to Lahinch.

He lives for the GAA. For Clare GAA specifically.

Which is why I really resented the efforts of certain clubs now to effectively shut him out of the conversation about local championship fixtures. And it wasn't as if I, personally, was trying to operate any kind of dictatorship here. I had already allowed the Clare players to play five or six out of maybe eight rounds of the League. Championship? Maybe two rounds, no problem.

But we were All-Ireland champions now, setting out on the defence of that title and the overriding energy I could feel coming my way from the clubs in Clare was one of hostility. They seemed to be organising endless meetings, adopting an aggressive stance against us.

We were training one night in Clare Abbey and, as we were doing the warm-up, you could see all these club representatives heading in to what was obviously going to be a bad-tempered meeting with the county board. This would have been before our first qualifier game against Wexford and it was clear the clubs had, by now, decided that they were calling the tune.

Now, this is maybe nine months after we'd won the All-Ireland and it was like county and club existed in two parallel worlds.

If they'd just come to me I don't doubt we could have found a compromise. The last thing I wanted was confrontation, but it was as if some of these people wanted nothing else. You could actually feel the tension at training that evening, the poison in the air. I asked Paddy Donnellan to canvass the players for their opinions on the basis that if we had a strong consensus that at least was something we could take to the clubs.

A message of 'Look, we're trying to defend an All-Ireland here ...'

But Paddy came out of the players' meeting afterwards announcing that the squad was divided 50-50. There was a split in the camp, basically. Maybe two weeks before that first Wexford game and, to me, half my squad was being put under pressure from their clubs to pull against me. Four All-Irelands won in our entire history and this was the dynamic in Clare now.

There and then, I knew it was a problem I couldn't solve. Too many different agendas pulling at too many people.

FATHER HARRY BOHAN: 'Davy feels he was entitled to more loyalty from different people at the time and I would agree with him. I feel he was very unfairly criticised after, but for some reason he seems to be a bit of a magnet that way.

'I would be a huge defender of his, not just because he won three All-Irelands for Clare, but because he knows the game. I don't know if anyone else thinks the game through like he does. He has superb knowledge, and I'd say hurling is what he thinks about nearly all the time.

'People underestimate him.'

Could we not have talked? I can say categorically that I have never been a dictator on this issue. I've never been dismissive of clubs, and, if anything, my view has always been that it's no harm to let your players escape that inter-county bubble every now and then and get back for a few games in a different environment.

But I remember that night specifically and the realisation hitting home that a fair raft of people in Co. Clare didn't give a fiddler's about how we got on in our All-Ireland defence. The thought struck, 'Fuck, I'm not going to get around this …'

And to this day I'd be very hurt by what the clubs did to us that summer. It felt as if they were pulling against us, almost willing us to fail. They just wanted to look after their own patch, irrespective of the impact it might have on the Clare senior hurling team. It was almost a case of 'We'll teach the Fitzgeralds!'

All this within less than a year of us winning the All-Ireland.

LOUIS MULQUEEN: 'Davy would be one hundred per cent right to say there were people advising me against getting involved with him in the first place. There's a kind of – bitterness is too strong a word, but the Clare team that won together, they're friendly, but then there's an element of indifference. They all have these strong, differing views on how the game should be played.

'They hurled together, they died together, they wouldn't wrong each other. And yet … I don't really know how to put this … I don't know did any of them want the other one to do well. Maybe it's Irish nature.

'I don't know … it's not begrudgery … but there was an element of nobody had succeeded prior to Loughnane, or after him, then Davy became the first success story. Then there was the connection with his dad in the county board. Was he getting more than other people? It was actually the opposite. Davy used to make me deal with Pat, because himself and Pat rowed continually.

'Pat mightn't be giving him enough sliotars. Pat might be arguing about a meal for the team. And Davy would be on to me. "Louis, get the meal off my dad, for fuck's sake!" He had people in his ear, saying it was his dad's "set-up". But it was never like that. Like, there's many a time himself and Pat didn't talk for weeks. Pat would say to me, "Say this to Davy …"

'And I'd be, "Okay, Pat." And Davy would be sitting beside me. I mean, these two men love one another to bits, but I've been in the car with Davy when he'd be on the phone to Pat and it'd be "Ya … okay … fine" – no chat between them at all. Could be a few minutes between each word.

'But he'd kill for his dad and Pat would kill for him. Their rows would be vicious. Yet anyone who wronged his dad was dead.'

Let me put it this way. Go back to the '90s and early noughties, back to Ger Loughnane's time as Clare manager, and there wasn't a club fixture played in the county until our championship race was run. Do you think we ever played Clare Cup games during Loughnane's time? Never.

I didn't operate that way, I never have. I'd always have taken the view that we should sit down and talk it through rather than being at one another's throats. So I'd be very disappointed with how certain people drove that in 2014. And that's what I was referring to, to the media after Cork beat us. The fact that it felt as if some of our own people were now pulling against us.

Trouble was, I suppose it didn't help when I'd say something along those lines. It just made people dig their heels in, deepened the divide. I was never drawn towards diplomacy when hurting and, in the years to come, efforts would be made to change that. We appointed a press officer to, I suppose, filter my language with the media, water down my message. I didn't particularly like that, but I understood it.

Sometimes maybe I just needed to bite my tongue. But make no mistake, I was entitled to my anger that summer as the clubs of Clare pulled against their senior hurling team.

Press officer or not, that fact wouldn't change.

Not long after our All-Ireland win, Colm Collins – Podge's father – was confirmed as new manager of the Clare football team. And, almost immediately, Podge announced that he was going to try to play both games for the year.

Now, maybe you had to understand the work Podge put in to get to where he got in 2013 to know instantly just how difficult he'd find trying to be a dual star. The truth is, before that year's championship Podge hadn't been hugely rated in Clare. I actually had people giving out to me for having him on the panel, but Podge was a real terrier, with an unbelievable work rate.

Paul Kinnerk and I were both massive fans of that work rate, but Podge's conversion rate was terrible.

I told him that during his early days on the panel. 'Podge,' I said, 'you're working great, laying off great scores, but I need you chipping in every game with at least 0-3 yourself. If you're not doing that, I can't justify leaving someone on the bench who will.'

You would not believe the work Podge put in on his own in 2013, spending endless hours down on the field in Cratloe, shooting from every angle, sharpening up his stick-work, turning himself into an All-Star effectively, someone who would end up right in the frame for Hurler of the Year. Everything Podge did in that championship was down to himself, to having the humility to put in those unseen hours.

But now, naturally, he wanted to give his father a commitment too and I just knew in my heart and soul that he was going to find it a struggle.

If I'm honest, I felt Colm should have advised him against it. Bear in mind that, almost overnight, Podge had become one of the country's best-known and favourite hurlers at a time when Clare footballers were operating out of Division 4. To me, it should have been a no-brainer that Podge just stayed with us, that he committed himself to a hurling career that suddenly looked like it could take him anywhere.

That said, this situation wasn't entirely simple. I understood that.

Podge wanted to play for his Dad, and Colm wanted to manage his two sons (Seán Collins was also a member of my squad). So both said they'd give the dual option a try, and though I disagreed from the outset, I knew too that this wasn't an argument I was likely to win.

Now Colm Collins is an exceptional manager, as his track record with Clare footballers since has shown. He's a fundamentally good man too and, when I met him to discuss it in the Radisson Hotel in Limerick, I could tell his intentions were entirely honourable. Colm said he was willing to compromise on the training load too, allowing the lads a roughly 60 per cent/40 per cent training split, in hurling's favour.

I knew the family figured that, because the dual option hadn't stopped Cratloe being successful on both fronts, they reckoned this model could be replicated with the county. But the levels were gone up so much at inter-county, they were trying to do the impossible now. And I said as much.

One thing that hurt me subsequently was how my views became conveniently interpreted in some quarters as evidence of Clare's hurling management being anti-football. Nothing could have been further from the truth. I was so proud to be a Clareman when John Maughan led the county's footballers to Munster final victory over Kerry in '92. It was an achievement that electrified every GAA person in the county, not just those in the football strongholds of the west.

But getting just a percentage of Podge for 2014 instead of the full deal just wasn't what I needed.

And that meant Podge was now a problem.

I just felt that he was putting himself under undue pressure and that the people around him should have recognised that and advised him against it. When that didn't happen, I suppose there was always going to be a breaking point. And, being honest, I didn't exactly handle that breaking point too well.

Trouble is, you sometimes say things you regret, and that would very much be the case for me immediately after we'd lost the replay to Wexford. I totally regret bringing up the dual issue in my post-match interview with journalists, because it seemed as if I was scapegoating Podge specifically for a defeat that just had the feel of death by a thousand cuts.

Our All-Ireland defence didn't end because Podge Collins was spreading himself too wide that summer. It ended because so many different strands seemed to be pulling against us and, in my view, the loss of a 100 per cent committed Podge was just one of them. But me bringing up the dual issue in the immediate aftermath was completely unwarranted.

I shouldn't have said that, because it made my comments seem personal. And I 100 per cent regret that.

My judgement isn't always the best when I'm hurting, I accept that. But the Podge I had exclusive access to in 2013 was a different animal from the one I shared in 2014. The first one would have gone through a wall for me if I asked him. The second one just seemed endlessly torn between two masters.

At the end of that year Seán Collins would be one of those I released from the panel, which maybe made it seem even more as if I had some kind of personal agenda against the family. Podge certainly wasn't happy with that decision and we'd have words over that too.

Again, that made me feel as if I was fighting an unnecessary fight here.

Seán would have been a captain of mine in LIT, a guy I had absolute trust in. I'd have considered us really tight, but he just wasn't getting anywhere near my starting fifteen now or, if I'm honest, even a place on the bench. He would have been just outside my match-day squad, and, given he was playing football too, I just felt he was better off committing 100 per cent to playing for his father.

And so this guy I once had a great relationship with, someone I knew believed in my way of playing, ended up bitter enough with me. And I found that incredibly hard to deal with towards the end of 2014. Here I was after completely alienating myself from a family with whom I'd always had a good relationship. One I massively respected.

But Podge just wasn't the same player in 2014. He was trying to do too much. When he was with us he trained as hard as anybody, but he was killing himself. And I was just trying to get the best out of him, a point I felt he kept missing. My job was with the hurlers and I needed everybody to be 100 per cent focused on a single target.

When that didn't happen, I knew I had to make a call. So at the end of that season I told Podge he had to make a decision. 'It's hurling or football, but not both, Podge,' I told him. And, maybe not surprisingly, he chose to go with his father.

Listen, 2014 was a million miles from the season I'd hoped we could summon as All-Ireland champions.

I made mistakes, no question. Historically, the season after an All-Ireland win has proved problematic for just about every county, bar Kilkenny. Look at Tipp in 2010. Within six days of Lar Corbett's three goals in the final, their under-21s took All-Ireland glory too, trouncing Galway in Thurles. There and then, the debate wasn't about whether that Tipp team would win another but how many.

Yet it was six years before they got their hands on the Liam MacCarthy again and, given the talent at their disposal, that probably felt like an eternity.

I knew 2014 was always likely to be a difficult year for Clare and even alluded to that reality within minutes of us winning the 2013 All-Ireland. But what I experienced really shocked me. The absolute sense of so many within the county pulling against us, maybe against me specifically, really jarred.

It seemed as if personal agendas held greater sway than any common desire to see Clare hurlers doing well.

Look, we definitely struggled on the field to re-create what we'd had going for us the year before. And we hadn't the physicality to do things any other way. We ended up moving John Conlon around like a deck-chair to win puck-outs and that wasn't entirely fair on John.

Maybe I didn't help myself either with that eruption against a local journalist in the dressing-room tunnel the day we drew with Wexford in Ennis. That was just grist to the mill of those looking to depict me as some kind of lunatic. There and then they had their 'sure what would you expect …' proof.

I was irrational. I was volatile. I was unpredictable. I was a hissing hand-grenade. I was almost a cartoon character in some eyes now and the really galling thing was I'd all but helped construct the image myself. But again, others I might have expected to be more supportive seemed only too happy to add fuel to the fire.

An example: immediately after the Cork defeat, Ger Loughnane sent Louis a witheringly dismissive text about the Clare players. It communicated a complete lack of any respect for a group that, bear in mind, were still All-Ireland champions. When Louis showed it to me it just made my blood boil.

What I did next probably wasn't right and I could tell that Louis was fit to kill me as soon as I began to speak. And that's one big regret I carry. Louis has been such a friend to me I probably shouldn't have put him in what became an invidious position.

But on the bus out of Thurles that day I made a point of reading Loughnane's text to the players. It was just so dismissive of these men who'd brought such glory to our county that I felt, if it riled them up now, that mightn't be any harm. How dare one of our own disregard them now as a bunch of losers!

I wanted the team angry going home. That's why I did it.

But a couple of weeks later the story appeared in the *Sunday Times*. It was written by Christy O'Connor, Jamesie's younger brother and someone who was sub goalie to me in Clare for a number of years. Christy, clearly, had someone in the group feeding him information.

This absolutely sickened me. Now, I'd never felt Christy had been especially supportive of me as Clare manager, but he was entitled to his opinion. What I couldn't accept was one of my players leaking information to him that couldn't in any way help the squad. Hard as I tried, I could never find out who that player was. I narrowed it down, for sure. I had my suspicions. But without proof, all I could do was grin and bear it.

To me, the person or people responsible needed to take a long, hard look at themselves. They couldn't be considered real Clare people when their intentions seemed only to undermine or damage the very group that they were supposed to be a part of.

But there was a steady trickle of information from our dressing-room that summer – private stuff appearing in newspapers and on forums – and all I can say is that those responsible are plain ignorant if, today, they don't look back on their disloyalty of that time with regret.

They were out of order in my opinion, people who showed zero loyalty to Clare hurlers at a time so many of their colleagues were working heroically to make things work.

And maybe the story of 2014 that was largely overlooked was just how magnificent the players had been. Because they were heroes to me every bit as much as they'd been the previous September. I mean we had Podge sent off the first day against Wexford, yet came back from the dead to force that draw.

The second day, Bugs and Jack Browne were both shown red cards by Johnny Ryan, meaning we had to play virtually the last half hour in Wexford Park with just thirteen men. I was furious with Johnny for about a year after that game, because I felt he'd given my players zero protection.

Two incidents stand out for me. One is of a Wexford player striking Tony Kelly across the helmet, with the ball nowhere near, and Johnny just waving play on. The other is of Aaron

Cunningham running in on goal, having his hand pulled and a free out being awarded to Wexford!

People might point to us winning only 19 of 35 of our own puck-outs, but look at the blackguarding of Kelly under those puck-outs. He hadn't a hope of getting the ball with the hits coming from every angle.

Yet, even with thirteen against fifteen, some of the hurling the lads produced was extraordinary. Honestly, I couldn't have been prouder of them. And I'm not saying that Johnny Ryan cost us our All-Ireland that day. Liam Dunne had Wexford in great shape, and, by Jesus, they were well fired up to take our scalp that day.

I said as much to the journalists after. I told them that all hurling people would wish Wexford well from here, specifically adding, 'Please print that!'

And I'll never forget the generosity of Wexford people towards us coming out of the dressing-room afterwards. They just stood there applauding, reaching out to us to shake our hands. That always stuck with me. They were on an absolute high with their own team now, but that didn't blind them to the respect that All-Ireland-winning players were entitled to, even in defeat.

If I'm honest, sitting on the bus that evening I couldn't help contrasting that attitude with what we'd encountered from some of our own people. I just felt we hadn't been given much help within the county, that any obstacle that could have been put in front of us invariably was. That really hurt me, the sense that personal agendas and petty jealousies seemed more important to some Clare people than trying to win All-Irelands. Little did I know at that moment that they wouldn't be going away any time soon.

14

TWO SIDES …

So it's a February night in 2015, we're training in the UL grounds and two senior Clare players want to talk to me.

We step to a quiet corner of one of the connecting dressing-rooms, where they let loose their frustrations. 'Davy, we're fed up to the teeth of this carry-on,' I'm told. 'These fellas are pulling down the whole group.'

The picture painted for me is probably as old as the GAA itself. A picture of players failing to meet the agreed standards of the dressing-room. In this instance three of them – Davy O'Halloran and Nicky and Cathal 'Tots' O'Connell – had been seen by a member of my management team out in a Limerick nightclub, the Icon, two days before our opening National League game against Galway.

Now, being honest, I needed this like a hole in the head.

We had a rule that players weren't to be out socialising the week of a game and this was a blatant infringement of that rule, irrespective of whether or not they expected to be involved that Sunday. In my view, everyone had to be seen to make the same commitment. We were either in this together or we weren't.

But there was a particularly personal dimension to this too that I could certainly have done without. For the previous couple of years the O'Connell brothers had been living with Sharon and me in Sixmilebridge, extended members of family, in effect.

Nicky had actually just moved out, having spent virtually all of '13 and '14 under my roof.

Their mother, Margaret, died young and I'd visited her not long before she passed. She was a wonderful woman and I was more than happy for the two lads to come and live with me. In fact Sharon all but became a surrogate mother to them, cooking them meals, organising their washing, basically filling a little part of the void that had been left in their lives by Margaret's death.

So to hear they'd been two of the three lads in the Icon that night really hurt a lot.

The news was only communicated to me after our second League game against Cork and I decided to deal with it in a way I thought would cause the least amount of disruption. We were now zip from two in terms of points and, with Tipperary next on the horizon, it seemed to me that the best option was to try resolving this internally.

I called them before the group and, without being remotely aggressive, told them that they owed the rest of the panel an apology. That done, I then said they would have to train on their own for a period of three weeks, during which time they'd have access neither to official training gear nor to the travelling party on a match day.

To me, that should have been the beginning and the end of it. It was these lads' fellow-players who'd brought the issue to my attention and, for O'Halloran specifically, it wasn't exactly a first offence. He'd been late for training a number of times and, when we'd played a challenge game in LIT the previous 23 December, it quickly became apparent that Davy was in no fit condition to play.

We subsequently discovered that he'd been out late the night before, so when we reconvened in Cratloe Woods the following day I tackled him about it in front of the group. And Davy, to be fair, apologised to everybody, declaring that it wouldn't happen again.

Now I thought this latest matter had been dealt with until I got a letter from himself and Nicky announcing their withdrawal from the Clare panel.

Tots took a different approach, chatting about it at home with me, admitting that he'd been wrong and, basically, taking his punishment on the chin.

Anyway, we lost to Tipp in Ennis next (our third defeat in a row), the pressure really beginning to build now. And that was the week I took a phone call from a journalist in the *Irish Times*. He'd been contacted by someone to complain about how Clare's management had tried to 'humiliate' three players over 'a disciplinary issue'.

The picture painted was of a total dictatorship. Basically, I wasn't even allowing them have any dialogue with the rest of the group for those three weeks (how I might police that was never explained) and – well, Davy and Nicky had decided they couldn't accept any further involvement with such a draconian regime.

There was also an allegation that the management had already turned a blind eye to an even more serious disciplinary breach, simply on the basis that the player involved was a regular starter and, accordingly, irreplaceable.

So I wasn't just being accused of being a bully here, I was also being accused of double standards.

Now, an absolute cardinal rue of mine in management is that everybody must be treated the same. If you don't have that sense of absolute togetherness, you've got nothing. So the insinuation that I'd let a more senior player off with something was completely untrue. I did learn subsequently that Louis had spoken to one player about something, not drink-related, and the matter was handled firmly without me even being told.

Maybe the lads got the wrong impression about that, thinking I'd just brushed one case aside but was now making an example of theirs.

The truth is, a number of our senior players weren't happy with the levels of discipline being shown by some and it was their patience that had snapped when the three lads were seen pitching up in the Icon.

I explained all of this now to the reporter, giving him plenty of off-the-record detail on the story from my perspective. To me, it scarcely amounted to a huge controversy. These lads were basically being asked to train on their own for a few weeks, after which they'd return to the squad, and, presumably, we'd all drive on together.

I made clear the fact that I didn't want to be quoted on anything but was happy to give him the full picture of a story that very clearly had two sides.

But pretty soon I got the impression that he was pressing ahead with the article regardless, that Davy O'Halloran's complaints would be given a national platform, one in which he would declare of me, 'Some lads are too scared to stand up to him.'

So the Friday before we played Dublin in Ennis this article appeared under the heading 'Clare hurler humiliated by "double-standard" treatment'. And it's fair to say its publication kicked off what I can only term a real shit-storm.

Suddenly I found myself accused of all manner of human rights violations. In the fall-out on radio and in newsprint I took serious abuse as some kind of madman treating my players like children. To this day I'm convinced that somebody else in Clare was pushing Davy to go public like he did, because I always felt I'd been decent towards him.

The irony was we'd more or less agreed to remove him from the panel at the start of 2015. Davy was a decent player, who'd scored 1-4 in the 2013 All-Ireland under-21 final, but he was well down the pecking order of our forward options now. And, if I'm honest, making little enough impression.

Why? I honestly believed he wasn't showing sufficient commitment.

That said, there was no denying his potential and, after Louis and myself went to watch him in a club game, we'd decided to give him another chance. Now I couldn't help thinking, 'If we'd just stuck with our gut instinct in the first place, none of this crap would be happening.'

LOUIS MULQUEEN: 'All of that stupidity about bullying was blown completely out of proportion. I was there, I saw it happening in front of my own eyes. It wasn't anything like what was conveyed. The three lads admitted they'd been out. Basically, all Davy got them to do then was run a few laps of the field.

'Next thing it was in the newspaper that they'd been treated so badly. It was all rubbish, in my view. This is where Davy maybe attracts too much media attention. If that was in Kilkenny no-one would have known. And that was where he got a bit paranoid. A lot of stuff was being leaked, and he never found out who was doing it.

'He'd say to me, "They're not important, fuck them!" But it'd be niggling him.'

Because of all the abuse suddenly coming my way now, an influential figure from outside Clare advised us that a players' statement of unity was probably advisable.

Paddy Donnellan sent out a text to the entire group, asking if anybody had a problem with this, and the vast majority were agreeable. I never expected 100 per cent. Players who aren't getting a game are never going to be happy with the management, but all the key men of the dressing-room knew that the abuse I now found myself on the receiving end of was completely unwarranted.

We were subsequently criticised for the release of that statement, Anthony Daly among those saying we should just have left things go. But what impression would that have given? That the depiction of me in the article had been fair?

It hadn't been and the senior players knew that.

I was fuming with the *Irish Times* for publishing it and made a point of ringing their sports editor, Malachy Logan. Now, it's fair to say that the conversation we had was less than conciliatory and ended up without any resolution. I got the impression that he regarded me as the bully depicted in the piece and maintained that I'd been 100 per cent in the wrong.

To be fair, I couldn't fault him for defending his journalist. I just felt he was completely deaf to anything that I said.

Later that evening, unable to let it rest, I texted him again. To my surprise, he texted back, saying that my persistence was making him think there might be a second side to the story. Again I protested, 'Malachy, that's all I'm saying, there's two sides to this. I'm not as bad as that article portrayed.'

In the end he suggested that we might meet sometime for a cup of tea and that's where we left it. Still nothing resolved as such but at least the feeling that I hadn't been completely ignored.

The big follow-up story was that Davy O'Halloran would be joining the Clare footballers now, an inference being that our loss would be Colm Collins's gain. And while Davy did indeed join the footballers, he didn't last too long there either. I never asked why.

As for Nicky, I agreed to meet him in Sixmilebridge one day but made a point of bringing Fergal Lynch along as a witness. Bruiser had been a massive factor in our All-Ireland win of 2013, even though he'd seen little enough game time. Just a hugely honest, positive presence in the dressing-room who I'd recruited to my back-room staff the following year. Himself and Seoirse took a lot of the training in 2015, two men I'd absolutely trust with my life.

I wanted him with me for that meeting with Nicky now so that I'd have a witness to what was coming. If that makes me sound paranoid, so be it. But I honestly felt there'd been so much misinformation put out about me at this stage I needed to protect myself.

And to say that some of the stuff Nicky had to say about what had happened was interesting would be an understatement. He apologised profusely, asking could he rejoin the panel.

I agreed immediately.

But it's fair to say there was a sour atmosphere building within Clare now and one of those who bore the brunt of it was Louis. Horrible rumours about his personal life, all 100 per cent untrue, began to circulate. He was hurting and watching him hurt absolutely disgusted me. No matter what we did now, we just seemed to be getting it in the neck.

Mike Deegan's departure, allied to the fact that we'd lost Paul Kinnerk to a year of travelling, had meant a big reshuffle of my back room. To that end I'd brought in Mike Browne, and Kieran 'Fraggy' Murphy from Cork.

Mike had helped Crusheen and Tulla win championships and going after him was a bit of a gamble, as I didn't really know him at the time. In fact I couldn't have been too sure even if he'd any time for me, but I was 100 per cent certain that Tulla wouldn't have won their senior title without Mike Browne. They'd come within a whisker of winning a Munster Club too and, though we'd have plenty of fights down the line, he would back up everything he did at club level with what he now gave to Clare.

I'd been trying to get Fraggy involved for a while, having coached him with LIT where I would have rated him easily in the top three of Fitzgibbon players that I've worked with. I never thought Cork got enough out of him hurling-wise because, while his ability was incredible, he also had this knack of bringing other hurlers around him into a game.

That game intelligence was what really appealed to me now. I knew Paul's absence would be felt by our forwards and, though Fraggy could only commit a day every two weeks, I was convinced he could still make a difference even in such a condensed time.

It would become a regret of mine that we didn't work together longer, as the imminent arrival of twins meant that Fraggy and his wife soon had more important business on their hands than focusing on getting Clare hurlers back to the top table.

With all this chopping and changing, Louis was more vital than ever to what we were trying to do now, but I knew he was really rattled by what was happening. The sense of unfairness was overwhelming.

LOUIS MULQUEEN: 'Letters were coming in here to the school to me, bullshit stuff. Not signed, of course, anonymous. Others were actually put through the letterbox at home. The only commonsense thing I could do was take them to the Guards and let them investigate it.

'Stuff about your personal life. You take it on the chin, but at the time it hurts. It's not fair. It makes you feel almost bitter that people can do this. I mean, these people don't know you to judge you. It'd be different if you were David Beckham or a pop star making millions. Let them take a shot at you then.

'But you're only an ordinary Joe Soap who has a job. You don't expect people to be sending you hate mail! It's this strange thing of being hurt by people you don't even know. And you had the "keyboard warriors" then who could say anything about you.

'That's the problem with profile. The GAA, and inter-county hurling in particular, is gone cosmic. It's an unnatural existence, and a lot of youngsters can't deal with it. You end up trying to fight people, but who are you fighting? At the time I wanted to machine-gun everybody. But you can't do anything about it. It's anonymous.

'The problem is that people think they have a right to knock you if you're successful. We were the kingpins after bringing Clare out of the wilderness, so people were looking for something.'

That was bad enough, but in the national media then Jamesie was having a go. Loughnane was having a go. It felt relentless. People kept telling me to ignore it, but when it feels as if you're getting a kicking every few minutes, trust me, it's hard to do that.

We lost our final group game in the League by a single point to Kilkenny in Nowlan Park, the same margin by which Galway had beaten us in Salthill. Our solitary victory had been over Dublin and so we were pitched into a relegation play-off, bringing us back to Nowlan Park for yet another tussle with Cody and Kilkenny.

Again they beat us by a single point, the fact that we'd put two really decent back-to-back performances against them now completely obscured by our plunge back into Division 1B. Put it this way: Kilkenny could just as easily have been relegated after two unbelievable games against us, yet would end the year as All-Ireland champions.

For all the doom and gloom around us then, I knew we hadn't turned into a bad team.

So relegation wasn't a reflection of how we felt about ourselves now, whatever the opinion of those on the outside.

The only League game we'd lost comprehensively was the Cork one. Otherwise we were competitive in every match we played. We just needed a break. Sometimes that's actually all you need. Something running for you that gives you a sense of momentum coming. Maybe of your luck turning, even.

But that didn't happen. Limerick beat us by a point in our Munster Championship opener, a ridiculous defeat in many ways, because the game always felt so winnable. This, of course, now meant we'd lost seven of our last eight competitive games. The fact that four of them had been by a single point seemed immaterial to the critics.

Though we then hammered Offaly in our first All-Ireland qualifier, Cork edged us out by three points in the next. Our season was over and, yet, all the time I felt we weren't that far away from really clicking.

Even in that Cork game there were times we looked like cutting them open. I genuinely felt that one Clare goal could have opened the floodgates that night. But little enough went right for us in the final third. We kept taking wrong options, a rash shot or a careless pass. The lads gave it everything and were always there or thereabouts.

But we came up short again. In two championships since winning the All-Ireland, our only win was against Offaly.

> SEOIRSE BULFIN: 'I honestly felt if we'd got over Cork that evening, things were really starting to come together again. I was on the verge of tears the whole way home from Thurles in the car.'

I knew that I had enemies piling up now and, sure enough, Brian Lohan came out with that call for an 'independent review' into Clare hurling. And, of course, his choice of chair was Ger Loughnane.

The premise of Brian's call was that clubs should have been able to have their say on whether or not I continued as manager. I still had two years left, but that seemed immaterial now.

The atmosphere within Clare was turning really sour, stoked in many cases by old comrades of mine. It was clear I needed a serious think about how I'd turn this round now. Paul Kinnerk would be returning, but I felt more than ever that we needed something fresh. That the players would benefit from hearing a new voice.

I had someone in my head too. Somebody from left field who, I was certain, nobody would predict. But, for all I knew, I might now be making a fool of myself by even asking.

15

THE END-GAME

D ónal Óg Cusack is a good storyteller and the one about the two of us on 2005 Railway Cup duty in Boston is decent, if a little embellished.

That was an odd enough trip, during which the Cork players didn't seem much interested in mixing with their Munster colleagues. They were the kings, dual All-Ireland champions and, reputedly, setting modern standards in terms of fitness and preparation that the rest of us couldn't imagine, let alone replicate. So to Clare men, Tipp men, Limerick men, Waterford men, they seemed aloof, a group happy to keep their own company.

I look back on it now and see things a little differently. The Cork lads went to America with a plan, the rest of us didn't. They had tickets organised for different events: a basketball match one night, a concert another. In other words, they always had somewhere else to go when the rest of the group seemed drawn by magnet to the nearest Irish pub.

As a non-drinker, no question I'd have been far happier immersed in the Cork arrangements, but at the time all I could see in them was arrogance.

That would have been the general vibe of the travelling group too, Dónal himself recounting how one night they almost found themselves squaring up to the Kilkenny contingent outside the hotel lift.

Anyway, I went to Boston as the All-Star goalkeeper and believed that that status should have been recognised in the Munster team selection. But Joe O'Leary, a Cork selector, who was Munster manager for the trip, told Dónal Óg and myself that we'd be getting half the final each. I was livid. To me he was just looking after his buddy and I told him so.

With hindsight I realise it probably wasn't the smartest thing to do for team spirit, but it felt as if all the top goalkeepers at the time – myself, Dónal Óg, Brendan Cummins, Damien Fitzhenry – were locked in an unspoken war, each one desperate to be recognised as the best. It's been spoken of since as a 'golden age' for the position and I suppose in that climate I was never inclined, willingly, to take a backward step.

So half a game each? Joe got it between the eyes.

I didn't really know Dónal at the time and had little enough interest in that changing. He was an opponent to me, nothing more. Wearing the Munster colours together now was, if I'm honest, an artificial union. He knew it. I knew it.

Anyway, Dónal Óg paints a picture of me acting the big-shot when we got to the pitch in Canton, standing in for pictures, signing autographs, carrying myself very pointedly as the Munster and Ireland number one. Honestly? There was probably a bit of that in my head all right and we certainly communicated a fairly mutual hostility in the warm-up, leading to a silent stand-off after he'd lashed a sliotar aggressively over my head into the forest behind.

But the story about me feigning injury just before half-time or, as he put it, 'limping like a fucking war veteran' – well, I'd take issue with that.

Anyway, you had Cork and you had the rest of us in 2005. That trip deepened an already significant divide and if you said to me as we flew home that, a decade later, I'd be looking for Dónal Óg to work with me, I'd have enquired what you'd been drinking.

For sure, there was mutual, if grudging, respect there. He got an All-Star in '99 that he admits should probably have been mine. And, if I'm honest, maybe I couldn't have begrudged him that one I got in '05.

I admired the role he played for Cork, a kind of quarter-back between the posts, directing operations with an accuracy of puck-out that, over time, came to preoccupy their opponents.

Were we buddies? You must be kidding. If you're a really competitive animal you're just not going to click with fellas you're playing against. The mentality is that you're going to war and I've always totally related to that. But there'd still be opponents you'd have massive respect for, fellas you can recognise as driven.

I saw Dónal Óg as someone who would do whatever it took to be the best and I've always admired that in people.

But I'd seen a different side of him in retirement too, specifically as a laser-sharp pundit on *The Sunday Game*, in which he wasn't afraid to pull hard on any controversial issue but, more importantly, consistently offered an astute tactical summary of whatever game he'd just seen.

When we won the All-Ireland in 2013, it struck me that Dónal Óg could read exactly what we were trying in every game. He was the only one. Others would blather on about the sweeper-this, the sweeper-that, when it was crystal-clear to me they didn't really understand the detail in a system.

To them, everything was one-dimensional. A sweeper system amounted to an extra defender and was, thereby, ultra-defensive.

Cusack was different. I've massive time for Cyril Farrell too, but in my eyes Dónal Óg was emphatically RTÉ's best hurling analyst over the last seven or eight years. He just got it. He understood. He saw the bigger picture of a system, in other words the total movement within it, as distinct from the obvious points of congestion.

I'd be sitting at home watching the programme and would find it uncanny just how clearly he'd read whatever tactics had unfolded. Like, Sharon's pretty clued in to what I do. Maybe her camogie background gives her a good hurling brain, but she'd know exactly how frustrated I'd become when someone would start bluffing about Clare in front of the camera.

Then Dónal Óg would come on and, regularly, I'd hear her say, 'Davy, that fella's the only one who seems able to cop on to what you're doing …'

The others? I honestly thought they just didn't understand it. They'd talk for Ireland when the red studio light came on but, if you analysed what it was they'd say, it was clear as day they couldn't quite figure out what we were doing.

So Dónal Óg was in my head now. I knew he had an ego and an abrasive enough personality (similar to me, I suppose), and there was every chance he'd now consider the idea of forsaking his pundit's chair for a back-room role with Clare as madness. I knew too that if, by chance, he agreed to come on board we could end up clashing like vipers.

But I just felt I had to take a gamble now. Even if this man hated my guts, he clearly knew his hurling. He seemed on the same page as me tactically. So that October, while on a golf trip in South Carolina, I dialled his number and left a message.

'Dónal Óg, it's Davy Fitz here, listen I'd love to sit down with you for a chat …'

Pretty quickly he rang back and we agreed to link up when I got home. He told me subsequently that, when he first heard the message, he instinctively turned to his father and said, 'This man could be ringing me to give him a hand.'

That amazed me. I remember prefacing my first sentence to him on the phone with 'You're maybe not going to believe why I want to talk to you, but there's something I'd really like you to seriously consider.'

DÓNAL ÓG CUSACK: 'I don't know why, but soon as I heard Davy's voice on the phone I guessed that'd be what it was about. Boston apart, we'd have had little or no interaction as people up to then, though I'd have come across him in a couple of Poc Fadas. I didn't really have any thoughts about him as a person.

'But, to me, he was one of the greatest goalkeepers to ever play the game. I remember standing behind him in Páirc Uí Chaoimh for the drawn Tipperary-Clare Munster Championship game in '99 at the Blackrock end. I was just a teenager at the time and, from a goalkeeping point of view, all the basics were just outstanding. He made this great diving save when Paul Shelly was clean through, but I also remember him catching this really tricky ball under the crossbar when the sun would have been in his eyes.

'So to do that stuff and then go up the field and score a penalty in the last couple of minutes to equalise the game against a goalkeeper like Brendan Cummins, more to the point to have the presence of mind to strike it to Cummins's supposed weaker side … you hear about great deeds in the game, but I couldn't imagine a greater performance by anyone.

'If you cared about the game, or were even just interested in it, you could only stand back in awe that day. I mean, I grew up on stories of Christy Ring, but whoever you want to talk about, that to me was a performance for the ages.'

I think it's a measure of Dónal Óg as a hurling man that it quickly became clear to me how the 'glamour' of television held far less appeal to him than the chance of being on the line with a serious group of hurlers.

We met in the Charleville Park Hotel a couple of weeks later, where I'd booked a room for privacy. And there, for maybe three hours, we just talked hurling. Funny, a good few of the people I'd run my idea by beforehand all thought it absolutely nuts. But, soon as we got talking, I can honestly say I wasn't going to let him leave that room without giving a commitment.

Pretty soon I realised he was just as enthusiastic as me. We just seemed to be on the same page all the time, knocking ideas over and back, exploring the options presented by one system or another. Even in that chat he showed himself to be smart and challenging, qualities we needed in Clare now.

But Dónal Óg was also ruthless. If I'd do anything to win, I knew he would too. And that night we more or less agreed that he'd be added to the Clare coaching ticket. I was thrilled. Just thought this could turn out to be the final part of the jigsaw.

LOUIS MULQUEEN: 'It was out of the blue to the rest of us, but Davy sat in my front room and explained his thinking to Mike Browne and me. His big challenge was to make sure there'd be no friction between Dónal Óg and Paul, who was returning, that neither one would feel threatened by the other. To that end he arranged a meeting between the three of them in Limerick.

'That's the intelligence of the guy.'

I also added Aonghus O'Brien, who'd done a great job with Limerick's minors, to the ticket, and, with Kinnerk agreeing to come back in February, the strength of our back room now was that any one of them could take an individual session and the quality wouldn't suffer. I've always said that a manager is only as good as his back-room staff and now, in my opinion, I had the absolute best in the business.

I mean, we still had Mike Deegan coming to games informally, sitting up in the stand with Liam Dowd. All bright, straight people.

We trained at 6 a.m. most days throughout January, hammering in the physical preparation through Kelvin Harold and Jimmy Payne on grass in LIT through the week, then concentrating on hurling sessions at weekends.

It wouldn't have been ideal for Dónal Óg, I suppose, that our first competitive game was against Cork in Sixmilebridge, his old Cloyne friend and teammate Diarmuid O'Sullivan on the line now with Kieran Kingston. There was, naturally, a bigger media presence than would be normal for a Munster League game, and Dónal's attitude was a simple 'We're here to do a job!'

We did it too, beating Cork for the first time since the 2013 All-Ireland final replay.

Pretty soon I decided that his rapport with the players was good enough to get Dónal Óg to take over the maor foirne's job from Seoirse. The change was no reflection on Seoirse, who I have always trusted implicitly. He's the one guy who's been with me all the time, someone who can coach as well as anyone I know and who'd still be in and out of the field as much with the hurleys.

I just thought putting Dónal Óg in the position might give us something different, and it says a lot about Seoirse that he had absolutely no issues with the change.

The abuse coming my way on forums and social media was pretty relentless now. I actually managed to find out the identity of some of those behind it. One chap from Tulla, one from Shannon, a couple from Ennis and one from north Clare. A clown in Scarriff especially, endlessly demanding that I step down 'for the good of Clare hurling.' None of them would put their names to the stuff, of course.

So these empty vessels just kept swinging from the dark. Cowards given the vehicle.

Very quickly, all my hopes for what Dónal would bring to the dressing-room came to fruition. I loved working with him. He was smart, spoke brilliantly when it was needed but, as much as anything, I thought our personalities really gelled.

Often after training he'd hang around for a game of pool, table-tennis, or whatever. He sometimes stayed in my house and we'd sit up chatting long into the night. Actually, if I could think of a single word that would best describe our time working together it would be 'fun'.

Honestly, we laughed a lot, sometimes in the absolute heat of battle.

After one of his earliest sessions with us he rang me to say his car was after running out of diesel. Dónal was driving a hybrid at the time, presumed the electricity would last long enough for him to find a petrol station open, but at that time of night everything was closed.

So I picked him up and we drove back to my father's house, where the only thing we could find was a watering-can with no lid. So we get it filled up with diesel and we're driving back to where his car is beached, Dónal Óg with this can between his legs. And, Lord Jesus, the diesel fumes!

I'm not codding when I say by the time we got back to his car the two of us were high as kites. He turns to me at one stage. 'Jesus Christ, this stuff is after going to my head!'

And sure I'm sitting there, driving, laughing so much I've nearly tears rolling down my face.

The early stages of the League passed undramatically. I thought Offaly were over-physical against us. Wexford were like bears with sore heads, having taken a heavy shelling from their local media after a non-performance against Limerick the previous week. And Limerick? They had Barry Nash sent off early against us so, while our main opponents were all trying hard, we were largely in a comfort zone coming through 1B.

That pitched us into a quarter-final against Tipperary and, hand on heart, we got lucky. Tipp were way better than us that day but leaked eighteen wides, and we edged the verdict on the back of nothing more scientific than a stronger will to win.

Naturally, Kilkenny the next day were an entirely different matter.

And we did something that nobody ever did against them. We went after them in the air. Actually, that's over-simplistic, because we did a lot of things differently that day in Thurles. One was to shove our two wing-backs up to our wing-forwards on puck-outs so that we'd have extra bodies in the landing zone. I remember talking about it with Paul beforehand, and our view was that Kilkenny wouldn't really have encountered this tactic before.

We weren't entirely sure if it would work, of course, but ended up looking at one another in the dressing-room and saying almost in unison, 'Let's just do it!'

Basically, it meant we could crowd them out on our puck-outs and one man with an absolutely key role in what happened from there was Podge Collins. I'd brought Podge back into the squad, if I'm honest partly out of sympathy for the nightmare year he'd just had with a cruciate injury, but also because we genuinely missed him on and off the field. He was still trying to be a dual player – a doomed pursuit he'd finally abandon the following season after I was gone.

But on this particular day I could almost have believed that he might make it work.

I'd phoned him a few days before the game, told him exactly what I wanted him to do. And now it was like having the old Podge back again. He was absolutely electric as a floating eleven, doing his job to a T.

Look, I know Podge will never openly agree with the stance I took on him trying to play both games at the highest level. And my decision to release his brother from the panel probably didn't help his perception of me at the time either. But that never showed in his attitude when he came back in. He didn't let it affect him.

That said, if he says he has no regrets about trying to do both, I think he's fooling himself. Because Podge made a big mistake, in my opinion. Just when he was at the very top of the game he put himself under unreasonable pressure. Never really gave himself the proper chance for a sustained run at that level.

I don't expect Podge ever to agree with that opinion. But I'd be surprised if deep down he doesn't have some degree of understanding for my perspective.

We scored 4-22 that day against Kilkenny, despite missing David McInerney, Shane O'Donnell and Conor Ryan through injury, while Cathal O'Connell, Colin Ryan, Aron Shanagher, Bobby Duggan and the returning Tony Kelly were all on the bench. The latter would come on to score points with his first two touches of the entire campaign, while Colm Galvin had a massive game in midfield.

I've always felt that the key to beating Kilkenny is that you've got to move their backs around and we did it brilliantly that day, using the ball really smartly. And the scoreboard surely gave the lie to any illusion that we were playing negative, robotic hurling. In fact Thurles that day blew a lot of myths out of the water.

Because in the other semi-final Waterford ran amok, scoring 3-23 against Limerick. Two teams now famous for the deployment of sweepers delivering an aggregate 7-45. And pundits telling Derek McGrath and me that we were ruining hurling!

They were at it again when the final ended in a draw between us, with no goal chances in the game and shooting on both sides poor. Waterford leaked twenty wides; we leaked nineteen. The reaction was, predictably, hysterical. It reiterated to me how so many former players and managers simply didn't (and still don't) understand the sweeper system.

A fundamental job of any manager is to limit the goal-scoring opportunities of your opponent. What do people think is the point of what we do? We're not in the entertainment industry: our only job is trying to get teams to win. That point seems frequently lost when it comes to post-game analysis. You'd swear we were getting grants for art.

Put it this way: based on the wides' tally, Waterford had at least 42 scoring attempts that day in Thurles, we had 41. Yet the game was crucified afterwards as some kind of eyesore.

It was sent to a replay by Maurice Shanahan's huge injury-time free and there was a picture in some newspapers the following day of me helping Maurice unclip his helmet at the end, even though I was gutted we hadn't seen the game out.

I was genuinely pleased for Maurice that he'd scored the free. He'd gone through a lot of personal stuff at the time, and I just thought it showed the character of the man to nail that score when he had to. We had a friendship too that overrode any hurling rivalry. Anyway, once the whistle goes it's over. I've no problem leaving stuff on the field and just moving on.

That last score was all about character and Maurice showed he had it in buckets.

His brother, Dan, said there was some heckling from our bench as Maurice lined up that free and all I can say is that, if so, it wasn't from me. But it's not golf we're playing out there and, trust me, some of the stuff roared at me over the years when I was taking penalties for Clare wasn't exactly gentle. So heckling in hurling? That's been around as long as the game itself, I'd say.

There were certainly plenty of verbals between the two benches all through that day, triggered – in my opinion – by a hugely inappropriate comment one of the Waterford back-room staff made to Dónal Óg. That made my blood boil and I'd let Derek know all about it.

Knowing him, he wouldn't have liked the comment either, but in those circumstances I suppose you feel an obligation to defend your own people. That's fair enough. I mean, I'll go to war with anybody, but if people start getting personal I'll have nothing to do with them.

Two days before the replay, Louis's mother, Patricia, passed away after a long illness. It was a devastating blow to him, an only child. He was in two minds about even coming to the game, but I felt it massively important that he did.

LOUIS MULQUEEN: 'When Mam died, Davy was first man up to the house, arranging the funeral with me. In my front room, going, "We need to do this, we need to do that …" This with a League final just two days away, but that's the kind of character he is. That's the loveable quality of the man.

'He'd visited Mam when she was sick and she had a picture of the two of them on her phone. My aunt from Cork, Mam's sister, couldn't believe how good Davy was around the time of the funeral and loves him to bits now. And this is a woman who would have had a very strong Cork image of him before that. It would have been "that little bollocks!"

'She hugs him when she meets him now. I suppose that's the thing with Davy. It's all extremes.

'I didn't know whether to go to the game or not. But he was, "Listen, you need to go! She'd want you to go!"'

There was a minute's silence for Patricia before the game in Thurles and I remember hanging on to Louis during it. It was a tough time for him and there was a picture taken of us, me kissing the cross around my neck and looking skyward.

And the game, of course, went down to the wire too, thanks – largely – to our concession of two really soft goals. Tony Kelly settled it with a magnificent injury-time point from under the

Ryan Stand just seconds after landing a 100-metre free. It was typical big-day stuff from a real big-day player.

But when that last point went over, I remember turning to Louis. 'That was your mam!'

Much was made in the media afterwards about a perceived foul on Jamie Barron near the end that had gone unpunished and, being honest, that really niggled me. Because, although there was clearly little between the teams, I honestly believed that we deserved to win both days.

The players had been magnificent, succeeding Waterford now as League champions from a Division 1B starting-base. And it meant that I was now the first Clare manager to win both All-Ireland and National League crowns, a big thing for me personally, given how so much of my early interest in hurling came from a love of the Clare team that Father Harry Bohan managed to two League titles.

That said, I dreaded the fact that we'd be playing Waterford again, just four weeks later, in the Munster Championship. You didn't need to be a genius to recognise how highly motivated they'd be now to get revenge.

So for all the emotion surging through me that day in Thurles, I was pretty sure a League win wouldn't put an end to the sniping. In my opinion, no matter what we did, that wouldn't be stopping now.

And maybe on some level that told me, even as we brought a national trophy back to Clare, that I was now pretty deep into the end-game.

EMPTY VESSELS MAKING NOISE

Maybe there are no real happy endings in GAA management, just the slow unravelling of once outwardly strong relationships.

I can say with absolute sincerity, though, that I never felt the dressing-room pull against me in my final year as Clare manager. Not once. A manager always recognises that the tail-end of any panel isn't ever going to be his strongest support base. Players who don't get game time are never happy. Nor should they be.

But I never got a troubled vibe that year. Everybody saw the character of the players in those two League finals and, all season, they did absolutely everything that we asked them to do. I did sense that some were being tugged in different directions by outside forces, usually fathers' voices pulling hard and low against the way we were trying to play.

One player in particular took to griping a little in the background, telling others that we should be going more direct. When I heard this I made a point of meeting him one-to-one, explaining the reasons behind our hurling style in great detail. I didn't need to do this, but I recognised that his head was being turned at home.

Another was complaining openly about not getting more game time, but he simply wasn't training enough. It never ceased to amaze me that he couldn't see any connection between the two. It was as if he believed he had some kind of divine right to play. That hard training was a requirement only of others.

That said, I believed then that it was a united dressing-room. I still do now.

We were doing everything we could to keep things interesting and different. After losing to Waterford in the 2016 championship, Paul Kinnerk and I took them for a walk up the Cliffs of Moher but, looking back, I think as a team maybe we'd become too good at talking now. There were fellas talking a good game but struggling to back it up.

Everything was about what we weren't going to let happen. How driven we were. Winning the League might have seemed to back that kind of stuff up, but deep down I felt we were trying to prod and poke something out of the players now that I wasn't entirely sure was still within.

On some level, you just begin to detect an element of bluffing, of bullshit creeping in.

We did the whole cliff walk, then stopped outside the castle, gathered in a circle and had a real soul-searching discussion about what we needed to do. Coming away, I felt it had been decent. But I suppose time changes your perspective and, given what was to follow, I recognise now that certain people were just talking the talk.

We also had a training break in Breaffy House two weeks before the championship and, again, there was a sense maybe of people just going through the motions.

SEOIRSE BULFIN: ''Twas horrendous. For me, the worst training camp ever. I didn't go for the full thing, but I remember there was a break after the first session the day I went up, and Conor McGrath was in the lobby trying to get work done. Some lads had taken three days off to be there, but there was just so much negativity around at that stage that you knew, if you lost to Waterford, you were in trouble.

'There was a lot of fellas talking the talk at that stage. Some younger lads even with egos. It's a lot easier to talk than it is to hurl!'

I'd always been sceptical about meeting Waterford so soon again, and, sure enough, they were much better than us in Thurles. They'd become a well-seasoned team under Derek now and were, naturally, right up for it on the day.

I was massively disappointed, but we'd put such effort into the latter stages of the League maybe it was inevitable that we'd end up a bit flat. And if you gave me a choice of winning that game or collecting a national title, I'd have taken the League all day long.

Because we needed to win something after flat-lining in '14 and '15 and, much as I love Munster Championship hurling, we'd won that 2013 All-Ireland through the back door. All we needed was a bit of momentum now.

That momentum never really came, though, and certain circumstance didn't help.

We hammered Laois, with Aron Shanagher getting a hat-trick of goals, then came from a slow start against Limerick to score nine unanswered points in a win that suggested we were hitting decent form. That pitched us into an All-Ireland quarter-final against Galway, a team Ger Loughnane had taken to ridiculing the week before for losing to Kilkenny in the Leinster final.

To this day, I've no idea why Ger did that.

Maybe as a former Galway manager he felt he had special licence, but he knew too there was a decent chance that we'd be their next opponents. So he took to describing Galway as a team 'made of absolutely nothing', one having 'no guts whatsoever', even likening their new manager, Micheál Donoghue, to the Dermot Morgan TV character Father Trendy.

I think hindsight shows just how ridiculous that comment was, Donoghue since proving himself one of the shrewdest managers around. It was an absolutely vicious attack that I felt hugely let down by. Ger will never be forgotten for what he did for all of us who won All-Ireland medals in '95 and '97, but I've never been able to understand one Clareman setting up another for a fall.

And that's absolutely how it felt to me back then. Why he did it I don't honestly know. Maybe it was just a lapse of judgement, but more likely, I suppose, Ger didn't particularly care either way.

But as soon as the final whistle went in that game against Limerick, I was basically firefighting. I talked about how Loughnane's views certainly did not represent the broad Clare view of that Galway team, though I pretty much knew the damage was already done.

And I subsequently heard that Donoghue, naturally, put great purchase on Loughnane's diatribe in the week leading up to the game. Why wouldn't he! A Clareman saying they had no guts! It was manna from heaven.

Look, Loughnane wasn't the reason Galway beat us.

We made a fair fist of that ourselves, conceding two goals that will forever haunt us as exercises in self-harm. The first one came in the 15th minute, when we placed a puck-out right down on top of Joe Canning, who was supplementing their half-back line, and he set in train a move that would lead to Conor Cooney finding the net. Even then I'd say Andy Fahy would admit he shouldn't have been beaten by Cooney's shot.

The second one?

We just didn't get our sweeper in place before the throw-in for the resumption and Galway, to their credit, spotted it, Johnny Coen cutting through us like a knife through butter. He offloaded to David Burke, who found Canning, and my old friend from LIT buried a great finish that put us ten points adrift and in big, big trouble.

We just hadn't been switched on for the restart. Unforgivable.

The boys kept hurling, winning the remainder by four points without ever suggesting that a big comeback was on the cards.

To this day I remain adamant that Galway were not seven points better than us. Their two goals came from terrible mistakes. Without those mistakes we'd have been right there. Maybe Clare people will see that if they look back honestly now. I wasn't even out the tunnel when that second goal went in. Didn't even see it. Just heard the roar as I came around the corner.

In the dressing-room afterwards I was non-committal about my future. Just told the players how proud I was of them and that, though I still had a year to go, I just wasn't sure if I'd be sticking around now. It was common knowledge that I'd needed coronary care that week in Dublin and I just had it in my head that I'd maybe had enough.

I remember the rest of the management team being concerned about me when I turned up to take our last session before the game. Dónal Óg telling me to be 'responsible', to remember that my health was more important than any hurling game. He joked that he had this vision of me getting so wound up inside the dressing-room the stents would pop out, hitting the ceiling like bullets, everyone ducking down so as not to be hit!

He knew – all the lads knew – I'd been taking knocks left, right and centre. It was only a small group of people who'd been relentlessly attacking me, but empty vessels can create a lot of noise. We'd won the League, won two games in the championship and, in my opinion, been far closer to Galway than their two-goal winning margin implied.

Two goals that had been giveaways.

But now familiar voices were depicting the defeat as some kind of catastrophe. And I was sick of that sound. Sick of the bitching, the petty jealousies and the faceless heroes spewing their bile again.

DÓNAL ÓG CUSACK: 'For some reason, in Clare I always had the feeling that there was an element just not happy at Davy being as successful as he was. One of my first nights with them, Davy asked me to go with the county chairman to present medals at a club away out in the west of the county.

'So I did it, said my few words, and as we were leaving, this fella stopped me. He was sitting at the bar counter, pipe going, arms folded and a pint balanced between his arms and his belly. And he started off, "What are ye going to do about these short puck-outs?"

So off he goes about a load of stuff about Davy, and he was just so feckin' cynical. And I remember thinking, Jesus Christ almighty! That was a typical example of what you'd come across. Any fella like Davy, who wants to drive on, who has no problem having a different view of the world, of simply being different, who is in "the boy done well" category, they always wanted to pick holes.

'Maybe it's human nature, but I would always say to him that he should try to stay away from getting drawn into it.'

There's only so much you can take. Maybe enough was enough now. Look, there's a huge amount of great Clare people out there. But there's a vocal few who, my God, the more I think about them the more disgusted I'd be with how they carried on.

If they looked at themselves honestly with hindsight they'd surely see they weren't doing Clare hurling any good. We'd won a League and All-Ireland in my time. What did Clare win over the previous sixteen years?

About two weeks after the game I spent the day ringing players, canvassing opinions. Rang about 20 of the top 22, on the basis that the last 12 to 15 guys were bound to want a change. The words I used with every player I spoke to were, 'Listen, you won't offend me if you think we need a change. Just say so!'

Eighteen of the top 22 told me there and then that they wanted me to continue. The other four were honest enough to say they thought they might benefit from a different voice. And I was fine with that. In fact my response to the four of them was something along the lines of 'You're probably right.'

Soon after this the guys I hadn't phoned began to kick up a stink, contacting the joint captains, Cian Dillon and Tony Kelly, and demanding they have a say in any further decisions taken.

So, Cian rang me. 'Davy, these lads aren't happy. We're thinking it's only right we ask them what they want.'

All of this was happening then as I was heading to America on a golf holiday. A players' meeting was called and I'm thinking, 'None of this would have happened if I hadn't phoned those top 20 players in the first place. I've brought this on myself!' And I started to consider that, irrespective of the outcome of their meeting, it was maybe time for me to hit the road.

I flew into Charlotte and on the drive to Myrtle Beach kept in contact with the situation on the phone. It was clear things were beginning to turn against me. I'll always remember Bugs, one of my most loyal supporters, saying, 'We know you're still the best man for us Davy, but, with some people doing what they're doing, maybe the best thing is not to give them the satisfaction …'

I respected that, but my mind kept changing. I knew I could have stayed, absolutely. I still had the majority of the dressing-room, the county board was backing me and people like Dónal Óg were encouraging me to go again.

So I was half and half, if I'm honest. One minute thinking the time was right to go, the next thinking, 'Fuck them, I'll hang tough here!'

In the end, I just didn't like the sense building of a dressing-room divided. The last few years had been hard enough without now trying to go again in an atmosphere lacking unity. Only a small number of the main players had indicated that they wouldn't support me and I sensed they were being pushed in that direction by people outside the group.

But I felt hugely tired now too. Maybe I'd been taking the abuse too much to heart, but it really does begin to eat into you over time. So I began ringing all the back-room staff, thanking them for everything they'd given Clare, telling them that a statement was imminent.

And, trust me, I took my time over that statement. It felt momentous to be sitting in a house on the far side of the Atlantic formally drawing the curtain down on my time in a job I'd always coveted. The statement ran to just over 300 words in the end, my head spinning as I put it together.

Mike Corry was sitting beside me as I pressed 'Send', and I'd say he almost saw me shudder as I did it.

But I knew the decision was right too and, the moment that statement was sent, I felt an incredible weight fall off my shoulders. Yes, a small part of me was hurt. Who wouldn't be? I'd given the players everything over the previous five years and, if I'm honest, I reckoned our achievements should probably have counted for more.

But I honestly held no grudges either. They were a serious bunch who, over time, gave me every bit as much as I gave them. And those achievements are carved into history now. We'd all meet in Lahinch in December 2017, at a function in the Aberdeen Arms for the presentation of those League medals.

That was important, I felt, an adult, civilised way of saying goodbye.

Because the Atlantic Ocean had been between us the day we went separate ways and, if anything, that was a relief at the time. I don't socialise very much at home and that golf trip with friends is something I hold very precious at the end of a long year.

In the circumstances, it was just what I needed. I think the other lads would tell you that I was a different person the moment my decision was made official. My golf certainly improved.

The day after stepping down as Clare manager I went around my favourite course in South Carolina, True Blue, in two under. The storm in my head had lifted.

17

THE 100 PER CENT TEAM

T he most basic human instinct is a need to feel wanted and, after three years of seemingly relentless negativity in Clare, maybe Wexford were pushing an open door now.

I was still in America when my father told me someone from the county had been looking to talk to me and, being honest, my first suspicion was that it might be a wind-up. But within a couple of days of touching back down at Shannon I was meeting their county chairman, Diarmuid Devereux, in the Clonmel Park Hotel.

To begin with, it felt like an out-of-body experience.

On arriving home I'd taken a call from Tom Doyle of Club Wexford, asking would I agree to the meeting with Devereux. Tom said they'd been on to Ger Loughnane about me and been given a glowing reference.

I smiled when I heard that. Typical Ger! He'll absolutely crucify you one day, be all about you the next. The moment you start trying to figure out where you stand with him is the moment you start wasting your time.

The truth is, I feel no bitterness towards Ger. What he did for all of us in Clare can't ever be forgotten, no matter how unfair he can be towards some of us at times. Ger is Ger. Expect nothing from him and you won't be disappointed.

Deep down, I knew I needed a rest now, and that the travelling the Wexford job would demand of me just didn't make any sense.

And still, within fifteen minutes of sitting down with Devereux I couldn't stop myself talking.

The more I thought about Wexford the more I recognised the possibilities. They'd just won three consecutive Leinster under-21 championships, beating Kilkenny in two finals. And I'd seen at first hand in 2014, when they'd ended our All-Ireland defence, that the senior team had a lot going for them.

But this was madness, and I knew it too.

Devereux and I talked for maybe an hour at that first meeting, after which he invited in two members of Club Wexford to, basically, back up everything he'd been saying. They were all unequivocal in their view that I was the right man to take over from Liam Dunne now.

Leaving for home that day, I told them I loved their enthusiasm but that I just didn't think I could do the job.

Devereux rang again the following day. 'Davy, you're the man for Wexford!'

Two days later, another call. 'I want you to meet a few people ...'

The pressure was relentless, but my response was always the same. 'Jesus, I'd love to, but, honestly, I don't think I can do this.'

At home, everybody seemed to be telling me the same thing. Madness. Last thing you need. Driving will kill you. They're not going anywhere.

And, on some level, all this negativity was actually beginning to stir contrariness inside me. That's almost a personal reflex, especially when people tell me I'd be wasting my time at something. It's like flicking a switch.

Meantime, Devereux kept ringing. He wanted me to meet the county board committee in the Killeshin Hotel, Portlaoise. Told me the job was mine, but that this was a formality. A box to tick.

Next thing I knew I was addressing maybe a dozen people around a table, selling my thoughts on a project for which, I suspected, I had far less energy now than the people listening to me.

You could say I had two voices at that moment. The first reiterating to that Wexford committee my feelings about the potential in the county, the second – somewhere inside my head – endlessly protesting, 'You're tired, you're bate, give it a rest, Davy!'

So why did I agree?

Definitely part of me wanted to prove something to those in Clare who'd been so hell-bent on getting rid of me for so long. But, critically, Sharon said she'd support me if I took the job. That was huge. She didn't want me going to Wexford, but she knew too just how difficult the looming winter would be for me at home if I didn't have a project.

So, roughly two weeks after stepping down as Clare manager, I was calling a meeting with Wexford's players in the Seafield Hotel and making a point of having my entire back-room staff lined up all around me from the get-go.

I wanted to get the message across immediately that this would be a professional operation, run by serious people. That we were getting straight down to business.

JJ Doyle was always going to be first on my list, a man who'd managed Wexford to three All-Ireland camogie titles, the county's under-21s to Leinster glory, and someone I'd done a couple of coaching sessions for over the years.

Páraic Fanning and Seoirse Bulfin were the next two people I rang and I was thrilled when Keith Rossiter and the former Kilkenny goalkeeper PJ Ryan agreed to come on board too.

And I wanted other familiar faces. Gazzy, who – inexplicably – had become surplus to requirements in Clare. Mike Corry on the stats. Bomber for a bit of everything.

I went for a kind of classroom vibe in the Seafield, sitting four players at each desk and getting them, immediately, to fill in a questionnaire that amounted to a mirror. What did they think of themselves? How did they rate their training, eating habits, everything?

Our first collective session then was on 6 November and I'll never forget it. We tested everybody for speed and mobility, the findings telling me that these lads were way off where they needed to be to play inter-county hurling. Some were far too bulky, for a start. They needed to be looser, more flexible.

But I was starting with a blank sheet here and told the board I wanted eight or nine games before the start of the National League to give me some indication of what I was working with now.

That would be my only way of finding out not simply what talent was available, but what style of hurling would now suit them.

Maybe people imagine I'm obsessed with a sweeper system, but the truth is I'm quite happy to send out a team to hurl orthodox if I feel I've the personnel to do so. In Wexford's case, I deduced pretty quickly that I hadn't.

Because we went fifteen on fifteen in our first challenge game against Waterford on the Astroturf in WIT that December and they were terrible at it. Soon after, we played Dublin in Bray – again going orthodox – and I'm not exaggerating when I say the Dubs beat us by about 25 points.

Afterwards, in this tiny Bray Emmets dressing-room, I made the players a promise. 'What happened ye here today will never happen ye again on my watch,' I told them.

I knew we'd be playing Dublin a month later in the Walsh Cup. And that was the day I decided we'd be doing it with a sweeper. To that end we spent the next four or five challenge games bedding in the system and settling on Shaun Murphy as the perfect man for the job.

Shaun's got a very good hurling brain, distributes the ball well and is well able to tackle, all qualities essential in the man buttressing your defence.

As our fitness improved, so did the players' understanding of the system. And by the time the Dubs came to Hollymount for a Thursday-night game under lights we were ready to show them a very different face.

PÁRAIC FANNING: 'We'd been all over the shop that first day in Bray, Dublin opening us up at will. But then that night under lights at the Shelmaliers Club we were a different proposition. We weren't bullied and there was this massive crowd really wiring into the hunger the lads were showing.

'That was the first night I remember thinking, "These people are absolutely crazy about their hurling …" A January night in Hollymount, where there's this long drive up to the field. You'd look down, and all you could see were these car lights that kept coming.

'We beat Dublin and it felt an important night, in that you could feel the crowd get right behind the team.'

Pretty quickly I realised that these lads had the humility to do whatever it would take to be successful. Kilkenny edged us out of the Walsh Cup on a miserable day in New Ross, but we should have beaten them, young Cathal Dunbar driving a late-goal chance straight at the goalkeeper.

He'd face plenty of good-natured slagging about that as the season progressed, but there was nothing light about my mood just before the start of the National League, when we let Cork walk all over us in a challenge game at Carlow Institute of Technology.

Wexford's was a dressing-room that had yet to see me in a temper, but they got it in stereo that evening. I went ballistic, flaking a hurley off gear bags, roaring at the top of my voice, 'Never fucking again!'

I could see the shock in faces, maybe even fear in some, as I gave the impression that if one of them moved during my rant I'd have levelled them with a belt of timber. We'd thrown in the towel that night and a team of mine doing that is guaranteed to make me vicious. 'As long as you're with me, we'll fucking fight!' I roared.

And they could see I wasn't bluffing.

All of this was happening at a time when, physically, I felt dreadful. The day we'd played Carlow in the Walsh Cup I was walking down the field with Mattie Rice after the warm-up when he said something that really jarred. Mattie is a kind of informal sports psychologist in the group. Brilliant in one-to-one dialogue with players. A really smart guy, whose opinion I place great weight on.

'Davy, you don't look well,' he said out of the blue.

Mattie could just see I wasn't in good form. I was flogging a dead horse here and something in my demeanour told him I was close to breaking-point. If I'm honest, he didn't even realise just how close. Because walking down the field that day I felt so bad I was almost in tears.

But it was around this time that I'd been introduced to Colin Smith, a reflexologist in Wexford who sets great store on nutrition. And it was through working with Colin that I would slowly but surely start feeling healthy again. He got me to cut out all soft drinks and sugary snacks. With all the driving I do, I was an awful man for grazing on filling-station temptations. Chocolate bars, sweets, chicken-fillet rolls. If you looked under the driver's seat of my car, the evidence was always damning.

Basically, I needed to take control of my own diet. To self-help.

Within a couple of months Colin had transformed me. I hydrated only with water. I brought packed lunches on the long drives to training. If I needed diesel for the journey home I'd despatch Gazzy to get it during the session so I'd have no excuse for a pit-stop.

Soon I was able to discard the mask at night and, psychologically, that was a huge moment. My energy levels began to rise. Wexford essentially now – finally – had the man they thought they'd been getting the previous October.

And it's fair to say our start to the National League pretty quickly lifted my energy levels even higher.

We slipped six points down in both our opening games, against Limerick and Galway, yet rallied to win each time. We'd been third favourites behind both for promotion from Division 1B yet now found ourselves in the box-seat. I'd told the players to just hang tough, stay honest, and see where it took them. They did that in spades.

The Galway game was crazy. We'd conceded three poor goals and seemed out of it, but the players just dug in. Galway's solitary score in the last 20 minutes was a point from a free and Wexford supporters came spilling onto the field in Salthill afterwards as if we'd just won the League itself.

That was the day I suggested people should maybe 'chill the beans'. I was just beginning to realise the passion of Wexford people now, something that was electrifying and worrying in equal measure.

Expected wins followed against Kerry, Laois and Offaly. But I was on guard against any hint of bad habits. Half way through the Laois game I went ballistic in the dressing-room. Just felt the players had become a little complacent after taking an early lead, allowing Laois to come back to within a couple of points.

If this group became too big for their boots, I knew we'd be in for a rude awakening.

And, of course, we then went to Nowlan Park for a National League quarter-final to secure Wexford's first away win in

Kilkenny since 1957. Sometimes you get a vibe from a place and, that day, we very much got the impression that Kilkenny weren't exactly welcoming the idea of a resurgent Wexford.

When we wanted to go out on the pitch beforehand we just seemed to encounter one locked door after another, with no sign of the groundsman to help us out. He seemed to have disappeared into thin air. Eventually the players had to navigate a way out through the terrace to get to the field.

I remember thinking at the time there might be an element of 'This Wexford team needs to be put back in its box now!' Maybe that was just reading too much into it, but that's how it felt.

Winning that game felt monumental and again the crowd poured onto the field at the end to celebrate what was only Wexford's third win in 21 meetings with a Brian Cody team.

There'd been a bit made of what looked like a managerial flare-up between the two of us on the line that day, but it was actually nothing. Brian just had early words with the referee and, to counter that, I made sure to give Alan Kelly the benefit of my opinion too.

Cody's response was to turn on me, but I was never going to respond. His animation told me we were getting under Kilkenny's skin. That was all I needed to know and the truth is that, only for Eoin Murphy's brilliance in goal, we'd have beaten them more comfortably that day.

So now we had Tipperary in the semi-final, reigning All-Ireland champions, carrying the obvious threat presented by what I considered the best forward line in hurling. Tipp can kill you in seconds with their goal-scoring ability and, maybe on some level, that was my biggest fear going back to Nowlan Park now.

And it's pretty much what drove me to a moment of infamy that would make me front-page news.

I had to do it.

I know that march onto the field to confront the referee, Diarmuid Kirwan, became a massive media story when it brought me into physical contact with a Tipp forward, Jason Forde. I know it looked terrible. I understand all that. And the fall-out, in Forde's case, is something I deeply regret.

But Diarmuid had just allowed two blatant fouls on our defender, James Breen, to go without a whistle in the build-up to Noel McGrath's 18th-minute goal. They'd already breached our defence with a John McGrath goal too so, nearly twenty minutes in, we were trailing 0-3 to 2-3. Clearly beginning to feel sorry for ourselves too.

And self-pity, I know from experience, is no defence against a goal-hungry Tipp. They're just programmed to destroy you. The way this game was going it looked like they could be out of sight by half-time.

So I basically went to war.

Now, I had absolutely no interest in making any contact with a Tipp player, but I did want to get my own players' attention. All our work of the previous few months was about to come undone here if we fell to a twenty or thirty-points hammering. And there was a real danger of that happening now. Of our confidence being torn to shreds.

The two fouls on Breen had been absolutely blatant. I needed to communicate that to the referee. And I went about it in maybe the most provocative way I could.

SEOIRSE BULFIN: 'Initially I was thinking, "Davy, don't!" Then when I saw Jason Forde coming for him I was half itching to go myself. Like, you'll fight on your back for Fitzy even though you know, at times, it's the wrong thing. But it's amazing how much you can process in that split second.

'The first thing is you want to back him up, but the second one is, if a second person goes in off the line there's going to be mayhem. You don't want that.'

After taking the first few steps onto the field I paused after about ten yards. I remember my sister, Helen, asking me about this afterwards. My answer was simple. Even at that point I knew I was in big trouble. I was already in a place I had no right to be.

But I knew too that I had to keep going now. So I kept walking. I had to change the energy around this game and, being honest, I couldn't blame Forde or his teammate Niall O'Meara for coming across and squaring up to me.

Jason told me basically to get the fuck off the field, and I told him to fuck off back in return. It really was that basic and that primitive. He should never have been suspended for what happened, because I was the only one in the wrong. Unfortunately, I wasn't the only one who paid for my incursion.

So I ended up with very mixed feelings after. The flare-up did bring my players to life, Aidan Nolan quickly coming across to square up to the Tipp lads and the whole team, generally, finding enough anger within to get us to the break trailing by just four points.

As it happened, Tipp still put us to the sword with an unanswered 2-4 between the 60th and 66th minutes, winning in the end by 5-18 to 1-19. But it actually could have been far uglier.

Soon as I realised afterwards that Forde might be in trouble with the authorities I rang the Tipp manager, Michael Ryan. 'Whatever you want me to do, I'll do it,' I told him.

I just felt that Jason was now paying for the high profile the incident had been given, something that almost always seems the case with me. There was a picture of the two of us on most front pages, the coverage just adding to pressure building for heavy punishments to be handed down.

A couple of days later I sat down with team secretary Dermot Howlin, county secretary Margaret Doyle and chairman Derek Kent in Enniscorthy for what, ostensibly, was a meeting to plan my appeal against suspension. They were 100 per cent supportive, but I'd already made my mind up that I was going to take my medicine.

I just felt that the optics of an appeal wouldn't have been great now. It would have looked as if I was trying to justify it, which I couldn't. And, honestly, I was far more concerned about Forde missing a game for Tipp, essentially because of something I'd pretty much dragged him into. He didn't hit anyone. He just gave me a little shove when he probably felt entitled to do far more than that.

There'd been nothing in it and, anyway, it had been 100 per cent my fault. Bottom line, I shouldn't have been on the field.

So I didn't even bother going to my own disciplinary hearing. The verdict was two months. Fair enough. The only thing on my mind now was how I'd delegate management chores for the start of championship.

A few weeks before our opening Leinster Championship game against Laois in Portlaoise we went to a warm-weather training camp in Portugal.

It proved exactly what I'd been looking for, four intense days of work – physical and mental – just to add clarity to what we were looking for from the players. On the second-last night I hired a bus to bring the players into Vilamoura for a beer. They'd no idea that was coming, but I knew a little blow-out wouldn't do them any harm now.

'Ye've two hours, boys!' I announced as we pulled up outside the bar. And, from that moment on, it was as if they were drinking against the clock.

To say they went for it would be an understatement. Let's just say not a single second of those two hours went to waste as the bar staff could hardly keep up with the thirst. I've never seen anything like it.

I had them doing a few laps the following morning, to run some of it out of their systems. And that's when I christened them 'the 100 per cent team'.

'Whatever I ask ye to do, in fairness, ye'll do it 100 per cent!' I told them. 'If I ask ye to train, ye give me 100 per cent. If I ask ye to buy in to a programme, ye'll do it 100 per cent. If I ask ye to fund-raise, ye'll do it 100 per cent. And if I let ye out on the beer, ye'll do it 100 per cent!'

That drew a big laugh. It just seemed to me that these fellas did nothing in half measure. They either went for broke or they didn't.

We had a sing-song on the bus journey back to base, and, honestly, the atmosphere was phenomenal. I couldn't have been happier with the unity in the group now.

And, as expected, that Laois game didn't hugely stretch us. They were competitive for a while but, once our lads found their rhythm, it was never going to be a serious game. Seoirse and PJ ran the line, with myself, JJ and Páraic above in the back of the stand.

Lucy Kennedy accompanied me to the game for that edition of *Living with Lucy* and, given that I was technically barred from the dressing-room, it was easy to keep the camera crew away from the team. Maybe that had been a small bit of a gamble on my part. I mean, imagine if Laois had beaten us and me being followed about the place by TV cameras! The fall-out would have been ugly, no question.

But I knew the players were in a good place, so I went with my gut. And, thankfully, I wasn't left with any regrets.

My suspension meant I couldn't do the line for our next game either, against Kilkenny. So they moved this little officials' box from one side of the VIP section in the Wexford Park stand to the other, fitting it with one-way glass. This meant that I could see out but couldn't be seen. Perfect!

The boys sensed a certain tension in the group that week – understandable enough, given that Wexford hadn't beaten Kilkenny in championship since the 2004 Leinster semi-final. So it was decided to put on a video of that Portuguese sing-song in the dressing-room at the very time people would have presumed it was all just high anxiety and raised voices.

I suppose that strategy mightn't have looked too clever when Kilkenny hit us with a goal inside 90 seconds from a TJ Reid penalty, but what followed was an incredible exhibition of fighting, chasing, blocking and tackling. This was the Wexford way and, with every defiant gesture, the crowd just roared their pride.

To see the excitement of the people made me hugely emotional in return. We went eight points up at one point, but another Reid penalty and a goal from Colin Fennelly made certain it would go right down to the wire.

Lee Chin was magnificent on the night, scoring as good a point as I've seen when we really needed it by spectacularly fielding a Mark Fanning puck-out and driving it straight between the posts.

When it was announced that there would be a couple of minutes of injury time I couldn't help myself but start banging the window of the box, the people outside now well aware of exactly who was on the far side of the glass.

Those dying minutes were incredible, Kilkenny typically striving to rescue a game they'd been beaten in all over the field. And they almost did that too, with a late Chris Bolger effort having to be stopped by a good Fanning save. But we should never have been in that position on an evening when every last Wexford man stood up to be counted.

The key to victory?

Neither Reid nor Richie Hogan managed a score from play for Kilkenny. Any day your backs achieve that, you're well on the way to taking the Cats' scalp.

PÁRAIC FANNING: 'I remember this period of about 40 seconds near the end and it was like the *Rocky IV* film, where there was just tackle after tackle, turnover after turnover, things we'd actually done in the middle of winter with tackling drills and that, high-intensity hits that would knock the stuffing out of you.

'The lads kept winning the ball back, and you could see we weren't flagging as much as Kilkenny. Wexford were winning those physical contests. We were stronger, and the place was just going bananas. I don't often notice the crowd, but you could definitely sense it that evening.

'I remember Matthew O'Hanlon running into Walter Walsh … like, lads were on jelly legs … I've actually watched that segment a few times since … The game is really in the melting-pot, but you could just see the lads were relishing it. Much as they were hurting, they were enjoying it.

'If you can be in control in that kind of chaos, we were. And yet there was that save from Mark Fanning at the end … As momentous as that night was, we could have blown it!'

To see the emotion afterwards was something I found very moving. Because of the suspension I'd been unavailable to give any media interviews but, the moment I went to leave the box, Liam Spratt nabbed me to do an interview with South East Radio. The giddiness was through the roof. Honestly, of all the great days I've had in hurling, this one was right up there.

We went down the town with the players after, Páraic and myself ending up in the Stores nightclub about 2 a.m., trying to talk hurling but not being able to hear a single word the other was saying.

Eventually we just got to hell out of there, settling down back in the hotel lobby, where I'd say it was well after 4 a.m. by the time we got to bed.

My biggest worry now was how the county's first Leinster final appearance since '08 would impact on the players' nerves. I think our only survivor in the group from that year was David Redmond. This game with Galway was always going to be played in front of the biggest crowd our players had ever experienced, though few predicted the record 60,000 who would turn up on the day.

I was back as a legal presence in the dressing-room now, and we decided everything should be as relaxed and low-key as we could make it.

The Killers' *Mister Brightside* is a favourite song of the group, and I went to Éanna Martin as the lads were getting ready with the suggestion that it mightn't be a bad time for somebody to sing it. There's just something in the lyrics that seemed appropriate to the day.

Next thing, Éanna and our physio, Joe Cullen, were in the middle of the dressing-room floor, belting it out. And within seconds the whole group had joined them, roaring out the lyrics at the top of their voices. It's just a song they've taken to their hearts, and at that moment it became a kind of anthem.

Jealousy, turning saints into the sea
Swimming through sick lullabies
Choking on your alibis
But it's just the price I pay
Destiny is calling me …

Anyone eavesdropping in the corridor would probably have thought we'd lost the plot inside, but the atmosphere felt perfect. Just a band of brothers absolutely ready to give their all.

And that's exactly what they did. The performance was actually brilliant for about 30 minutes, but then we just tightened. It was as if the players started to think to themselves, 'We can actually do this!' and went back to the old Wexford way of just horsing ball aimlessly up the field. Leaving things to chance. Once that happened, Galway had our number.

Conor McDonald had a 39th-minute penalty saved too, and though the players kept fighting, we really only hurled the way we planned to hurl for that first half-hour. That's what disappointed me. On some level too I think we ran out of legs, although I suspected that was more a mental than a physical thing in the end.

There were a few little things that went against us each side of half-time too, and we just didn't handle them the way maybe a more mature team would have done. Shaun Murphy had a poor day at sweeper, making good use of maybe only four of the 24 balls he got. That kind of statistic was never going to be good enough, and he didn't need to be told.

Look, it certainly wasn't all down to Shaun, most of the players under-performed and, on some level, maybe that was inevitable. It was the biggest game they'd ever played in, the atmosphere incredible. I'd watched the first fifteen minutes above in the stats box, but our communications system broke down, so I went down and watched the rest with Keith and JJ on the line.

After that game I had a fair idea our race was run. The season had taken its toll and Waterford just had too much in the tank when we squared up to them in an All-Ireland quarter-final at the spanking-new Páirc Uí Chaoimh. I just felt we spent that day kind of waiting for things to happen rather than seizing the opportunity ourselves.

It was tight all through, but once we gifted them a Kevin Moran goal the writing was on the wall. Four points separated us at the end, probably a fair reflection.

And that was the day I was seen to have a go at the TV pundits afterwards, specifically Henry Shefflin and Michael Duignan, for their continuing criticism of the sweeper system. It wasn't entirely a solo run. I'd pretty much decided I'd go that route if asked the appropriate question. But, in a quick chat with Derek McGrath before heading into the press conference, he actually suggested it'd be no harm for me to address it.

Both of us were sick and tired of feeling the need to justify a system that made absolute sense to our teams. Anyway, my comments kicked off a little firestorm of controversy, with Duignan especially taking exception.

Our season might have been over, but mine still had a few days to run.

18

LAST WORD

LIAM DOWD: 'I remember Davy ringing me about ten days after Teresa's funeral, asking how I was doing. "Are you at the house?" he asked. "I might call in for an hour."

'"Why? Are you up?" I asked.

'He said he was but that he was tied up with people for a couple of hours. And, of course, next thing he's at the door. Ended up staying for hours, copious amounts of tea drank. He was no more in Dublin when he rang than I was in Mars. He was at home in Sixmilebridge.

'Those moments you never forget!'

DANNY CHAPLIN: 'Look, the man is vilified in this county. We're the greatest shower of ghouls in Ireland. We can't wait to knock our own. He was nearly ran out of the county in 2016, but I think people are starting to wonder now, "Did we get rid of Davy a small bit too early?"

'He had a game plan, he knew what he was doing. Okay, you mightn't have liked the game plan, but all the players looked like they knew what they were doing. They won an All-Ireland and a National League. And we hounded him out of the job! Like, some of the local media gave him an awful time.

'Then you had social media and these message boards. The personal abuse he got was incredible. Ferocious. People take shots at Davy and they don't know the man from Adam. And he takes a lot of that stuff to heart.

'He's not a messer, he's not a drinker, he's not a trouble-maker, yet we can't wait to knock him in this county. It wouldn't happen anywhere else.'

SEOIRSE BULFIN: 'Look, I often say Fitzy's the human version of Marmite. People either love him or hate him. In Clare, they love cutting the back off him, which I could never figure out. I often say to him, "Fitzy, if you were from Limerick they'd have a statue of you outside the Gaelic Grounds …"

'It beggars belief how he was treated in Clare. In his time they won a League and the All-Ireland. Yet the way it turned so quickly against him … Like, I'd be very cross with some of the Clare players. I get on well with all of them, but there are certain guys I'd have no regard left for, to be honest. Because of the way Davy was treated.

'I know how some of them were looked after from a college point of view, how guys who would have struggled a bit, for different reasons, I know how Davy made sure that they were looked after. He didn't get that same loyalty back. The last two years were toxic in Clare. It's only looking back that you see the effect it had on him.

'It was all so negative for a team that had just won the League.'

FATHER HARRY BOHAN: 'There is huge goodness in Davy. He's very good with people who are sick, and so on. He gives people that kind of time. And that's why a lot of the criticism hurts him as well. I would definitely say that a lot of the criticism he got after 2013 was unfair.

'Like, I'm steeped in the GAA, but I've never known a man to put such thought into hurling. He has broken the mould in a lot of ways in terms of how hurling is played.

'Now, I would be one of those people who'd say the short puck-outs would drive you crazy at times. When they go wrong … But he brought them in because of the make-up of the team, and Derek McGrath did the same with Waterford.

'It's Ireland, in some ways. There's a lot of begrudgery ingrained in people. I saw it here with the late Brendan O'Regan in Shannon. There's thousands of people in this area wouldn't have jobs only for him.

'In many ways, the same thing would apply with Davy in hurling. Like, we all grow up in Clare yearning to win All-Irelands, and there's a fella just down the road from us who's won three of them.

'And the human side of him, the fact that he gets so deeply hurt by criticism, almost draws it more. People know that they're getting under his skin. And the fact that he gets such massive adulation from all kinds of people, that makes the criticism – especially from his own – seem worse.

'But it isn't. It's natural. That's the world.

'By the way, I have a theory that the bullying of his childhood eventually worked in Davy's favour. It made him determined not to be put down. It hurt him so badly, it gave him defiance. Nobody would best him again.'

◄◊►

PAT BENNETT: 'The problem with Davy is that he'll tell you something straight out. A lot of guys don't like that. Look, personally, I don't particularly like it when I've someone telling me that I'm wrong. Sometimes he can be too blunt, and people don't like that.

'But he doesn't rant and rave. He's got a very good hurling brain. You can have arguments with him, and if your point is good enough he will listen. He talks things through. If you look at his record going through Waterford, Clare and Wexford, his record is unbelievable.'

LOUIS MULQUEEN: 'Davy'll have a game thought out meticulously for weeks. Some other managers I've worked with in the past wouldn't have a plan B. But Davy would have a plan C, D, E and F.

'He has serious hurling intelligence. He would tell you himself that he never liked school, that he was bullied. But he's one of the best men I've worked with to sum up something on the pitch as it's happening.

'Other people just wouldn't have that sharpness on match day. That's his biggest asset, I think. Sometimes the charisma can be a problem, because it brings too much shite. But he always had the right people with him for a battle.

'People who'd be loyal to the end, who'd come out swinging ...'

DÓNAL ÓG CUSACK: 'I think people have a one-dimensional view of him that's unfair and a bit lazy as well. He's a man of depth, innovative, someone who thinks a lot about the game.

'We were competitors as county hurlers, and when you're on opposite sides it's easy to fight against that person. You try to prove you're better than them, but that doesn't mean you don't respect them. It's actually the opposite. If you didn't respect them you wouldn't care about that.

'I found him very caring and loyal to work with. And I'm very comfortable and happy in his company. There was a lot of bullshit when I went to Clare, along the lines of "Jesus, these fellas will never get on ..." But that's not the way it works.

'I used love the fierce detail he'd go into before a game. I loved the way he cared so much. I suppose we're very alike, in that we both nearly have to win, even if it's only a game of cards.

'So I was very disappointed when he stepped down as Clare manager, because I believed he was on the right path. The incoming managers made it clear they wanted me to stay, but I felt torn, if I'm honest. I didn't like the idea of not going with him.

'But at the same time I didn't like the idea of leaving something after just one year either. I did worry for him then going to Wexford, just in terms of the challenge and the stress, and the distance he'd have to travel. I mean, if you look at hurling counties, with the exception of Antrim there's probably no longer journey you could make than that between Clare and Wexford.

'Yet here's this man who's got so much feckin' drive ... I've never met a person with more drive in them for the game ... now going to dive headlong into this challenge. And at a time his health wasn't great.

'But that's the man. I would say that my time with him did finish too early.'

◄◊►

SEÁNIE MCMAHON: 'It was always intense with Davy but my God we'd have some fun too. I remember one training camp we had in Dangan in Galway, the players flat to the boards. Louis and Davy had two bikes with them, they were big into the cycling at the time. So didn't Davy come up with a challenge. He said if Hego could cycle two circuits of the field in a set time, the players would be let off the evening session.

'Anyway, off Hego goes like a bullet, and he's well on course to meet the time when doesn't the bike puncture. So you had all the boys running down the field, trying to push Tommy over the line in time, and he comes in just outside the mark. So the boys ended up having to do the session, everyone wondering had Davy sabotaged the bike!'

DEREK KENT: 'I would have shared the perception of others before he came to Wexford. Davy Fitz? That crack-pot? But it's a perception that is so far from the truth. He's actually the complete opposite when you get to know the guy.

'I'll put it this way. He was supposed to present medals at a junior club one Friday night, but pulled out because of sickness. Drove down two weeks later, when he wasn't due in Wexford for training, a meeting or anything else, just to honour that commitment. A six-hour round-trip to present medals to under-14s! Who else does that?

'Who else gets into a van at five in the morning and drives down to Wexford Park from Clare for a church fun day and drives back home that night? The man has a big heart.

'And this stigma about Davy Fitz breaking county boards is so far from the truth. He gets travel expenses which, to be perfectly honest, are modest. The plain truth is he puts any hurling county he gets involved with on a far better financial footing than they'll have been on when he took over.

'What people forget is the income that Davy generates. Put it this way, if hurling was a business in Wexford, these last two years that business would be profitable. My experience of him is that his number-one priority is the players. But he's acutely aware of budgets too.

'He brings a business approach to looking after a team and he gets maximum return from anything that's spent. I can't speak highly enough of him. I started off as a chairman to him, but I'd like to think I became a friend too.'